Advance praise for

Adaptive Fashion

Kolko has crafted a groundbreaking, essential look at the world of adaptive fashion from the perspective of entrepreneurs and designers who clearly see the intersection and importance of inclusivity, accessibility, empathy, and mental wellbeing and how the time for fashion forward thinking is now.

—Janeane Bernstein, EdD, Founder of Outside the Box, author of *Better Humans - What the Mental Health Pandemic Teaches Us About Humanity*

A must read for anyone passionate about creating a truly inclusive and equitable fashion industry. This book is a call to action for designers, brands, and consumers alike, urging us to re-think how we define beauty, style, and accessibility.

—Brenda Cooper, Costume designer and Emmy Award Winner The Nanny, author of *The Silhouette Solution*

There is finally a book acknowledging that adaptive apparel design should be included in the vocabulary of all fashion studies. The physical and emotional benefits of stylish, well-fitting clothes should be accessible to all, and through Susan Kolko's research, this underserved market is brought forward.

—Lorrie Ivas Professor Fashion Design & Merchandising Santa Monica College, author of *Pencil to Pen Tool: Understanding & Creating the Digital Fashion Image.*

This book serves as a reminder that the development of personal style is an important part of identity, and applies to everyone. Making this analysis part of a fashion curriculum will add yet another dimension to any designers understanding of the customer.

Susan Kolko has opened a new perspective for people in the fashion industry, as well as disability activists. Adaptive Fashion stimulates innovative thinking about the aesthetics, functionality, and marketing of fashion. It is well-researched and full of great information.

Susan Rothman Kolko

ADAPTIVE FASHION

How People with Disabilities Experience Clothing

Fashion and Personal Style Studies

Collection Editor

Joseph H. Hancock II

LPP

First published in 2025 by Lived Places Publishing

The author and editor have made every effort to ensure the accuracy of the information contained in this publication, but assume no responsibility for any errors, inaccuracies, inconsistencies, or omissions. Likewise, every effort has been made to contact copyright holders. If any copyright material has been reproduced unwittingly and without permission the Publisher will gladly receive information enabling them to rectify any error or omission in subsequent editions.

British Library Cataloguing in Publication Data
A CIP record for this book is available from the British Library

ISBN: 9781916704732 (pbk)
ISBN: 9781916704756 (ePDF)
ISBN: 9781916704749 (ePUB)

The right of Susan Rothman Kolko to be identified as the Author of this work has been asserted by them in accordance with the Copyright, Design and Patents Act 1988.

Photo: Lauren Wasser
Credit: Richard Phibbs / Trunk Archive

Cover design by Fiachra McCarthy
Book design by Rachel Trolove of Twin Trail Design
Typeset by Newgen Publishing UK

Lived Places Publishing
P.O. Box 1845
47 Echo Avenue
Miller Place, NY 11764

www.livedplacespublishing.com

Abstract

Adaptive Fashion introduces readers to this new field in clothing design and fashion by exploring disability and special needs, some recent creative developments in meeting those needs, the relationship between self-image, appearance, and fashion, and some essential business considerations in market development. Case studies, vignettes, and personal stories throughout illustrate the experiences of designers, marketers, people with disabilities, and their caregivers, enabling readers to gain both professional and personal insights into this special fashion field. Keywords and study questions are included in each chapter. The author, Susan Rothman Kolko is a professor in the Fashion Design and Merchandising program at Santa Monica College. She believes that if advocates plant the seeds, policymakers, industry leaders, and consumers will grow the roots, and that adaptive fashion will become both accessible and affordable for all.

Keywords

ableism, accessible, adaptive apparel, adaptive clothing, adaptive fashion, adaptive space, adaptivewear, dexterity, disability, ease of dressing, impairment, inclusive, magnit, paralympics, Runway of Dreams, social model, Universal Design, VA clothing allowance, Velcro™, wheelchair, Easywear

Acknowledgements

A special thank you to those who contributed to this project and are spearheading the advancement of adaptive apparel:

Asiya Rafiq	Adaptive by Asiya
Billy Price	BILLY Footwear
Chamiah Dewey	DEWEY Clothing
Charlie Dorris	
Cindi Seifert	Preventa Wear
Conner Lundis	Rollettes
Dana Zumbo	Zappos Adaptive
Deborah Carabet	Elevate Multi Sport&Elevate Women 4 Tri
Dr Juliet Rothman	
Emma Butler	Liberare
Fox	Eightfold Fox
Francisco Postlethwaite	
Harry Thal Insurance	
Heidi McKenzie	Alter Ur Ego
Helya Mohammadian	Slick Chicks
Izzy Camilleri	IZ Adaptive
Jane Fainberg Ivanov	Megami
Janina Urussowa	
Jessie Provoost & Sofie Ternest	So Yes
Julie & Bill Buck	Buck&Buck

Lucy Jones	FFORA
Lynn Brannelly & Alexander Andronescu	Sewn Adaptive
Maria-Lousia Mendiola	MIGA Swim
Marta Elena Cortez-Neavel	Abilitee
Mindy Scheier	Runway of Dreams
Nancy Peters	MagZip/Ankhgear
Natalie Itrube Jackson	Melrose Trading Post
Quaysean Willams	Manikin
Ram Sareen	Tukatech
Ridhwan	Santa Monica College
Ryan Ringholz	PLAE
Stephanie Thomas	Cur8able&Disability Fashion Stylist
Susan Donohoe	Kozie Clothes
Talia Goldfarb	Myself Belts
Tracy Vollbrecht	Vollbrecht Consulting
Veronika Ivanova	
Victoria Jenkins	Unhidden

Contents

Preface

Why this book? Why this title? Why this topic? Who is involved?

As a college professor who has taught fashion merchandising for over 30 years, it has become apparent to me that there is a category of clothing that is currently very underrepresented in both fashion design and production. Over the past 15 years, academics in this field have stressed the importance of sustainability, technology, ethical business practices, and the green scene in the world of fashion. Vegan leathers, recycled and upcycled clothing, made in the United States, and production waste have been the focus of education for future designers and merchandisers. I myself have been stressing the importance of these values in my own classes. I am also aware that current events, projects, discussions, and field visits leave students with lasting impressions, and pave the way for career decisions, and in the direction of business strategy.

I was initially inspired by my mother, who taught disability at the School of Social Welfare at UC Berkeley. We had many conversations about disability, aging, and fashion, and what it meant to have to adapt to sizing changes, address comfort needs, and try to avoid dependence on others. During COVID-19, my classes were on Zoom, and I invited my mother to speak on fashion and disability to my students. She did not know too much about high fashion, but, more importantly, she knew about optimizing the functioning of people with disabilities. Students were interested and open to the topic, and by the end of the class, they were considering ways to incorporate adaptive clothing into their designs and business plans. During the next couple of years, I started to really explore the role fashion plays in disability, and realized that I wanted to learn more. I also decided this was also the time in my career to contribute a piece of work that would inspire learners, provide essential information, and advocate for an important unmet need.

In December 2021, I started interviewing anyone and everyone possible who had a connection with, or was involved in, the field of disability fashion. Of course, there were some designers and brands with whom I was unable to connect, but I am confident that I have been able to interview a well-rounded group of fashion disability advocates to prepare myself for creating this book. Designers, merchandisers, consumers, community representatives, policymakers, and people both with and without disabilities have all been essential components of this project, and it is my hope to create a piece of literature that promotes inclusivity, accessibility, and acceptance, and encourages further development in the field of adaptive clothing and fashion.

Susan Rothman Kolko, M.A. Organizational Management

Introduction

From the beginning of time, clothing has been an important part of the development of culture. Early humans used animal skins and natural resources to protect and embellish their bodies, primarily to provide a barrier between themselves and whatever element they might encounter, and to communicate some sort of group identity. From weather to symbolic rituals, clothing has addressed the most basic of human needs. Clothing is considered a "soft good", meaning that it is made of either natural or human-made fibers, processed into cloth materials, and sewn or manufactured into finished goods. "Soft goods" can be found not only in clothing but also in interior design, and as components of many other products. Historically, cloth and fabrics were mostly used to provide a barrier between human skin and the outside world. Culture dictated the appropriate style, purpose, and use of the clothing. Over time, clothing became an important indication of social status, religion, gender, and culture. As civilizations developed, so did individual styles that represented culture. Most fashions were reflective of natural resources and lifestyles that were valued in the population's geographic region. Fibers, colors, patterns, and accessories became a form of identifying culture. It was not until fourteenth-century Europe that tailoring and trimmings began to make clothing individualized and form-fitting. A short while later, Renaissance clothing was designed to be suitable for unique occasions as well. The costs related to wardrobe ensembles became representative of class distinction. In the nineteenth and twentieth century, human-made fibers and machinery provided advanced production efforts that helped to lower costs and make clothing styles available to the masses.

The demand for clothing that satisfies needs, from basic to extravagant, will continue to be a multi-billion-dollar global commodity as long as humanity exists. From Third World cultures to advanced technological societies, from thrift to haute couture, and from recycling to luxury, clothing plays an important role in identity, and access to fashionable clothing should be an equal opportunity for all.

This book has been researched and written to fill a gap in the fashion industry—a gap in both the design and the marketing of clothing for a significant section of our population—people with disabilities—who need clothing designed for their special needs, clothing which supports a positive self-image, and clothing which is on trend with contemporary styles. The apparel industry has the skill set, and the toolbox, to facilitate the development and marketing of adaptive clothing. The goal of this book is to create awareness of both the needs of people with disabilities for functional, affordable clothing, and the opportunities these needs create for fashion businesses to develop and market a new clothing category.

The production of this specialized clothing, titled "adaptivewear", requires specific expertise and knowledge in both design and marketing, and in the special, specific needs of people with a wide variety of disabling conditions. As with "plus" and "petite", large and small, and niche market specialties, adaptive clothing is increasingly permeating ever-broader areas of the apparel industry, where special attention can be given to the design and provision of functional products for a previously underserved segment of the population. Cost factors, social acceptance, and understanding of specific needs have made the adaptive category of clothing a challenge to traditional business models. Case studies, included in each chapter, provide the reader with the real-life experiences of designers, producers, marketers, and, of course, users of adaptivewear fashions.

This book will explore and discuss the various elements essential to the development of clothing adapted to serve special needs. It begins with an introduction to the world of disability, and with a brief history of disability and the disability rights movement, which, like civil rights and the women's movement, served to bring attention to the challenges faced by this societal group, and to create changes in laws and practices to support equal rights and opportunities for people with disabilities. People with disabilities themselves, their caregivers, families, medical advisers, educators, and community advocates have played an essential role in drawing attention to the inequities, the potentially dehumanizing effects of disability, and the rights of people with disabilities to the same opportunities as non-disabled people. As a result of this advocacy, new standards have been set, both in the United States and globally, for physical environment, education, job opportunities, and basic income levels. "People First" language was developed, to define first personhood, and then disability—so, not a "disabled person", but a "person with a disability".

The major groupings of disabilities, such as mobility limitations, dexterity, and vision limitations, are explored, with discussions of the specific adaptations that can enable ease of clothing selection, dressing and undressing, and other special adaptive needs. Businesses and individuals who have designed and marketed this clothing share their stories, both their challenges and their successes.

As all are aware, clothing is an essential element in an individual's personal self-image. Clothing itself is a basic human need, but many people desire to go beyond meeting just that simple need, and prefer clothing, which is fashionable as well as functional, and well-designed. Several types of clothing adaptations will be included, with accompanying discussions and case studies to illustrate design and methodology.

The book includes a special section on the social model of disability, which currently has superseded the previously dominant medical model. The role of fashion, fashion that moves beyond the simple functionality of adaptivewear and into current trends in style and materials, is an essential element in the social model, and the stories included here will serve as examples of the development of fashionable clothing for people with disabilities.

Clothing also plays an essential role in the development of individual self-image and has a strong influence on the way the individual is perceived by others. The challenges that supporting positive individual images has presented to the industry, not only in design but also in marketing—especially in terms of fashion, choice, cost, and market accessibility—will be explored, presented, and discussed through the stories of innovators in the field.

Market considerations are an essential aspect to consider in providing adaptivewear that is both functional and fashionable. The apparel industry has taken on the responsibility for meeting these special needs, but retailers, brands, and designers have observed slow increases in sales despite their business efforts. Research has been done in this area, with a focus on statistics that address the sizable number of people with disabilities. All potential consumers of clothing designed for special needs have been included here, as research on trends assists in the understanding and addressing some of the potential causes of marketing challenges, as well as some potential methods and resources to address these. Marketing efforts can increase awareness of the existence of this special resource, and accessibility can enable greater exposure to potential purchasers. Today's marketing has already begun to increase awareness about this growing market segment, the demand for products, and the potential for increased business opportunities. Again, the stories of people who have developed brands and markets will illustrate their routes to success and inspire creativity and exploration.

The final section, which supplements the previous discussions, shares stories of notable people with disabilities and their experiences with clothing and fashion. It also includes a listing of additional educational resources and programs that will enable readers to continue to explore and develop skills in both design and marketing to this special segment of the population.

It is hoped that this book can serve to educate, to create awareness of the need for functional, affordable, and fashionable
clothing for people with disabilities, and to expand the interest
and the opportunities for growth of this new clothing category
within the fashion industry.[1]

Part I
Understanding the adaptive clothing market

It is essential to consider several key factors in designing and marketing clothing to meet the specific needs of people with disabilities. The first of these is awareness of the major developments in the field of disability and accessibility, which will be addressed in the first chapter. The next chapter presents the groupings of specific conditions which require a variety of clothing adaptations. These adaptations enable individuals to function optimally in society, minimizing differences and enhancing function. Case studies included in this chapter provide personal insights and illustrate some of the specific ways in which clothing challenges have been addressed.

1
The disability movement and adaptive clothing

Introduction

It is important to be aware of the history of disability in order to understand how current laws, policies, and advocacy affect the everyday living experience of people with disabilities. Understanding the disability rights movement, with its emphasis on equal rights, ethics, inclusivity, accessibility, and affordability, can provide a practical framework for both present and future decision-making related to adaptivewear and the apparel industry. History has shown that every law has several interpretations; hence, amendments and court systems are often needed. The Americans with Disabilities Act of 1990 (the ADA) specifically develops laws related to disability and accessibility but leaves some decisions to the American people for interpretation, which may be affected by both the free market and the capitalist economy. Disability is still often stigmatized as a potential cause of business losses, as marketing and store accommodations require extra effort and planning, and extra funds, which must then be absorbed into business and community budgets. The integration and acceptance of people with disabilities into the societal system, and all of the accommodations and expenses that this has incurred, has initiated a paradigm shift in the American psyche, and in the American economy. Clothing is necessary for survival, while fashion is not. However, in our society, clothing does not define who we are: fashion or fashionable clothing does. As an example: A poorly assembled garment given to a person with a disability at the time of discharge from a hospital that must be worn due to a new disabling condition, serves its purpose, and meets the basic clothing need. However, that garment, associated with so many negative impressions, can create an identity for that wearer that can develop into a lifelong "I am less, I need help" self-image.

Now, over 30 years since the passage of the ADA, the field of disability, and society's knowledge and understanding of the challenges and needs disability can create, continues to broaden, and clothing, related to survival and mental health, has become a topic of awareness and may even be linked to sustainable business practices.

Figure 1 IZ Adaptive

Learning objectives

Upon completion of this chapter, the reader will be able to:

- Identify major developments and laws related to the disability movement;
- Analyze societal changes that have occurred as a result of the disability movement;
- Judge the implications of these changes related to disability and fashion;
- Assess the special considerations and thoughts behind the development of adaptive clothing;
- Identify key figures leading to the development of adaptive clothing; and
- Make reasonable predictions regarding the future of the category of adaptive clothing

A. Disability and the disability rights movement

From the earliest recorded history to post-war America until the mid-1950s, people with disabilities were considered different and inferior to others in some way. As a result, many people with disabilities were hidden away, separated from the general society in large institutions, where they were kept isolated and received minimal care and attention. Parents who had given birth to a child with disabilities kept that child at home, hidden from others. Children with disabilities were often considered shameful, a punishment visited upon the child due to the parents' or the child's misbehavior. Formal education was generally not possible for these children. If a disability impeded what was considered "normal" day-to-day functioning, people with disabilities were treated as medical patients, categorized and "labeled" according to their medical condition only. If they were unable to function in mainstream society, or posed a threat or burden to others, they were placed in facilities, segregated from the rest of society, and provided with minimum care and very marginal conditions. These conditions prevailed until the 1970s, when, with more awareness of the rights of people with disabilities, these large, isolating institutions were closed.

Soldiers returned from wars with all kinds of physical and mental conditions, and they and their advocates found the conditions for those who needed care to be unacceptable. The voices of the wounded, who had served in the US military, their families, and their communities began to advocate for better care and accommodations. It was felt that these veterans, who had sacrificed with both body and mind for their country, were owed care and consideration, post-war and as long as needed, sometimes for their entire lifetime. In 1946, the Paralyzed Veterans of America (PVA) was formed, and it still serves as a sounding board for veterans and all people with disabilities regarding healthcare, benefits, rights, and research. The PVA has been directly involved as an advocate, both in legislation and in ensuring benefits. Along with other organizations like the World Institute on Disability, National Council on Disability, the United Nations Committee on the Rights of People with Disabilities, and The ARC (Association of Retarded Citizens) and others, it has served as one of the key resources for change. The US Constitution itself was used as the framework by which lawmakers and disability advocates created amendments and outlined the legal rights to treatment for people with disabilities.

An eminent early leader of the disability rights movement, Ed Roberts, who was diagnosed with polio at 14 years of age, was a major force in the deinstitutionalization of people with disabilities. He was the first student in a wheelchair to attend UC Berkeley, and, finding that no dormitory could accommodate his needs, was forced to live in the university's hospital. He founded the Independent Living Movement, co-founded the World Institute on Disability (WID), and was one of the most influential figures working to change legislation and promote a new social world of acceptance for people with disabilities. The Ed Roberts campus at UC Berkeley stands today as a fully accessible campus for students with and without disabilities to gather and learn. Other disability rights advocates include Justin Dart, who founded the American Association of People with Disabilities and was awarded the Presidential Medal of Freedom, and Judy Heumann, who organized sit-ins in support of the passage of laws for people with disabilities. They were also active in the passage of the ADA (see below).

Significant issues in disability rights have been addressed though both court cases and laws focused on ensuring justice and rights. Landmark court cases have been used a "sounding board" for new policies, and for procedures that protect the rights of people with disabilities.

B. Major disability rights court cases

These cases, listed in order of dates resolved, have had a major impact on the lives of people with disabilities. As can be seen, four of the six cases are related to education, and to the rights of children with disabilities to public education with accommodations to meet their needs with individualized programs, supporting the key role that education has in the lives of all people. The Olmstead case supported deinstitutionalization and the development of community support systems, while the United Airlines case addressed correctable vision.

- **Brown v Board of Education,** (1954), a case addressing segregation that is also used in an effort to mainstream people with disabilities into the community at large.

- **Mills v Board of Education of District of Columbia** (1972), which stated that public schools cannot exclude people with disabilities from education.

- **Southeastern Community College v Davis**, (1979), which outlined the laws of reasonable accommodation.

- **Sutton v United Airlines** (1999) focused on the definition of disability, and what that definition meant for the workplace, through the process of considering the use of corrective glasses to enable required visual acuity.
- **Olmstead v L.C.** (1999), which determined that people with mental illnesses have the right to live in the community, rather than in institutions.
- **Andrew F. v. Douglas County School District** (2017), which determined that public schools must offer individualized programs for students with disabilities.

C. Major disability laws

Disability laws seek to address discrimination, affirmative action, and the rights of people with disabilities. As can be seen, the original Rehabilitation Act addressed disability specifically, a category that was not included in the landmark Civil Rights Act. It served to motivate and inspire advocates and leaders of the disability rights movement and, 17 years later, resulted in the passage of the American with Disabilities Act, the signature law which currently guides programs, institutions, employers, and others in meeting non-discrimination standards. Building on the court cases listed above, the Education of All Handicapped Children Act moved laws and policies regarding the education of people with disabilities from the individual state level to a more inclusive, federal level.

> **The Rehabilitation Act of 1973** requires affirmative action in the workplace, and assures that people with disabilities cannot be discriminated against in programs that receive federal funding. The Rehabilitation

Act is often compared to the Civil Rights Act. The Civil Rights Act addressed discrimination based on race, religion, color, sex, and national origin. The Rehabilitation Act focuses on disability specifically, and has laid the groundwork for the American with Disabilities Act

The Education of all Handicapped Children Act of 1975, now called the **Individuals with Disabilities Education Act**, ensures that children with disabilities have the same access to education in all public-school systems.

The Americans with Disabilities Act of 1990 prohibits discrimination against individuals with disabilities in all aspects of public life. The ADA has created increased accessibility for people with disabilities, as well as increasing social awareness for the non-disabled.

Two key advocates for the passage of the ADA:

- Judy Heumann – Judy was diagnosed with polio at an early age and has been in a wheelchair her entire life. As a disability rights advocate, she played a significant role in the signing of the ADA, leading protests, and sit-ins, and speaking at events all over the country. She has dedicated her life to advancing rights and promoting policies and legislation that protect people with disabilities both in the United States and internationally. She has served under the presidencies of Clinton and Obama and, with Ed Roberts, co-founded the World Institute on Disability.[2]

- Justin Dart Jr – Referred to as "the father of the ADA", Justin has polio, and, in a wheelchair,has traveled the country to gather information and date in order to compile statistics related to the treatment of people with disabilities. He has served under both the Regan and Bush administrations and has spent his lifetime advocating for equal rights and the inclusion of people with disabilities in all aspects of life.[3]

D. Disability rights and clothing

Adaptive clothing to meet special needs has not,been considered a specific category of clothing historically, and often is still not considered so today. There are no court cases, laws, or policies mandating the production and availability of adaptive clothing, even though clothing is considered a basic human need for all people. As such, the design, production, and availability of clothing to meet special needs has been initiated and produced by private individuals and companies, and there are no laws or standards that guide production and distribution.

Adaptivewear is produced in regular sizing, with mainstream materials, and often needs to be altered, either by the person with the disability or by someone else, in order to be functional. Adaptive clothing has always been individually designable and creatable. However, with the Industrial Revolution (1760–1840) and the development of machinery enabling mass-produced clothing, the individual needs of people with disabilities could not easily be addressed. Often, people with disabilities simply wore larger sizes to allow extra room for movement and fit, tied material together, or cut holes in garments to accommodate special needs. Customized tailored clothing was expensive, and did not fit into the budgets of most consumers with disabilities. It was during this time that one of the first adaptive features was introduced by Gladys Reed, who was hearing impaired, and designed a belt with hip pockets to carry her hearing aid battery, rather than hand-carrying it or having it in a handbag. She also developed a woman's bra that had storage compartments, allowing smaller disability equipment to fit closer to the body.

Notable fashion designers and business planners had begun to create fashionable adaptive clothing long before the American disability movement. Between 1955 and 1976, more than 30 well-known clothing designers created adaptive garments under the brand "Functional Fashions". Helen Cookman, a businessperson with a hearing disability, realized that there was a sizable market in adaptive clothing for injured soldiers, who needed easy-to-reach pockets, as well as hidden adaptive openings and closures. Cookman co-authored *"Functional Fashion for the Physically Handicapped"*, and Virgina Pope, a NY Times style editor, gave her the "stamp of approval", with a foundation to run her business. The business flourished for over 20 years, and designers such as Pauline Trigere and Joseph Love collaborated with Cookman to create men's, women's, and children's clothing for special needs, with easy-to-reach pockets and hidden adaptive openings, both not too complicated to build into a design. Vera Maxwell, one of Cookman's most notable collaborators, designed the "Speed Suit", with adaptive textiles and features. The "Speed Suit" was a dressing ensemble specifically for people with disabilities. The suit had easy slip-on and slip-off features for anyone with hand dexterity issues that wanted to dress quickly. Maxwell also takes credit for the "Rugby Suit", a luxury suit that included a robe for wheelchair users. Maxwell was also one of the first designers to use "Pressure Tape" for closures, which developed into modern-day Velcro™. The most memorable collaboration, one with Levi's™ jeans, would be Cookman's last.[4]

The functional Levi's™ jeans included useful features such as stretch denim and full-length zips in the side seams that opened from the top or bottom. The zips also stopped anywhere along the seam. Another useful design feature was a special inside half belt buttoning on either side to hold the jeans in place when the seat dropped. The belt could also be reversed for a front drop. A roomy seat and easy-to-reach pockets were added benefits.[5]

After 1976, adaptivewear almost disappeared: it was expensive to produce and also was focused on a part of the American population that was not included in the "Liberalism" of the post-war era, where women's rights, gender-neutral work, and independence became the focus of attention. Then, in the 1980s, caregivers began to advocate for fashion-focused adaptive clothing to enable easier dressing and caring for people with disabilities. Manufacturers and designers were on board, but the focus of clothing design was related primarily to functional utility, and many of the adaptations were tagged as "medical". With a medical identity, garments were not recognized by the fashion world, and served as an indication of a person's disabilities rather than abilities.

It was not until 2014, 30 years after Cookman had passed away, that Danielle Sheypuk took her wheelchair and turned heads at New York Fashion Week. It was at that moment in time that celebrities such as Selma Blair opened the door to the field of acting and entertainment for people with disabilities, and that activists like Mindy Scheier both founded the Runway of Dreams and collaborated with Tommy Hilfiger on adaptive clothing designs. The fashion disability movement began then, in 2014, and continues until the present day, as people, both with and without disabilities, continue to engage with every moving part of the apparel industry to create awareness and promote inclusivity. Many of the adaptations in today's designs, such as side-open pants, easy-to-reach pockets, and alternatives to buttons and zippers, are remarkably like the adaptations from Cookman's original designs. As the adaptivewear movement continues today, its current intensity is fierce, and its spokespeople are unwavering. Victoria Jenkins, Stephanie Thomas, and collaborations with other high-profile activists and celebrities are key elements in initiating change in adaptivewear and fashion.

This intensity and activism do not mean that everyone studying fashion design or merchandising must create adaptive designs or market adaptive designs. What it does mean, however, is that to be present in the fashion world today, it is necessary to be educated and sensitive to the needs and rights of all people, including people with disabilities. Whenever there might be an opportunity to make a difference, whether by incorporating an adaptive feature in a design, accommodating shoppers with disabilities, supporting a cause, or simply passing on individual knowledge to the showroom next door, all contributions are vital. Fashion is expression, fashion is freedom, and fashion is identity, and those who are a part of the industry owe it to both the general population and to people with disabilities to be culturally aware of the shift in focus and the movement toward a more inclusive industry.[6]

E. Where society is today

Technology plays a key factor in communication. It allows messages to transmit instantly and connect with an accurate intended audience. Stephanie Thomas is an example of someone with a disability who is driven to instill awareness and create change for businesses and consumers. As a disability stylist, she has created unique ways to focus her entrepreneurial skills on both the business and consumer marketplace. The Podcast with Stephanie Thomas offers a pioneering voice in the world of fashion—one that speaks from personal experience, professional expertise, and a vision for true inclusivity. Born with disabilities herself, Stephanie brings over two decades of experience to the microphone every Tuesday. As the creator of the award-winning Disability Fashion Styling system, Stephanie has not only shaped her own career but has also defined an entirely new approach to fashion styling. It's crucial to note that Stephanie coined the term "Disability Fashion Stylist" to describe her specialized focus— serving the disability market as a fashion stylist. This distinction underscores her innovative approach to inclusive fashion. With graduate degrees in Communication and Fashion Journalism, coupled with her background as a Top 5 Nielsen Rated Radio Personality, Stephanie doesn't just talk about fashion—she provides actionable insights that empower her listeners to express their personal style confidently. This podcast serves a community often overlooked by mainstream fashion: disabled fashion enthusiasts. Additionally, Stephanie has conversations with fashion lovers from the tech, academic, and fashion industries, bringing diverse perspectives to the discussion. Stephanie's approach isn't about dictating what's "right" in fashion. Instead, she's creating a space where her audience can explore, learn, and grow in their personal style journey, guided by someone who truly understands their experiences and challenges. Two weeks a month, listeners get direct access to Stephanie's expertise and her award-winning Disability Fashion Styling system. She shares practical strategies for navigating the shopping experience, making confident style choices, and advocating for one's needs in the fashion world—all informed by her firsthand understanding of living with disabilities and working as a stylist for Tony, Emmy, and Independent Award–nominated actors with disabilities. On alternate weeks, Stephanie brings in guests who are passionate about fashion and equity within the industry. These conversations go beyond surface-level discussions, diving deep into the future of inclusive fashion and providing listeners with valuable insider knowledge. Most importantly, this podcast is both fun and culture-shifting, highlighting the voices of disabled and non-disabled fashion lovers. From analyzing the work of groundbreaking photographers to dissecting the innovations of iconic designers, the show connects the dots between fashion history and the present-day push for inclusivity. Stephanie's focus isn't on fleeting trends but on equipping her audience with the knowledge needed to fully participate in the world of style.

"Disability Fashion Stylist: The Podcast" isn't trying to appeal to everyone. It's for those who want to be part of a movement toward true inclusivity in style, led by someone who lives this reality every day and has developed a system to address it. By tuning in, listeners aren't just consuming content—they're joining a community of forward-thinking individuals, who refuse to be sidelined in the fashion conversation. They're gaining access to Stephanie's groundbreaking Disability Fashion Styling System, acquiring tools to change how they interact with fashion, and in turn, how the fashion industry interacts with them. This isn't just a podcast. It's a movement toward a more stylish, more inclusive world—one episode at a time, guided by a pioneer who's not only walked the path but has paved the way for others with her innovative approach to disability fashion styling.

Contributed by Stephanie Thomas
Case study: Zappos

Dana Zumbo has had a lifetime career in the retail industry, starting in Miami, Florida. During her 15-year career in Miami, she found herself challenging her co-workers to volunteer with some of the organizations that her company supported in the community. She became incredibly involved with the Special Olympics and supported their events for multiple years while living in Miami. She was also a Big Brothers/Big Sisters volunteer, for ten years with the same family. The relationships she built with the community kept her motivated toward making a positive impact on others' lives. She found this to be fulfilling, both emotionally and professionally.

After moving to Las Vegas, Nevada, Dana became involved with the local disability community—kick-starting an Adaptive Splash Swim program at her local community center that continues to thrive today. Through this swim program, she reconnected with the Special Olympics and became a swim coach for a team of athletes. She worked directly with the autism community, eventually joining the Board of Directors for Families for Effective Autism Treatment (FEAT), a local organization that supports families who are affected by autism.

Dana has been at Zappos for over 15 years and has focused on disability inclusion for the past 8 years. At Zappos, everything revolves around customer engagement and experience. The business has been "customer-obsessed" for over 25 years. She has helped to bring the curated shopping experience, Zappos Adaptive, to life on the Zappos site. The goal was to offer everyone options that were functional, that fit their needs, and that were fashionable—so that they could express themselves through their own personal style.

The sole responsibility of the entire department of the Zappos customer service agents is to take very special care of their customers. The retailer's attention to service and to the customer has been their differentiator in the world of retail. Dana notes the reality of multiple retailers, carrying the same products, and the need for Zappos to have a differentiator to make their business stand apart from the competition. Zappos employment practices include an immersive training program for all new hires, which, when first launched, was unheard of in the retail industry. In this training program, employees learn the importance of customer engagement and acquire the necessary skill set that enables them to provide the level of service that continues to drive Zappos' success.

Zappos Adaptive evolved from their experiences with a customer, Tonya, who called in to return a pair of shoes she had bought for her grandson, Gabriel. Tonya shared that Gabriel has autism and cannot tie his own shoelaces. She was looking for a Puma shoe that was designed with a hook-and-loop closure instead of traditional laces, but it was not available in the size Gabriel needed. Hearing about Gabriel's needs, Saul Dave, a Senior Director at Zappos, began to do research and came to understand both the need for adaptive and universally designed footwear, and the scarcity of the product in the market. Determined to find a solution, Saul reached out to Zappos' employees.

Dana saw an email with the story of Tonya and Gabriel, explaining that Saul was looking for a solution to better serve all customers, and she wanted to help. Her problem-solving strategy began with research. The retailer then conducted in-person and remote focus groups, compiled relevant statistics related to the population, and learned as much as possible about the competition. They studied disability, diversity, culture, ethnicity, demographics, psychographics, geographics, and any other market category the Centers for Disease Control and the Census Bureau could identify. At the time, there were no retailers who had products that filled this void in the marketplace. Tommy Hilfiger had just launched Tommy Adaptive, and Silverts catered mostly to an older demographic. Through their research, Zappos learned that the disability population was the largest minority population both in the United States and worldwide. This presented an opportunity for Zappos: to take its company mission of exceptional customer service and to dive into an untapped market segment. At the same time, Tonya commented on her own experiences, saying, "I am honored, and so proud, that we still have companies who care about changing lives, and that put their customers and employees first above the bottom line."

When Zappos Adaptive launched, the primary goal was to pro-vide options for easy dressing. Billy Price, the founder of BILLY Footwear, was launching his namesake brand at the same time, and it became one of Zappos' first suppliers, filling a specific need in footwear. With Zappos as leaders in the footwear industry, and with the relationships that the Zappos Adaptive team had, and were continuing to build, with their customers, they also con-tinued to work with other big brands and in discussing how to incorporate more accessible designs within their footwear. This led the Zappos team to do focus groups that included fit-and-wear testing and to ensure that people with disabilities were included in the process from beginning to end. Zappos worked with influencers, and models with disabilities, to share the stories behind their products, to ensure that their voices reflected an authentic point of view.

The Zappos website is curated to provide the customer with the ability to shop for features, functions, and fit. It is important to note that Zappos Adaptive does not produce its own brand of shoes. Rather, it is a multi-brand retailer that carries a wide selec-tion of footwear, along with complementary apparel, accesso-ries, and more.

One of Zappos Adaptive's goals is to provide options that can enable everyone to be able to express themselves through fash-ion. Dana expresses that Zappos Adaptive has had much suc-cess with its brands over the last five years, but there is always more to do.

Dana Zumbo interviewed by Susan Kolko

Discussion: What are some of the key factors in Dana Zumbo's career path that led her to Zappos Adaptive? Why would these factors be relevant for the Zappos brand? How does Zappos increase brand value by offering an adaptive line?

Case study: Runway of Dreams

Mindy Scheier is the founder and CEO of Runway of Dreams and GAMUT Management. With her background in fashion design and merchandising, she created the Runway of Dreams, a foundation with the goal of empowering people with disabilities by providing them with access to fashionable clothing. She was inspired by her son Oliver, who has muscular dystrophy but wanted to wear jeans like everyone else. Runway of Dreams raises awareness, educates consumers, advocates for industry change, and helps to develop the next generation of innovators and leaders in the field of adaptive fashion. Mindy's fact-driven, emotional TEd talk has made an impact on more than a million viewers. In the meantime, Oliver, who had struggled during COVID to keep his physical self healthy, has blossomed into a young adult with character and style!

Mindy feels strongly that the next generation of innovators will regard the category of Adaptive clothing no differently than plus sizes and petites. Her foundation enables educational programs that support the development of adaptive clothing, fashion, style, design, marketing, business, technology, and event production. She works closely with designers to modify tech packs, ensuring modifications that will make these products accessible and functional for people with disabilities. She believes that education plays a pivotal role in change and works closely with Dr Kerri McBee Black, a professor at the University of Missouri, currently one of the leading academics in the field of adaptive clothing. Mindy also works regularly with students in the textile and apparel management program at the University of Missouri. She collaborates with Dr McBee-Black in efforts to bring awareness and to share expertise related to opportunities and needs in the adaptive clothing market. Mindy supports the University of Missouri's capstone program and praises their efforts in developing Adaptive collections. Mindy is also aware that Parsons and FIT are working to include adaptive apparel in their curriculums. She comments on the value of education, and the role it plays in advancing adaptive clothing into mainstream apparel categories. Her methodology is focused on ease of dressing, and she feels confident that the apparel industry, through exposure and education, will move toward treating disability fashion as an opportunity.

Mindy feels strongly that everyone engaging in conversations about marketing, or consumerism should speak the same language, and use the same vocabulary for the adaptive space. While she recognizes that Universal Design and inclusivity are very important, she believes that adapative design should really focus on the inclusion of people with disabilities in the design thought process. The word "adaptive" itself, she says, implies using or choosing something that already exists, and modifying or "adapting" it so that it is easier for more people to wear. However, she believes it is essential to recognize that, for example, pants specifically designed for someone who uses a wheelchair generally wouldn't work well for someone who is ambulatory: they cannot be worn comfortably while standing and walking. Hence the term "Universal Design" is not applicable to all of the clothing needs of all people. There are too many possible tangents that could be interpreted with a vocabulary that is not disability-specific. The word "adaptive" defines a resource that is specifically for people with disabilities. It is an easily understood term that can serve as a category, and people with disabilities are responsive to its message.

Mindy is also well aware of the barriers to entry in social media. The algorithms do not understand people with disabilities, which affects the ability of a specifically designed product to reach the people who need it. The algorithms can also prevent people with disabilities from reaching the product. The push/pull marketing strategy cannot be applicable, because the current algorithms do not enable either side to move forward. Hopefully, software and technology, with the help of brand and disability advocates, can raise awareness so that social media will join forces and create space for the algorithms to connect, rather than disconnect, people with disabilities from needed resources.

Chapter 7 expands on government support for adaptive clothing. In the United States, this support is non-existent, with the exception of a small budget allotment for veterans. Mindy feels that adaptive clothing should be part of flexible spending which would allow people with disabilities to use pre-tax income to pay for clothing. A major challenge is that the category of adaptive clothing exists in the world of fashion, rather than in the world of medicine and healthcare. Without the medical label, which Adaptive designers, brands, and marketers do not want, financial assistance will not be available in the foreseeable future. In addition, there are no available benefits for adaptive clothing businesses importing goods. Tariffs and taxes apply to this category the same as to other clothing categories. However, a magnet that enables ease of dressing costs a lot more than a button, and magnets are generally produced overseas. If the entire industry shifts toward magnetic closures, quantity itself would drive the price down. Another potential way to drive the price down would be to use innovative design in manufacturing to minimize cost differences.

The more brands, awareness, innovations, and technology are developed to exist in the Adaptive space, the smaller the gap will become between Adaptive apparel and cultural acceptance. Mindy also launched GAMUT Management in 2019 to help companies find authentic ways to create products for, engage with, and represent people with disabilities. The progress she has initiated and fostered along her path has no limits.

Mindy Scheier interviewed by Susan Kolko

Discussion: Consider the multiple ways Mindy Scheier is initiating public awareness for inclusion of adaptive clothing in the world of fashion. What are some of the biggest challenges? Why does she believe that education plays such an important part in the adaptive movement? Why or why not is it realistic for adaptive to be included as a category of clothing?

Summary

The disability movement is a recent one in American history. Policymakers and disability advocates have paved the way for social change. Court cases and laws have mandated rights for people with disabilities and supported rights to a place in the general society. General Civil Rights laws as well as specific laws currently protect these rights, especially in the areas of education and employment. The disability population is aware of their legal rights, and businesses are also aware of their obligations to meet compliance standards. Adaptive designers have produced accessible, functional clothing since 1950. However, it has not been until recent years that consumers utilizing the category of adaptive clothing have demonstrated a demand in the marketplace for stylish, affordable fashions. Today, customers with disabilities, their families and caregivers, and the businesses that provide specific adaptive products have entered into mainstream American marketing efforts. Zappos Adaptive is one of the brands of adaptive clothing and is striving to address special needs, including providing a special website for easy accessibility for all. It is the responsibility of designers, manufacturers, wholesalers, retailers, merchandisers, consultants, trade associates, and marketers to use the ADA as the foundation—not only for the normalization of the clothing labeled adaptivewear but also for the creation of fashions, shopping environments, and business plans that facilitate, support, and promote comfortable and fashionable clothing for people with disabilities.

Learning activities

- If you were a policymaker or disability advocate, what issues might you see on the horizon?

- Create an apparel industry timeline of the disability rights movement and adaptivewear. This can be either in a visual interpretation or in written format. Consider vocabulary, brands, and styles.

- Review 2–3 recent news publications and/or video content related to fashion and disability. Identify common issues and options for solutions.

- Research government agencies and fashion resources that might be able to collaborate to ensure that people with disabilities have equal access to fashionable, functional clothing.

- Discuss possible reasons why the Civil Rights Act was not simply amended to include people with disabilities.

Adaptive talk

- Civil Rights Movement
- Americans with Disabilities Act
- Handicapped Children Act
- Rehabilitation Act
- Paralyzed Veterans of America
- Danielle Sheypuk
- Helen Cookman
- Vera Maxwell
- Levis™
- speed suit
- pressure tape

- *Functional Fashions for the Physically Handicapped*
- *Disability Fashion Styling System*
- Stephanie Thomas

Case studies

- Zappos Adaptive – Dana Zumba
- Runway of Dreams – Mindy Scheier

2
Defining the adaptive market

Introduction

A "market" has a wide variety of definitions. In the field of "*Adaptive Clothing*," "market" is defined as the consumer market, and it consists of customers who want, and need, adaptive clothing. These potential customers may include the actual end user, or an individual or organization that is purchasing the product for the end user. Adaptive clothing is often purchased by others on behalf of the person with the disabling condition. It is considered a market segment of the broader apparel industry market, one that serves the clothing needs of people with disabilities. The customers for this market segment have various characteristics that define the specific needs for the market's products, similar to the market segment of people who purchase the special size clothing which serves big, tall, large, and small specialty sizes.

Markets also identify potential consumers by considering environmental, economic, and lifestyle factors. For example, as a result of the COVID-19 pandemic, it is a known factor that people are working and spending more time at home. As a result of this change, apparel needs have shifted. There has been a clearly trackable movement toward the purchase of sportswear and active wear. The challenge for the apparel industry then becomes: how does this general trend affect individual consumer segments? For example, how has this trend affected the clothing for people with disabilities? What might this mean from a design and marketing perspective? The most common, relatable, and calculated characteristics for identifying market size and function are demographics, psychographics, geographics, and behavior.

Data sources

Several sources of data have been accessed for this chapter and may also be accessed by readers. The United States Department of Labor and Statistics, the Bureau of the Census, and the Federal Trade Commission are three of the most widely used resources for general data on populations. Data related to disability may be found on the U.S. Bureau of the Census, National Health Statistics, Bureau of Health Statistics, and the World Health Organization websites. Specific data related to the apparel industry may be found in both trade associations and professional organizations that track statistics, such as the National Retail Federation, RetailNext, Nielsen, and the Kantar group.

To access specific data effectively, it is important to be able to define the consumer segment based on characteristics that will best serve the end user. The disability consumer market can be defined as the segment of the population that purchases products adapted to their specific needs. As people with disabilities have a variety of conditions, and a wide range of limitations within these, it is a challenge to meet needs on a mass-market scale. Another consideration in the adaptive clothing market is the number of people without disabilities, who might find the accessibility and inclusivity aspect of the product or brand comfortable and desirable. Therefore, even though the world's population living with some level of disability is 15 percent, the potential market for products is greater. Statistics related to the disability population are key factors driving business strategy, and should be considered essential knowledge for any business or design team that caters to the adaptive market.

As stated above, statistics compiled by the World Health Organization and the Centers for Disease Control in 2023 note that 15 percent of the world's population lives with a disability, but this is not equally distributed by age, and the proportion of people with disabilities in the population increases as people become older. The older portion is a huge market segment, amounting to over 1 billion people.

The one in four adults in the United States living with a disability includes both people with a documented disabling condition and people living with a disability without seeking specific medical attention for their condition. For example, footwear tends to be one of the more common challenges as one ages, and many shoes no longer fit comfortably. Fashionable shoes, especially for women, are exchanged for shoes that are comfortable, safe, and practical. This is not necessarily considered a disability, but it creates a consumer demand for a product that satisfies needs, and that is not often at the forefront in advertising or considered "fashionable" according to the traditional standards of fashion. Billy Shoes, Friendly Shoes, Zappos Adaptive, and PLAE are examples of footwear companies that have created products addressing many of the needs of this market. From young children to seniors, market research is a necessary component in producing a shoe that satisfies adaptive needs. All four of the shoe companies mentioned have been interviewed for this book, and their experiences and business models will be explored in later chapters.

In the United States, disabilities are often grouped into specific categories, such as mobility, cognition, hearing, and vision, which may range from severe to mild. Individuals may be affected by one or more disabilities in these groupings. A disabling condition may necessitate modifications and changes in the affected individual's daily routine. In addition, the disability may be intermittent or episodic, stable and constant, or progressive. These categories, based on studies of the adult population, can be broken down into numbers and percentages to enable strategic business planning. For example, if a business knows that the largest percentage of disability among its actual and potential customers is related to mobility, it can create shopping experiences, and seek designers, who create fashions catering to the needs of this group, and, as a result, capture and satisfy a broader consumer base.

Figure 2 Rollettes wheelchair dance team

Learning objectives

- Understand the characteristics of the disability market segment
- Understand disability groupings and some of the special needs these can create
- Understand the distinct types of market research that apply to disability and fashion
- Understand how to meet the needs of consumers with disabilities from the direct experiences of business owners
- Identify attributes related to products for people with disabilities
- Understand the role technology plays in closing the accessibility gap
- Understand how a business can best strategize marketing efforts and ensure best practices

- Define the common groupings of characteristics for consumer markets based on demographic, psychographic, geographic, and behavioristic qualities.
- Understand that the number of people in the market changes in relation to environmental factors

A. The market, fashion, and disability

It is essential to consider the statistics noted above—that 15 percent of the world's population has a disability—and to be aware that this rate increases markedly for adults over 65, the aging population. The World Health Organization reports that disability varies from region to region, and is dependent upon income. These are essential considerations in both the development of marketing strategies and the fashionable design of adaptive-wear. The United States Centers for Disease Control specify the nature of disabilities by percentages: the two largest numbers are 12 percent with cognitive disabilities, and 14 percent with mobility limitations, which can include inability to ambulate, and limitations in arm and hand movement, head movement, general body positioning and dexterity, while 8 percent have independent living limitations. Additionally, 6 percent are hearing impaired, 6 percent are vision impaired, and 4 percent are unable to manage self-care.

These numbers indicate that the market size of consumers with disabilities in the United States is considerable, and that market size increases with age. Therefore, the largest proportion of this consumer market is aging adults. Aging baby boomers and the advances in medical research and care directly impact these statistics. As noted above, there is also a demand in the market for products that address disabilities by the non-disabled population. As a result, the general adaptivewear market segment becomes even larger. The challenge for the fashion industry is to design, manufacture, advertise, and provide a retail experience that promotes inclusivity, values diversity, and supports sustainable business practices to address the specific needs of the disability population.

1. Demographic data

Demographic data can be defined as researched, quantifiable information, compiled by legitimate sources and not limited to government agencies, trade associations, or marketing groups. This data may also include customer tracking, benchmark studies, and internal organizational sources such as sales reports.

Historically, demographics have been defined by age, income, gender, education, family size, home ownership, marital status, occupation, and race. However, environmental and cultural changes have prompted a need for category adjustments. For example, gender demographics may no longer be defined simply as the male or female category assigned at birth. Race is no longer clearly defined due to the blurring of traditional racial markers and the sizable portion of multi-racial people. Rather, race currently tends to be defined by the culture with which an individual identifies. Education is not limited to high school, two-year, four-year, or graduate degrees, and today can include on-the-job training, certification programs, independent studies, and experiences. Disability as a demographic category is a recent addition as well.

People with disabilities as a market segment may be defined both by the disabling condition and the degree, or severity, of that condition. For example, people who are visually impaired may be near- or far-sighted, have blurred vision, double vision, loss of color-identifying ability, poor night vision, blindness, or vision limitations as a symptom of another illness. When designing or selecting products for people with disabilities, certain attributes are particularly essential in ensuring that the products are usable, accessible, and meet the specific needs of this very diverse group. The importance of these attributes varies, depending on the type and severity of the disability, as well as individual preferences and needs. However, some key attributes are universally recognized as essential in product design for people with disabilities.

Current statistics from The United States Census Bureau state:

- 40 percent of adults aged 65 or older report having a disability.
- 5 percent of children under the age of 14 have a moderate to severe disability.
- Women have more disabling conditions than men.
- Regions with lower incomes have higher rates of disability.
- In the United States, 20 percent of the labor force have a disability.
- Mobility impairments are the most common disabling condition.
- People with disabilities are less likely to receive an education.
- People with disabilities tend to have short life expectancies.[7]

Demographics, fashion, and disability

Market research plays a vital role in creating brands and shopping experiences that satisfy the disability market. It is essential to explore all the demographic data available. Demographic data can also assist businesses to understand the potential impact of specific disabilities by utilizing data such as age, gender, income, race, education, and stage in the family life cycle. Gender-specific demographics have changed drastically in the past ten years to include non-binary consumers. Considerations for the non-binary adaptive consumer may be a smaller market segment, but exploration of gender-neutral styles and fashions can enable the manufacture of these in larger quantities, leading to lower production costs and retail prices for consumers, thus making the styles more affordable.

2. Psychographic data

Psychographics are another form of consumer segment identification, providing quantifiable data in relation to lifestyles, values, and consumerism. This is particularly important as a consumer's personality, interests, and habits often drive purchases. Psychographics focus on why consumers buy what they buy, shop where they shop, and spend what they spend. Marketing plays a significant role in guiding businesses toward the creation of an optimal, customer-specific atmosphere for consumer segments in response to psychographics. For example, demographic information may note that there might be only a certain number of potential buyers for a particular line of products, due to cost. With strategic marketing tools derived from psychographic studies, businesses can capture a larger market segment for these products by advertising and promoting them in a more financially attainable manner, through offering long-term credit, or frequent sales.

Psychographics related to the population with disabilities provide additional considerations that are pivotal for business strategy. These include health and wellness, pain points, interests and goals, and cultural values and beliefs, as well as communication methods and strategies—all high priorities in developing markets. Generally, people with disabilities

- want to be independent
- are very health conscious
- value community support
- appreciate disability activists
- do not like to feel alone
- struggle with mental health and esteem issues
- value accessibility, diversity, and equal rights
- desire to work and be creative
- obtaining higher education can be challenging
- find that working remotely is agreeable.[8]

Psychographics, fashion, and disability

Fashion is a visible, physical representation of psychographics, often indicating individual lifestyles, interests, personalities, attitudes, challenges, goals, and emotions. The public, including people with disabilities, value honesty, sustainability, and beauty, but people with disabilities are often especially aware of costs, an essential consideration in business planning.

In relation to certain customer characteristics, clothing brands are especially able to illuminate and represent individuality from a psychographic perspective. Knowing what the consumer values enables accurate product placement and marketing. In fashion, brand loyalty, accessibility, empowerment, and cost are key components of clothing and style choices for people with disabilities. Both a brand's transparency and its accessibility to consumers can influence product choice. IZ Adaptive and ASOS Curve brands have tapped into all aspects of psychographics in creating accurate product selections coupled with customer experience that promotes brand loyalty.

Psychographics may also include a consideration of the special importance of pets in the lives of many people with disabilities. Pets provide emotional support, as well as assistance with daily routines. They are also a form of expression, a key to broadening socialization opportunities, and are especially important in that they can enable a person with a disability, sometimes personally dependent, to provide care for another living creature. In recent years, clothing for pets, sometimes referred to as "pet couture", has become a distinct way for pet owners to express themselves: dressing their pets can illustrate personal interests and tastes, and many pet stores now carry extensive lines of fashionable clothing. Hair accessories, collars, jackets, booties, and seasonal costumes for pets are mass-marketed, as well as designed with high-fashion styling. The fashion needs, tastes of the pet owner, and the owner's ability to dress their pet are important to consider when designing clothing for pets!

3. Behavioristic data

Behavioristic data reflects how and why a consumer purchases a specific product. Consumer markets can be tracked by considering average spending, days of the week and time purchases are made, return percentages, and average prices per item, as well as brand-driven analytics. The most accurate resource for behavioristic data is consumer-based analytics. For example, adaptive clothing may more often be purchased online than in stores, simply due to accessibility. This information can inform business planning and ensure the creation of a website which uses adaptive software and is user-friendly, customer services that minimize returns, payment options that are realistic, and product design that is in the queue with trends. The adaptive market differs from the larger market, especially in relation to certain characteristics, such as adaptive behaviors, social behaviors, health and wellness, lifestyle, self-advocacy, and financial management. It is also important to recognize that the ability to utilize a specific item may vary, depending on the nature of the disabling condition, and whether it is constant, or varies with time, physical activity, or other factors.

The Centers for Disease Control reports that people with disabilities

- are brand loyal
- have accessibility challenges
- have sizing challenges
- enjoy outdoors
- participate in sports
- are concerned about safety

- are interested in the latest technology
- prefer online shopping
- are concerned about health and tracking health
- enjoy gaming
- are concerned about costs and budget
- prefer brands and retailers that are inclusive[9]

Behavior, fashion, and disability

There are several specific areas where trackable behavior related to disability and fashion cross paths. Practicality and usage are predominant, and functional needs, such as magnetic closures and modified pattern proportions, are a high priority in adaptivewear design. Accessibility considerations related to availability and affordability continue to be a marketing challenge. Social media, or flagging a marketing effort of an adaptive brand with a photo of someone in a wheelchair, does not help to make products accessible to people with disabilities. The high price of magnetic closures often makes retail prices too high for many adaptive consumers. In addition, the desire for self-expression and inclusivity are guiding motives for consumer behavior in general.

While the average consumer may be able to easily find fashions from luxury to budget, and from high fashion to fast fashion, this broad range of fashion is often not accessible to people with disabilities. Aside from universal accessories, such as handbags, sunglasses, jewelry, and make-up, people with disabilities often find that fashion comes with a high ticket price, due to its specialized nature and more limited market. One recent, and still developing, response to this problem is the emergence of Universal Design, which expands the more restricted consumer base by introducing special sizing, more adaptable textiles, and price points that are realistic for both the general public and people with disabilities. Nike FlyEase shoes are a noteworthy example of Universal Design.

Trendy, sustainable brands that cater to niche markets, such as Lululemon, Patagonia, Reformation, and Supreme, have retail prices which are not realistic for most people with disabilities. From a strictly business strategy perspective, it might not be profitable for these brands to create adaptive lines. However, the concept of Universal Design allows brands to potentially take a beginning step toward expanding product selection, including a larger consumer population, and recognizing the need to consider moving beyond simply standard sizing and styles.

4. Geographic data

Geographic data helps businesses to plan locations according to segmented populations. Cities, states, regions, and zip codes are common categories utilized in determining geographic information. Businesses can track where potential consumer markets are located based on delivery and transportation reports, which are generated as products are shipped. For example, Silverts, one of the largest online adaptivewear retailers, tracks their consumer market by product purchases related to delivery locations. Geographics can also be useful in planning retail locations for people with disabilities by considering population size and distribution, accessibility, economic and financial status, and living conditions.

There are population clusters of people with disabilities in certain regions, often related to general accessibility and the availability of health care for particular conditions. Craig Hospital, in Denver, CO., for example, serves patients with all levels of paraplegia and quadriplegia, and major limitations in mobility and their families, offering in-patient and out-patient care. This creates a greater special needs population density and provides a more concentrated market for adaptivewear than the general population.

Geographics can also be identified within an organization by analyzing which stores, in which areas, have sold specific adaptivewear items, to whom, and at what price. This allows a business to have a clear picture of the year ahead, enabling planning for the entire omni-channel system.

The World Health Organization reports:

- Wealthier nations have lower rates of disability (Europe and N. America)
- Poorer nations have higher rates of disability (South Asia and third world Africa)
- In Latin America and the Caribbean, 12 percent of the population has a disability
- Urban areas report higher rates of disability
- Rural areas report lower rates of disability
- In lower-income areas, children with disabilities have a higher rate of not attending school
- Employment varies by region but lower-income nations have higher rates of disability
- Higher-income countries can provide more access to transportation, education, employment, and support

- Culture varies by region and the values that are attached to culture directly affect people with disabilities
- Higher-income regions have more laws, policies, and legislation that support people with disabilities.[10]

Geographics, fashion, and disability

Certain regions in the United States tend to have higher numbers, or clusters, of people with disabilities. These areas are generally related to healthcare access, aging populations, environmental conditions, work hazards, and economic conditions. Statistics illustrate that there are higher poverty rates, as well as larger aging populations, in the southeastern United States. Due to lack of readily available healthcare, rural areas and farmlands tend to have fewer people with disabilities. Coal mining areas and other hazardous working environments tend to have more health-related issues among the population, so more people with disabilities. Most post-industrial areas, such as Flint, Michigan, where the auto industry once thrived, and the areas around the Great Lakes called the "Rust Belt", where factories and manufacturing were dominant a century ago, have populations with many disabilities related to conditions experienced during those early years. Areas near military bases with high deployment rates, such as the U.S. Army's Fort Bragg and Fort Hood, and areas where military veterans tend to retire due to tax exemptions and healthcare benefits, such as Virginia, Florida, and Texas, also tend to have higher numbers of people with disabilities.

Geographic clusters like these can be found all over the world, often related to job opportunities, family history, and economic factors.

What do these geographic data mean for adaptive fashion? The combination of aging populations, health issues, and low income does not necessarily enable the purchase of high-fashion adaptive clothing. However, this is clearly an excellent potential business opportunity for adaptivewear.

5. Income data

Income plays an important role in segmenting populations around consumer spending, social class identification, and healthcare expenditures. Historically, in the United States, income has strongly influenced an individual's opportunity for higher education. However, in recent years, state governments and new legislation have prioritized the availability of higher education for lower-income people. Similarly, healthcare is now more widely available to all. Income is an essential factor to consider related to people with disabilities. Often, the ability to fulfill job requirements includes high-functioning physical as well as cognitive skills. Depending upon the severity and the nature of a person's disability, work performance and productivity may be strongly affected. Standards and laws passed in recent years, detailed in Chapter One, have assisted people with disabilities to have equal access to employment, but jobs available are often minimum-wage or part-time positions, many of which do not lead to advancement, often due to an individual's limited ability to perform tasks at a higher level.

There are several essential factors to consider related to income and people with disabilities. Employment rates are lower, and income is lower. Lower income may create barriers to education, and a lack of education may limit optimal financial planning. In addition, poverty levels are often higher because low-income people with disabilities have higher healthcare costs in proportion to their income. Two government-subsidized programs provide the greatest support for income-related challenges for people with disabilities: Social Security Disability Insurance (SSDI), and Supplemental Security Income (SSI). The Americans with Disabilities Act (ADA) helps to protect and ensure employment and equitable pay scales for people with disabilities. In addition, employers are required, and often reimbursed, for expenses incurred in the provision of reasonable accommodations for people with disabilities in the workplace.

The World Bank reports that people with disabilities:

- poverty rate is higher for people with disabilities
- unemployment rate is higher
- 20 percent of people with disabilities have jobs
- employment is more challenging due to lack of skills
- employment rate is lower due to lack of education
- have higher income in nations that have laws and policies in place
- lower-income nations have a larger gap in earnings for people with disabilities
- have higher cost of living
- face discrimination and exclusion which impact income
- technology provides for accessibility in income
- start their own businesses to be financially independent[11]

Income, fashion, and disability

Chapter 4 will explore the need and the desire for people with disabilities to "fit in". Clothing plays a significant role, as it provides a clear, visible representation of personal values, and of the culture with which individuals identify. The ability to purchase mass-marketed, brand-named fashion is affected by both the limited availability of adaptive clothing and the costs of brand-name fashion. Adaptive clothing tends to be higher priced due to several factors: the lower quantities produced, the need for attention and detail related to design, the high prices of the textiles and materials involved, the need for customization and size fitting, and the higher amount of research required in the design process. Target, Tommy Hilfiger, Zappos, Kohl's, and J.C. Penney are some of the mass-market retailers currently carrying adaptive clothing lines.

It is important for a business to know the general income level of its consumers in order to provide affordable products and services. The Department of Labor and Statistics and the U.S. Bureau of Census both provide these statistics. The average person over 16 years of age, with a disability, earns $23,000 a year, as opposed to the $35,000 earned by the average person without a disability. Approximately 20 percent of people with disabilities are employed, as opposed to the 63 percent who are employed without a disability. In addition, people with disabilites have a higher poverty rate. Approximately 27 percent of people with disabilities live in poverty, as opposed to 13 percent of people without a disability. Factors driving these numbers relate to lack of education, as well as to the higher proportion of people in lower-level and part-time employment. Social Security Disability Insurance and Supplemental Security Income programs, subsidized by the government, assist people with disabilities by providing additional income and resources, but a substantial income gap remains between the average person with a disability and the average person who is not disabled.

B. Typical product attributes

As noted above, people with disabilities regularly participate in two clothing market segments: the larger, general apparel consumer market, and the smaller, or niche market of adaptive clothing consumers, specifically designed for special needs. Frequently, the adaptive clothing consumer's goal is to be able to wear fashions that are on trend in the mass-market segments. However, a person's disabling condition and the frequent lack of style in adaptive clothing may limit this possibility.

Attributes are the specific qualities that make a product desirable and include price, quality, brand name, variety of services, functionality, customer service, exclusive offers, promotional campaign, packaging, convenience of purchase, location, guarantees, store/office décor, and payment terms. These attributes may be prioritized differently for people with disabilities. For example, the brand name of a clothing item might be more important than its actual functionality, and the special guarantees offered related to product performance might help to alleviate the stress related to cost. Some attributes can be abstract, and not directly within the control of the marketer, such as receiving a compliment from a friend about a particular clothing item. Compliments about appearance are positive experiences, which increase the perceived value of the item for the consumer. Similarly, the number of "likes" one might get on a social media post increases the perceived value of an item.

Often, the apparel industry uses Universal Design to assist in streamlining the adaptive market. Universal Design aims to promote accessibility for all, by considering flexibility, simplicity, and ease of use, in addition to design itself. Universal Design products have unique product features that can meet the needs of niche markets as well as the broader general market. Nike's Fly Ease shoes are an example of a global brand with a product line that can be worn by a niche market within a product range. Trimming, such as magnetic strips and Velcro™, are often used in both Universal Design and adaptivewear.

Adaptive clothing uses much of the same universal approach. However, the design of the product must also include the features or qualities tailored to the needs of specific disabling conditions. For example, pant measurements are proportioned differently for the person in a seated position for extended periods. This design would not be of use to anyone who does not need a wheelchair, or otherwise confined to a seated position. Conducting this research can be challenging, as the goal is to have both function and fashion in the same product.

C. Market research

The term "market research" describes the activity of compiling data and information related to a particular subject matter. The results of this research are then converted into workable content to enable accurate business planning. Types of market research include: previous sales, surveys, consumer panels, focus groups, computer databases, electronic feedback, virtual reality, and intelligent retail technologies. It can be challenging for a business to separate mass-market research from research on specific market segments. Technology plays a major role, as software and information systems are used to gather to both gather information and process consumer demand. Companies with the latest technology are able to pinpoint specific needs related to people with disabilities.

Some specific topics to consider in market research related to fashion and disability include an awareness of current laws and ethical practices related to disability. It is important to be aware that legislation varies from nation to nation, state to state, and community to community. The Library of Congress, government, and legal websites, social media, and academic research can provide accurate, up-to-date statistics, laws, and policies related to any sizable market.

Considerations, such as "made in USA" awareness, ethical and social responsibility, and environmental sustainability in relation to the market segment are also important. For example, there has been a substantial movement toward more sustainable clothing on a mass-market level—but how does this affect the disability market? In many instances, adaptive clothing must be custom-made to meet specific needs. This might create more options, such as utilizing sustainable brands, which can be altered, as well as clothing upcycled from thrift and consignment shopping. The following are external resources for market research:

1. Magazines and trade publications

There are several notable magazines and trade publications that emphasize fashion for people with disabilities. Some focus exclusively on disability, such as *Disability Horizons, New Mobility,*

Ability, and *Wearable Therapy by Tokki.* Other magazines are also inclusive of disability and regularly post articles and interviews on adaptive clothing, such as Vogue, Elle, and Fashion Revolution. Trade publications, such as *The Journal of Fashion Marketing and Management*, occasionally cover adaptive clothing topics too.

2. Fashion Forecasters

Fashion forecasters are business consultants who help to predict trends in consumer demand. This is a very specialized field, and adaptivewear requires knowledge of both the fashion and the disability markets. The most accurate sources of trends for the adaptive clothing market are the brands and designers who are at the forefront of the adaptive movement. Brands and retailers like Tommy Hilfiger Adaptive, Disney Adaptive, Target's *Cat & Jack,* and Kohls' *Nine West Adaptive* are lines specifically designed for people with disabilities. Market niche designers such as Chamiah Dewey, Billy Price, Maria Luisa Mendiola, Lucy Jones, Izzy Camilleri, and Victoria Jenkins create designs to meet specific customer needs.

3. Stylists, social media influencers, bloggers, and disability advocates

Stylists, such as Stephanie Thomas, are at the forefront of adaptive fashion promotion. As an advocate for inclusive clothing, her styling philosophy revolves around fashion, function, and accessibility. She is the founder of Cur8able, a platform and resource that advocates adaptive fashion.

Social media influencers and bloggers Jillian Mercado, Chelsea Hill, Jesse Sadler, and Louis Boyce also work to raise awareness, build community, and counter stereotypes related to adaptive fashion. They regularly post on Instagram, YouTube, and Twitter to share both their collaborative work, and their ideas related to design trends.

4. Fashion and inclusivity

Since adaptive fashion is a developing category of clothing, the emergence of stylists, influencers, and bloggers help to create a change in basic assumptions regarding inclusivity, fashion, diversity, and awareness. As noted in Chapter 1, Mindy Scheier, the mother of a child with a disability, has dedicated her life to creating awareness related to the importance of clothing in the process of human development, and is the founder of Runway of Dreams, a foundation that coordinates fashion shows for people with disabilities, hosts podcasts, and participates in education through college clubs and scholarships. Mindy's TED Talk has over a million viewers.[12] Conner Lundius, also a disability advocate, had studied fashion merchandising in college. After a car accident, she found herself using a wheelchair for the rest of her life, and was determined not to let that define her as a person. She is a designer and a dancer for Rollettes, a seated dance team that is invited to perform regularly at a wide spectrum of events, including a recent performance at a half-time Celtics basketball game. Conner's story will be shared more fully in a later chapter.[13]

5. Laws and government policy

One of the unique features of the apparel industry in the United States is the absence of any laws or restrictions on any type of design, as this would be a violation of the First Amendment, which protects freedom of speech as well as other constitutional rights. There are some restrictions related to dress, which have been developed to promote public safety, such as requiring certain types of soles on shoes, and others, such as work policies, which limit the wearing of clothing to work that has writing on it. There are no direct laws designed specifically to protect people with disabilities in the area of clothing. Current laws address the needs and rights of people with disabilities related to accommodation and accessibility only. However, the ADA prohibits any form of discrimination based on disability, and employers are required to provide reasonable accommodations for people with disabilities regarding clothing in the workplace. A flexible dress code that addresses disability challenges, as well as adaptive designs in uniforms, is supported by the ADA.

Currently, health insurance does not cover adaptive clothing unless it is required for medical purposes. Disability advocates are working to try to change this policy and turn to countries such as Australia, where adaptive clothing is included in health coverage, as examples. In certain cases, it is possible to file a tax exemption for adaptivewear; however, this tax exemption is the only monetary incentive the government provides for the public needing adaptive clothing. Consumer protection laws, in place for all products including clothing, provide extra consideration to safety and quality issues in considering adaptive clothing. Adaptive clothing for veterans is often covered by government insurance.

6. Technology

Technology plays a vital role in market research related to the disability population and accessibility. Often, when people become disabled, they rely on technology to assist them in bridging the emotional differences they experience in moving from considering themselves non-disabled to considering themselves disabled. Social media, virtual fitting rooms, online platforms for shopping, and apps that assist in selections such as color choice allow people with disabilities access to the same trends and styles as the mass-market population. Textiles, such as temperature-regulating fabrics, trim that uses Velcro™ and magnets, 3D printing, and adaptive designs make fashion a wearable reality for people with disabilities.

In addition, technology has advanced the possibilities for employment in clothing production for people with disabilities. Ergonomic cutting tools and voice-activated machinery are allowing people with disabilities in the apparel industry to play a significant role in manufacturing and production, as well as in consumption. Tukatech is a global company that specializes in fashion technology. Their goal is to streamline fashion production systems and simplify the development process by using efficient software. They were the first in the fashion industry to create a fully automatic pattern making and grading system. Ram Sareen, Head Coach, and founder of Tukatech, is confident that all of their technology is ready to go for any adaptive designs and measurement specifications.[14]

7. Sustainability

Sustainability has become a major consideration for the apparel industry. From manufacturing and production to packaging and recycling, the focus on sustainability has increased awareness related to ethical business practices. Consumers are currently making purchasing decisions that support green fabrics, and brands that promote sustainability as an important part of their image are favored. These trends have also made local production, which usually involves the production of smaller quantities at higher prices, an important priority. In addition, local production also increases opportunities for customization. People with disabilities often need custom garments, as standard-size grading might not be sufficient to meet their needs.

One of the most sustainable responses to the excess amount of clothing currently in our society is the purchase of secondhand items, recycling, and upcycling. Using secondhand clothing to create adaptive designs is very appealing to the disability market, as new purchases often must be cut, pasted, and/or jerry-rigged to meet specific consumer needs. In addition, secondhand clothing is much less costly, which is key for those living on low incomes.

Case study: Slick Chicks

In 2014, the founder of Slick Chicks, **Helya Mohammadian**'s sister, faced a tough recovery after an emergency C-section and needed help with everyday tasks, like getting dressed. Seeing her struggle inspired our founder to find a solution. What started as a personal mission grew into something much bigger, touching lives far beyond what we ever imagined.

The brand's mission is to empower individuals by making everyday dressing easier for those with limited mobility. We believe everyone deserves clothing that offers a sense of self, dignity, and independence. By enhancing the accessibility of apparel, we champion the voices of people with disabilities and ensure that everyone can experience the freedom and confidence they deserve.

Slick Chicks goes beyond being a brand; we are a community where the voices of people with disabilities are amplified, advocating that everyone deserves the support of products designed with their dignity and independence in mind. This mission underscores our commitment not just to sell but to connect, empathize, and solve genuine issues. Each purchase is a testament to our vision, a nod to the real people, stories, and needs it represents.

At Slick Chicks, the design process is rooted in our commitment to innovation, quality, and inclusivity. We set ourselves apart from competitors by embracing innovative technology (magnetic closures, multi-directional stretch fabric blends, etc.) that enhance the functionality and comfort of our products, helping our customers feel empowered when getting dressed.

The designs prioritize both style and practicality; we believe that functional clothing shouldn't compromise on aesthetics. Every piece is thoughtfully crafted with premium, comfortable fabrics that elevate the everyday experience.

Inclusivity is at the core of Slick Chick's mission and design process. We offer a wide range of sizes (XS–5XL) and partner with manufacturers who share our values of equality and inclusivity. This collaborative approach not only empowers our customers but also reflects their dedication to making a positive impact in the community.

Through this intentional design process, Slick Chicks delivers smart, stylish solutions that empower individuals to navigate life's daily challenges with ease and confidence Content provided by Helya Mohammadian Founder

Discussion: Ease of dressing plays an important role in adaptivewear. How does Slick Chicks prioritize ease of dressing while making products that are stylish and affordable? Consider some of the obstacles Helya Mohammadian most likely faced in launching her brand.

Case study: Melrose Trading Post

Natalie Iturbe Jackson is a special events and marketing manager whose skills and interests have led her to a career with Melrose Trading Post, an open-air Sunday market in Los Angeles that sells antiques, vintage goods, and collectibles. Natalie suffered physical trauma in the womb. When she was born, one of her hands was not fully developed. She knows that trauma was the cause of her disability, but she is unaware of the details. Her left hand has a thumb, but not the other four fingers. Psychologically, she accepts her disability but finds herself physically challenged daily. She describes herself as a woman with a short, curvy body which can create clothing difficulties regardless of a disability but finds that her hand makes dressing a daily challenge. She finds herself always looking for clothing with easy-to-attach buttons or zippers, and simple designs with pockets. She loves wearing t-shirts, but, because she is on the petite side, they "tend to look like long night gowns". She does not have a sewing machine, but, due to her height, she has learned how to hem her pants. Natalie believes that women's sizing in general is different from brand to brand, making it very hard to gauge size accurately. Adding a physical condition to sizing differences and then finding something that works is a real challenge.

One of her biggest clothing challenges is gloves, because she is an avid gardener. She must usually buy a pair of gloves, reconfigure the design, and sew it back up again so that they fit her hand properly. Mittens and winter gloves end up being the same process. Natalie recalls that her grandparents were always mending clothing, and she learned how to sew from them as well as from her mother. As she works with roses, she needs particularly good gloves to protect her hands from the thorns. She finds it challenging to sew thick leather gloves, but considers that it is a necessity for proper protection.

She is aware of technology that could enable her ability to have more use of her hand, but she is not so interested in seeking it out. She was born with her disability and feels that it is a part of who she is as a person: she accepts her physical challenges. However, she would be interested in tools to help her dexterity, such as a gardening tool that she could grip better. She favors her right shoulder, arm, and hand because it is easier and faster to manipulate. Her left side, she says, does not suffer from underuse, but her right side does feel the impact of doing the work for both sides.

Originally a vendor curator for Melrose Trading Post, Natalie now focuses on marketing to local designers who are interested in designing for every body type. Her disability allows her a special perspective, helpful for representing an inclusive trendy, retail platforms, and notes that some of the companies that are onsite are open to customizing their items for people.

These companies include:

CAYA "Come as You Are", a local company from West Hollywood that specializes in leisure, hip-hop, and punk styles. They have many clients that are gender nonconforming, or that have physical disabilities that require the kinds of designs and styles they carry.

"Rojas Clothing", a company owned and operated by Freddie Rojas, is known for adapting clothing to meet special needs. Freddie makes designs that "would fit anyone". In addition, he also uses vintage dead stock fabrics, which promotes sustainability in the apparel industry.

Other companies at Melrose Trading Post also sell vintage clothing, and can customize and create hybrids out of two pieces of clothes. "Grandma's Closet" is an online vintage retailer that uses skilled sewers to create innovative designs with vintage apparel.

On the topic of departmentalization….Natalie feels that it would be important for adaptive clothing to be available along with traditional clothing and sizing. Fashion is an important part of identity. If the goal of adaptive clothing is to provide apparel for everyone, to create inclusivity, people shopping for it should be able to associate themselves and their clothing with the general population. Natalie also comments on the importance of brands and retailers specializing in adaptivewear to satisfy a niche market with a deep assortment and choices.

Natalie feels that people with disabilities are still not a part of the conversation in the fashion industry, and is hopeful that education and awareness will create a new impression and foster new values.

Natalie Iturbe Jackson interviewed by Susan Kolko

Discussion: What are Natalie Iturbe's biggest challenges in clothing and dressing? What could the apparel industry do to make clothing more accessible for her?

Case study: Unhidden

Victoria Jenkins is both a designer and a disability advocate. She studied design in college and worked with fashion brands such as All Saints, Sweaty Betty, and Victoria Beckham. Her career skills evolved from pattern cutter to garment technologist, where she obtained enough experience and confidence to start her own business. Twelve years ago, Victoria was diagnosed with digestive disorders, and, while in the hospital, found herself identifying with others facing similar dressing obstacles. She connected with one particular patient who, as an ovarian cancer survivor, had several conditions requiring clothing that enabled access to medications through a chest port. Fashionable clothing would have been a luxury: functionality had to come first. Victoria herself, physically uncomfortable in regular clothing, realized that she didn't want to spend all day dressed in pajamas, or wear medical-grade garments that simply served access needs. She founded Unhidden, an adaptive fashion brand.

Unhidden is suitable for people who use wheelchairs, amputees, people with gastrointestinal disorders, and others with additional needs, and Victoria is well known in the apparel industry for her attention to sustainability, and for making use of dead stock fabric. Her clothing items are small production runs, by female seamstresses in Bulgaria, and she intends to hire workers with disabilities in the future. She is a talented writer and a public speaker, and who also produces workshops on inclusive design and workplace culture as learning tools for anyone interested in adaptive clothing, or in starting a niche market business.

In a recent article, Victoria mentions that her sense of humor, ability to remain calm under pressure, creativity, and organizational and multitasking abilities have proven to be important strengths, allowing her to manage her disabling condition as well as her personal life and career. Her failures have been disappointing, but she believes that learning from them is an important strength. She continues to work with children and parents to develop innovative design concepts, and participates in fashion weeks and disability events.

Victoria is an example of someone with lived experiences, who was ultimately moved by someone else with a disability that sparked her passion for creating sustainable fashionable clothing for people with disabilities.

Victoria Jenkins interview by Susan Kolko

Discussion: How has Victoria Jenkins turned her challenges with disability into a life of ability? Why would she choose to call her brand "Unhidden"?

Case study: IZ Adaptive

Izzy Camilleri has been a Canadian designer for 40 years. She is the founder and chief designer at IZ Adaptive, a fashion brand catering to the disability market. Her design career changed focus when she was asked to design clothing pieces for someone who uses a wheelchair. This experience made her aware of the need for fashion in the adaptive space. Izzy is an example of a designer whose personal experience in working with someone with disabilities inspired her to want to make a difference. With her expertise, her knowledge, and her newly found interest in satisfying an underserved market, IZ Adaptive was born. Izzy explored all of the research she felt was necessary in order to create a brand that would become innovative, practical, and fashionable. As there were few adaptive brands, Izzy felt that she was venturing into uncharted waters, but knew that she was on a mission—to bring stylish clothing to a population who had had few choices. She felt that the existing clothing options tended to be depressing and certainly not fashion-forward.

Izzy's design for a seamless back pant was introduced during the pandemic, and enabled expanded function for the entire seated population which, during the pandemic, generally also included the population at large. Izzy recognizes the importance of education, and she is often invited as a speaker at colleges and universities, where she emphasizes the need for more designers, brands, and businesses in the field of adaptive fashion. Izzy has won many awards for her innovations and her impact on the fashion industry, including the CAFA's Designer of the Year Award. Her adaptive collections have been curated at the Royal

Ontario Museum, her designs have been featured in *Vogue* and *InStyle* magazine, and her clientele includes celebrities Meryl Streep and Angelina Jolie. In 2020 she hosted a TEDx talk entitled *Redesigning Fashion*.

She is widely known in the adaptive community as a leader open to new ideas, and ready to take on new challenges.[15]

Discussion: How did Izzy Camilleri's experience with disability impact her career? Why is it important for people with disabilities to have designers and advocates like Izzy? Why would pants be a focus of design during the COVID-19 pandemic?

Summary

The disability and adaptivewear market is growing every year, and inclusivity and accessibility have become pivotal words for businesses seeking to provide goods and services for people with disabilities. In general, consumers with disabilities are both supportive and loyal to the businesses that address their needs. Consumers also place their brand loyalty with those brands and markets that support and share their personal values. The demographics, psychographics, geographics, and behavior characteristics of the disability market are quantifiable. Market research uses traditional marketing tools to strategize production and sales tactics.

Learning activities

- Select 3–5 specific clothing items, such as jeans, sweaters, shirts, undergarments, and sneakers in both standard and adaptive styles, and examine the adaptive features.

- Compare standard apparel retail price and adaptive apparel retail pricing.
- What causes adaptive clothing to have a higher retail price
- Research an adaptive line of clothing, and identify the consumer in terms of demographics, psychographics, geographics, and behavioristic characteristics.
- Discuss why technology plays an important role in the design, production, and consumerism related to adaptive clothing.
- Consider what sustainability means to people with disabilities. How might this play a role in clothing choices?
- Review 3-5 disability influencers on social media. What are the commonalities and differences among their posts? Why is it important to have differences among them?

Adaptive talk

Market
Market segment
Market research
Demographics
Psychographics
Geographics
Behavioristics
Fashion forecasters
Sustainability
Veterans Clothing Allowance
Technology

Case studies

Slick Chicks – Helya Mohammadian

Melrose Trading Post – Natalie Turbe

IZ Adaptive – Izzy Camilleri

Unhidden – Victoria Jenkins

Part II
Addressing special clothing needs

The clothing needs of people with disabilities vary, depending on the disabling condition. In considering the design, production, and marketing of adaptive clothing, it is essential to consider some important aspects of disability. For example, a person with difficulties in finger manipulation may need clothing that does not require buttoning, zippering, or lacing. This may be *caused* by losses due to age, or to specific medical conditions, such as Parkinson's disease, multiple sclerosis, or paralysis. The *level of impairment* may be minor, moderate, or severe. The *course* of the disability may be progressive, constant, or intermittent, potentially requiring various kinds of adaptations in clothing at different times. The effects of the disability of the individual's *activities of daily living* (not only bathing, dressing, and eating but also employment and leisure activities) may create varying clothing needs.

Because most adaptivewear is mass-produced and marketed, it is important to understand various groupings in order to assess the level of need and the specific adaptations necessary. This will enable effective design and provide information about potential markets. Chapter 3 will explore several different systems of grouping disabilities helpful in planning for an adaptive clothing market. In Chapter 4, several of these groupings will be utilized to explore specific experiences, adaptations, and marketing strategies. Vignettes of the firsthand experiences of designers and businesses specializing in these fields will help to illustrate the process, challenges, and rewards of addressing these special needs.

3
Understanding disabling conditions

Introduction

One of the most helpful and important tools people use to help them understand the world is the creation of groupings, or categories. In the field of disability, groups are used for a wide variety of purposes: to determine eligibility for special education, to receive benefits from SSDI (Social Security Disability Insurance), SSI (Supplemental Security Income), and other government agencies, to qualify for special programs, for housing accommodations, travel accommodations, and many other purposes. In the field of adaptivewear, categories are both necessary and helpful—however, they may need to be more specific, and categories within categories may need to be created to address special, specific clothing needs.

The groupings addressed in this chapter have been selected as helpful in defining and determining the types of clothing needs that are most prevalent among people with disabilities. The first, most basic grouping divides disabilities into three groups: physical, cognitive, and sensory. This most basic division may be brought into each of the following systems, providing additional information and organization to each.

Because disability groupings may contain many conditions that do not create a need for adaptive clothing, the specific listings included here for medical, World Health Organization, and the U.S. Department of Education are focused especially on groupings that may require adaptive clothing.

The final category, Rolland's Courses of Disability, groups disabilities by the condition itself, which may be constant, progressive, or episodic. Each of these categories has major implications for adaptivewear fashions and must be carefully considered in marketing and business planning.

Figure 3 Adaptive by Asiya, Jessica Smith Australian Paralympic Swimmer. Photograph by YULIIA.

Learning objectives

- Understand the reasons for disability groupings
- Recognize the difference between physical, cognitive, and sensory disabilities
- Identify the difference between impairments and disease/disorders
- Understand the role the Paralympic committee plays in setting the standard for sports at all levels of play
- Create an analysis of a disabling condition according to the groupings
- Identify characteristics of disabling conditions

A. Three basic groupings

The three simplest, most basic groupings of disabilities are:

Physical disabilities, affecting movement and dexterity related to the physical self.

Cognitive disabilities, affecting comprehension, behavior, learning, communication, and social skills.

Sensory disabilities, affecting one of the five senses, most often sight and hearing, but also sensation.

Many, though not all, people with disabilities can be placed into one of these three groupings. Some have multiple disabilities, and may be included in more than one group. Of the three, people with physical disabilities tend to have the greatest need for adaptive clothing, but cognitive disabilities, such as autism, and sensory disabilities, such as blindness, also have adaptive-wear needs.

Case study: Buck and Buck

Buck & Buck was founded in August 1978 by **Julie and Bill Buck**. Upon receiving her master's degree in education in 1973, Julie became Social Services Coordinator in a skilled nursing facility near Boston. She and her husband moved to Seattle two years later, where she became Assistant Administrator for a 177-bed nursing home, working with nursing staff and residents to ensure all their needs were met.

Julie immediately recognized the need for an adaptive clothing source that would make dressing her residents easier, but after searching thoroughly, none were to be found. She decided to have a few things made for her patients, such as rear closures for dresses for the women and elastic-waisted pants for the men, making the dressing and undressing process easier for aides and residents alike. Since then, B&B has grown to become the national leader in quality adaptive clothing for nursing facilities, guardianship services, veterans' homes, group homes, individuals, and more. While B&B does not market directly to foreign countries, they receive orders from many European countries, as well as Canada, Australia, and New Zealand.

The special qualities of B&B include:

Original Designs: All B&B's designs originate through long-term relationships with nursing facility staff throughout the Pacific Northwest. For over 20 years, the business has scheduled personal, semi-annual visits to hundreds of facilities, and worked directly with nursing staff and residents to develop designs that solve many of the common dressing challenges.

Unlike many businesses in the adaptive clothing industry today, which began as traditional clothing retailers wishing to expand their market and meet a need, Buck & Buck was created from extensive experience in understanding the special clothing needs of people in nursing facilities and in the healthcare industry. This experience has guided the design and the refinement of garments, making self- and assisted dressing easier for all seniors, both those living in a facility setting and those being cared for at home.

Customer Service: Most of B&B's customer service staff have been with the business for decades and are able to act as knowledgeable personal advisors to anyone needing guidance as to which garment will best answer the special needs of the wearer, whether that person works at a nursing facility or is a family member ordering for a parent or loved one.

Custom Alterations: Unlike many other adaptivewear companies, B&B offers garment customization, and their onsite sewers can perform most special alterations in less than a day, enabling shipments to go out the following day. Many customizations are included in the cost of the garment, while others incur a slight fee.

Made in USA From the start of the business, B&B has prioritized working with American manufacturers, and Julie and Bill feel that this enables them to fulfill orders more easily, reduce supply chain issues, and improve quality control. The manufacturers with whom they work appreciate the need to keep costs down, which, they say, enables them to meet, or even beat, competitor pricing on their items made overseas.

Services Geared toward Facilities: Julie and Bill note that their services have been streamlined to anticipate the needs of facilities and their staff to make ordering, distribution, and payment as easy as possible. Orders can be phoned, faxed, or placed online. They have found that many facilities prefer to order by phone, which also allows any questions to be immediately addressed. Invoices are enclosed with each person's order, facilitating payment, and labeling of all garments with the resident's name is offered at no charge, ensuring their return to the rightful owner after laundering. Thirty-day terms are offered to all facilities, and monthly statements are provided, indicating which residents' orders have been paid and which are still outstanding.

The Buck & Buck Brand: B&B uses high-quality fabrics that are laundered well in a facility setting and has established long-lasting relationships with sewing contractors to minimize quality control issues. The owners say that nursing facility staff calls B&B from all over the country, confident that pricing will be competitive, shipping will be timely, and easy payment options will be offered, and the business received many positive customer comments about both the garment quality and the excellent customer service. Most staff in the industry, they say, have worked with B&B at one time or another, and trust the brand name. The Adaptable Designs® brand, a line of walker and wheelchair accessories, is a subsidiary brand.

Interviewed by Susan Kolko and adapted by B&B

Discussion: Consider Julie Buck's career before Buck & Buck. Without a background in the apparel industry, what do you think some of the challenges were for her in product development and marketing?

B. Medical groupings

The Disability Statistics Center groups disabilities into two major groups by causative condition. The first of these, impairments, includes:

orthopedic impairments
learning disabilities
visual and hearing impairments
paralysis
deformities
absence of a limb or other body part
speech impairments.

It is easy to see how each of these may require adaptations to meet clothing needs, and this listing offers a potentially practical way to consider and design clothing to meet these specific needs. The medical groupings listed here focus strongly on physical disabilities and needs.

The Center's second major group lists causes, diseases, and disorders, such as diseases of the musculoskeletal system, digestive system, and respiratory system, and provides information, but little guidance, in addressing adaptivewear needs.

Case study: DEWEY clothing

Chamiah Dewey, founder and designer of DEWEY, explains: "As a designer, my goal has always been to create something with real purpose, which is why I set out to establish DEWEY—the world's first fashion brand dedicated to adults 5 ft and under. We've created a unique size chart featuring carefully crafted proportions that also includes varying arm and leg lengths, allowing customers to find their perfect fit off the rack."

"We've also commissioned the world's first 5 ft.-and-under mannequins, which will be used to display DEWEY collections in retail spaces, starting with Selfridges. This innovation ensures that our pieces are displayed exactly as they were designed: to fit and flatter extra petite frames."

The majority of Chamiah's clients are "extra petite": 5 ft and under without disabilities that affect their height, but one in five of their community fit into this "short stature" demographic. DEWEY recently launched its first high street retailer, Selfridges' flagship store, on London's fashion central, Oxford Street.

The first drop—an athletic-leisure collection—features 16 thoughtfully designed women's wear pieces and 6 unisex styles, all created to flatter and fit extra-petite frames. A mainline collection was launched in winter 2024, incorporating accessible design features to ensure inclusivity for everyone 5 ft and under. And that's not all—a men's collection is planned for early 2025, demonstrating DEWEY's commitment to serving the full spectrum of customers within this overlooked demographic.

With one in ten adults in the United Kingdom and United States measuring under 5 ft, DEWEY's mission is to boost the confidence and self-esteem of its global community by providing stylish, well-fitting clothing for extra-petite individuals. Chamiah's passion for this mission stems from her own experiences, and those of people close to her, who have struggled to find stylish, well-fitting clothes. These personal connections drive her dedication to making a tangible difference in the lives of extra-petite individuals.

DEWEY was founded in 2020. With First Class Honours from the London College of Fashion (UAL). Chamiah was inspired by a personal connection to this overlooked demographic, and discovered that in the United Kingdom and United States alone, there are over 43 million adults who measure 5 ft and under. While DEWEY refers to itself as an "accessible" fashion brand, rather than placing itself in the "adaptive" space specifically, Chamiah's designs are always informed by access, comfort, and style.

While Selfridges marks DEWEY's major retail debut, the brand will shortly launch its own direct-to-consumer website, offering worldwide delivery, with plans already in place to roll out further high-street retail presence, giving accessibility to millions of customers struggling to find clothes that fit off the rack. In addition to its retail and direct-to-consumer expansions, DEWEY is committed to sustainability, incorporating eco-friendly materials and ethical production practices.

DEWEY Sportopia athleisure wear collection highlights:

- Ultimate fit off the rack. Allowing women 5 ft and under to purchase clothing off-the-rack with no costly alterations needed.
- Accessible designs for all. Thanks to DEWEY's unique sizing, items are available in a range of leg lengths, ensuring a proportional fit for petite frames.
- Versatile designs. Stylish items that transition seamlessly from Yoga class to running errands.

- Easy to wear. Mindful design features make this unique collection easy to wear for all women 5 ft and under*.
- Confidence boosting. Helps extra-petite women feel empowered and confident with clothing that truly fits.

* Accessible features include: elasticated and drawstring waists; rubber zip tabs for sensory stimulation and ease of grip; slightly raised, heat transferred care labeling across stretch fabrics for visually impaired people and to avoid sensory irritation from regular tab labels; pocket placement in accessible position for reach (higher on the body); super-stretch, buttery fabric; flat seams across all stretch items, avoiding pressure sores or sensory irritation; cotton rich sweat shirts with super-soft brush back for sensory and heat regulation.

It is also important to note that the reason for expanding their range from the short stature space to include a much wider demographic and simplifying their size chart conventions was to purposely improve ease-of-shopping for customers; adults 5 ft and under have never had the option to shop off-the-rack specifically for their bodies. Now that this is possible, they are looking for ease, accessibility, and style.

Chamiah Dewey is not just a designer but is also an advocate for the extra-petite community, engaging in numerous public speaking events and sharing her insights as an authority in the sector. Dewey has received significant media attention, has been featured in over 50 publications, and has won 13 awards. This recognition underscores Dewey's impact and the growing demand for inclusive fashion. Customer testimonials also reflect the brand's positive impact, with many praising the perfect fit and stylish designs that boost their confidence and self-esteem.

As DEWEY continues to grow, the future includes expanding its range and collaborating with other designers to create more innovative and accessible fashion solutions for extra-petite individuals. Chamiah's vision for DEWEY extends beyond clothing, and aims to foster a community where extra-petite individuals feel seen, valued, and stylishly empowered.[16]

Interviewed by Susan Kolko and adapted by Chamiah Dewey

Discussion: Why might Chamiah Dewey choose to be considered an "accessible" brand as opposed to an "adaptive" brand? How does this relate to inclusivity in marketing? World Health Organization groupings

The World Health Organization adopted the International Classification for Functioning, Disability, and Health (ICF), which groups disabilities into three categories:

> body functions and structure
> tasks and actions by individuals and participation and involvement
> severity and environmental factors.

While this system offers groupings, these appear broader and more general than the medical groupings. However, exploring and understanding a disabled person's body functions and structure may provide needed guidance in clothing design.

Body functions and structure appear, again, to focus on physical aspects of disability, while tasks and actions might involve not only physical but also cognitive and sensory conditions. The ICF groupings provide an additional very essential dimension with a part of their third grouping, severity, which suggests that disabling conditions range from mild, to moderate, to severe. The degree of severity might support the possibility of various designs.

Case study: FFORA

Lucy Jones grew up in Cardiff, the capital of Wales, U.K., a small city of approximately 350,000, compared to the 3 million in Wales as a whole. She had no exposure to fashion design, but with a single Textiles class at high school, and had no idea that this field could be a career or a source of income. As a child, she had always customized her clothing, "hacking and sewing" to make a garment that worked for her, and she got her first sewing machine at the age of 12. For many years, she took the clothing her mother no longer wanted and cut them into fashions for herself, a hobby that she loved. Lucy shares that Wales is "a very creative county" and that "most careers either lean toward singing and acting, or you become a lawyer". Alexander McQueen was the first designer she learned about, and he "opened (her) eyes to fashion, and helped define what fashion meant for (her)".

From a young age, Lucy was fascinated with Japan and with Japanese culture. Japanese designs and architecture "spoke to (her)", and helped her to understand that clothing could be more than just "something that hung on a hanger", or walked down a runway. Clothing was transformative, and she was inspired to learn more. Initially, Lucy wanted to go to school in Japan, but she was also eager to be in the United States, where she was accepted at the Parsons School of Design. At Parsons, she was "overwhelmed by the saturation of the fashion industry": there were so many students, and, coming from a small city, she felt she couldn't possibly do anything that had not already been done. Lucy initially felt that other students were more advanced in "everything from global issues to social behavior". She didn't feel creatively productive. School was draining both will and energy, and she felt that her opportunity to invent herself was slipping away from her. One day, one of her professors, aware of her discouragement, told her to "break away from the negativity, and start thinking about solutions to change the world". Her professor told her that all of the greatest designers had an individual point of view and something to say. "Sure, there's a lot of cutthroat competition, but competition is going to be everywhere you go, in any career you choose," her professor told her. Lucy was also aware that she did not have the resources that would enable her to create her own collection or support her career. She wanted to create something real, not fantasy fashion, or "landfill". She didn't want to contribute to waste and to the many unsustainable practices of the apparel industry. She didn't want her garments to "come off a conveyor belt": she wanted them to have a higher level of meaning.

Lucy has a cousin, Jake, who has cerebral palsy. He is independent, but she realized she had never asked him or spoken to him, about his disability. Although no one had told her specifically that she should avoid this clearly normal conversation, she felt "society" would somehow tell her it was best not to raise this subject, even though they were very close, until, one night on "skype", during a typical catch up: "He was fourteen and I was nineteen. I decided to ask if he had any difficulty with clothing and dressing. The answer was, yes, a lot "mostly buttons". Lucy was dumbfounded and had to hold back her tears because she was angry that she had never asked him about his accessibility preferences, or even about his needs. She experienced an "epiphany" at that moment and felt a sense of shame when she considered that she was in the best fashion design school in the world, and this entire category of clothing and clothing needs was seemingly non-existent, and not discussed. There was no way to even see or design for people who had disabilities because every mannequin was a standing typical size 6!

This inspired her to do her next project: creating a pair of trousers with Jake's comments as the motivation. The project taught her so many things, from fit and measurements to the need for adaptations related to dexterity. The fly, the zippers, and the buttons were all a challenge, as she needed to create adaptations that would accommodate different levels of mobility and dexterity in each hand. Lucy's professors encouraged her new-found purpose, and she turned to them often, for both design and motivational advice. The fact that she was creating something for a real person, that had a functional purpose, and that could make a person's life easier, became the most meaningful way to imagine her future. Reaching her cousin for fittings became difficult, as he lived in Dubai, so she began to connect with people with similar interests in New York. Lucy realized that she needed help conceptualizing her business concept, and needed to learn more about the consumer market that she had decided was her calling.

She met a lady called Ronnie who had responded to the project request and welcomed Lucy into her home. As Ronnie was a power wheelchair user, Lucy began to design clothing for her needs. She had never realized that the seated body was different from the standing body in terms of clothing design: this was neither in her design pattern construction books nor in her education. While her peers were designing collections, she was focused on learning about alternative fitting approaches and having conversations about it. This created much stress, but she was aware that she was learning new things to consider every day—new ways of addressing clothing needs for people who use wheelchairs, including those who may have difficulty transitioning from one position to another, a process very much impacted by clothing design. She began to think not only about the body and movement but about other external factors as well—the wheelchair itself, tables and chairs—and realized that accessories are also vital for people who have disabilities. Addressing the necessity of ensuring security over personal belongings, phone, and credit cards for people in wheelchairs was something that excited her.

Lucy felt she was falling short at school because she had not created a collection, as her fellow classmates had done. Instead, she created a textbook she called *The Advantage Block*, which, she felt, was the most productive manifestation of her learning and her studies. She wanted to pass all that she had learned on to others so that "they would not have to start at ground zero", as she had, in designing clothing to meet the needs of people with disabilities. Lucy created her 200-page book in a few months, a book that allowed a standard block size to be adjusted for a seated position. She was thrilled with her work, and the potential value that her contribution could make to the apparel industry. She gave copies of her book to judges at her round of judging, such as Vogue.com and Aimee Mullins (yes, Aimee, who walked in the wooden Alexander McQueen prostheses!). None of Lucy's peers recognized Aimee Mullins at first, but Lucy was well aware the moment she walked in of the impact she made as an athlete, actress, and model who wears prosthetic legs. Lucy had also been studying prosthetics in an effort to learn as much as she could about disability and design and was ecstatic to be in the presence of someone she viewed as her hero.

When she won an award for her book from Kering, they flew her to Italy to meet other artisans, celebrate her achievements, and inspire more material creativity, Lucy was part of a graduating group of students who paved the way for a new curriculum at Parsons School of Design, where she has also taught. Her contributions have changed the way in which the school prioritizes design, currently including the increasing need for inclusivity in design. She also continues with her special projects, In the realm of product innovation, she has continued to focus on creating designs for the seated position while working on various jobs that, at the time, seemed unrelated, but in retrospect were laying the groundwork for her business concept. Lucy wanted to create a product that would appeal to all genders, incomes, and occupations, and that would serve a purpose that paralleled both the Lego and the Apple business strategy. She envisioned the building blocks of Lego creating something specific, like an attachment for a product, and the customization that was possible with Apple, so that even if consumers had the same product, they would feel as though no one else had the same exact one, because the software and the applications enabled each item to be uniquely tailored to the individual consumer. She wrote a realistic business plan, that enabled scale, often a challenge for designers, and her family assisted by contributing enough money to get her business started. Her focus, she decided, would be accessories.

Accessories, Lucy feels, enable each person to create a unique identity from something that appears to be generic. She wanted to begin her business with accessories, and then potentially expand. Different disability needs require customization—for so many different types of wheelchairs, and prosthetics, and individual usage and preferences! By jazzing up her handbags and cup holders with color and style, Lucy was able to find a market niche within a niche market. Using her background in design, her ability to connect moving parts from other businesses to create her own concepts, and working first hand with individual consumers, she was able to build a business with the kind of purpose she had envisioned.

Fora is the Latin plural for the word "forum". Lucy felt strongly that the creation of a fashion brand required listening and speaking to people who had lived the experience and the need directly. The brand name FFORA is built from the concept of a fashion forum. Often FFORA is mistakenly considered to mean "Fashion for All". The brand has designed bags, cup holders, and attachments for wheelchair users, including athletes such as Steve Serio, the Team USA Wheelchair Basketball gold medalist, and Bri Scalesse, a New York based model. Lucy's designs have been displayed in the Museum of Art, and she has been featured in Forbes under 30. She was Womenswear Designer of the Year at Parsons in 2015. Lucy continues to live in New York, where she remains in touch with other adaptive fashion advocates and works closely with models, both of whom assist her in communicating her passion for inclusivity and accessibility. She still believes that a lack of education is to blame for the lag in the fashion industry's efforts to prioritize adaptive fashion, but feels that, in recent years, the gap has been closing.[17]

Lucy Jones interviewed by Susan Kolko

Discussion: Why did Lucy Jones feel that accessories are so important for people with disabilities? What might be considered another niche market within a niche market. U.S. Department of Education groupings

The U.S. Department of Education utilizes 13 categories to define disabilities to ensure equitable and appropriate public-school education for all children. Many of these do not seem to require adaptive clothing. Potential categories which may require adaptivewear include:

learning disabilities
autism
visual impairments
orthopedic impairments
traumatic brain injury
emotional disturbances

Although some physical disabilities are addressed, such as visual impairments, orthopedic impairments, and traumatic brain injury, the Department of Education appropriately focuses on disabilities that might impact learning, such as learning disabilities, autism, and emotional disturbance.

E. Uniforms for educational and military settings

Uniforms create special challenges for people with disabilities. Uniforms, by their very nature, reflect the goal of unity and standardization – goals which are difficult to attain with and for people with disabilities. Uniform designers must balance the goals of uniformity with the needs of individuals within groups.

1. School uniforms

Private schools often require that students wear uniforms, while public schools in the United States do not require them, as they are an infringement on the fifth amendment, which allows for freedom of speech and expression. There are several reasons why a uniform is the choice of apparel for students in a private school setting. First of all, clothing and fashion can be a distraction for students, faculty and staff. Loud colors, funky prints, revealing necklines and body parts draw attention that might more effectively be spent on schoolwork. In addition, clothing often defines personality and character, and can indicate both social status and values, all of which can be a distraction from the goal of learning specific content, and can stimulate destructive or harmful emotions in young people. A uniform ensures that everyone appears visibly equal. No one person has nicer shoes, luxury brand labels, or offensive artwork on a t-shirt that defines them as a person. Students must define themselves by their behavior and their performance in school. There is little agreement about the issue of school uniforms, but, as they currently exist in private school settings, merchandisers have developed lines that specifically meet the standards and requirements for clothing to be worn in schools. A student with a disability, subject to the same requirements for clothing, needs to be able to be comfortable and blend in like everyone else. In the past, this has meant having garments custom-made or tailored specifically to their needs.

More recently, adaptive school uniforms have become available for young people with disabilities. This has helped to relieve family and caregivers of the stress of reconfiguring a wardrobe every year as students grow and develop. Target, one of the largest mass merchandisers in the United States, has an adaptive line, Cat & Jack, which includes school uniforms. The uniforms are sensory-friendly and accessible, come in traditional uniform colors, such as white, khaki, and blue, are affordable, and can be ordered in a timely manner online. Lands' End, a niche market catalog retailer that specializes in representing a conservative, New England lifestyle and values, has a line of adaptive school uniforms. The brand calls the line their Universal Collection, and features MagnaReady technology and sensory-friendly fabrics. French Toast is an adaptive brand committed to making school uniforms affordable and accessible, with wide necks, flat seams, label-free comfort, easy closures, extended pull zippers, and lift loops. It has sizing that extends through young adults and offers a wide selection of styles, colors, and patterns that allow for adaptive individuality within a dress code.

School uniforms are an example of specialty apparel that might be overlooked when thinking about the needs of people with disabilities. Uniform needs extend into adulthood with employment requirements, company apparel, safety and service apparel, and military uniforms.

2. Military uniforms

The military has a history of employing people with disabilities, both veterans and civilians. San Antonio Lighthouse, a nonprofit agency, has coordinated employment for people who are blind, with jobs sewing combat and other uniforms for troops in Iraq and Afghanistan.

The Ukrainian army has announced that every wounded soldier will be given an adaptive uniform kit that allows for accessibility, sensitivity to skin, and comfort. T-shirts, shorts, pants, and a sweatshirt will be the basics available for both men and women. Zippers will be on the side seams with accessible fasteners. The concern is that the adaptive uniform should be functional for soldiers returning to their stations, as well as those requiring longer hospital stays. Currently, the Defense Military is testing various manufacturers for durability, fit, and function of their accessible clothing.

In the United States, *Sew Much Comfort* is a brand that has been serving injured service members for over 20 years. Specifically, the brand is known for t-shirts that have an easy-access opening that allows for convenient dressing. However, other garments, such as pants and wheelchair pants, will soon be part of the collection. The company caters to military hospitals primarily, and their mission is focused on providing service members access to adaptive clothing. Their free adaptive clothing is funded through the Elizabeth Dole Foundation, which provides services that support the well-being of veterans from all branches of the military, their families, and their caregivers.[18]

F. Paralympic Committee groupings

Several sports organizations, such as the International Paralympic Committee, group athletes by their degrees of limitation. They also recognize that different sports require different abilities, so participation categories must be sports-specific. The Paralympics include athletes who have physical disabilities or visual impairments. The allowable disabilities are divided into ten eligible impairment types:

impaired muscle power
impaired passive range of movement
limb deficiency
leg length difference
short stature
hypertonia
ataxia
athetosis
intellectual disabilities for some classifications (added recently)

Deborah Carabet is the owner and founder of Elevate Multisport Coaching & Training as well as Elevate Women 4 Tri. She is the coordinator for Athletes with Disabilities for the Los Angeles Marathon. She coaches physically challenged and visually impaired athletes as well as age groupers in the endurance sports arena. Coach Carabet's expertise and leadership was instrumental at the 2024 Paralympics in Paris, France. In a recent interview, she shared some of the most important things to consider in clothing for athletes with disabilities.

- the impact the disability has on movement and clothing
- the challenges related to changes in clothing during a race
- bulk and additional attention related to incontinence briefs
- the body measurements and disfigurements not necessarily equal on both sides
- getting in/out of a wetsuit. The extreme tightness of the neoprene is extremely complicated to manipulate alone or with a handler.
- the need for moisture-wicking soft fabric
- the need for easy on/off access and adjustments

She advised that an adaptive wetsuit designed specifically for athletes who have limited body movement would make the sport of triathlon more accessible for people with disabilities. In addition, Coach Carabet explains that the body position in a hand cycle and a race chair (aka push rim) is hugely different from the body position on a road bike. Attention to adaptive clothing design would make cycling a more accessible sport as well.

Case study: Francisco Postlewaite Munos

Francisco Postlethwaite Munoz was born with spina bifida. While the exact cause of spina bifida is not known, it is clearly a condition related to the spine and nerves, which affects both mobility and the function of body parts. However, Francisco doesn't spend much time thinking about the how or the why, or whether his condition is genetic or environmental, or any of the other what ifs. He has been determined since childhood to embrace life despite the challenges. He understands that people staring at him are simply curious and concerned, not judgmental.

Francisco is an only child, raised by his loving parents in Mexicali, Baja California, who have been by his side every step of the way in his medical treatments, his education, and his activities. Their focus on his health has been crucial to his growth and development. Over the years, he has transitioned from using braces on his legs and occasionally a wheelchair to using a wheelchair only. Using a wheelchair, he feels, gives him more independence, allows him to get to where he needs to be, and do the things he wants to do in a much timelier manner. He has a bachelor's degree in visual merchandising from UABC (The Autonomous University of Baja California) and currently works in technology.

Recently, Francisco became interested in the sport of triathlon.

Triathlon is a sport with many moving parts because it's three sports in one event. One can train for triathlons focusing on one or two of the sports at a time, but eventually one must put it all together to compete. A triathlon can be many different distances and can even be completed as a relay, but the event always consists of a swim (usually in open water, not a pool), a cycle course, and a run. Francisco decided that he wanted to compete as a para-athlete in triathlons. His coach, Christopher O'Driscoll and the Tower 26 Triathlon & Swim Program provided him with the training support he needed to compete in many races. Recently Francisco qualified for the most competitive triathlon in the sport, on the island of Kona, Hawaii. Francisco shared that in swimming he uses neoprene shorts to help with buoyancy in the water and that the rest of his wardrobe consists of basic, over-the-counter apparel that he can adjust for his needs.

The most challenging part of his wardrobe, he shares, are his shoes. When he wore braces, wearing shoes was close to impossible, because he could not get his foot *and* the brace to fit into the shoe, due to the shape and size of his foot in the braces. He no longer uses the braces, but he still cannot find shoes that work properly for him. He is either in socks or in Crocs that have a shape and mold that works and allows for wiggle room. When asked Francisco if he was familiar with any adaptive shoe brands, he replied that he had no idea that these even existed. This raises a critical issue, the vital importance of consideration and assessment for both marketing and accessibility.

Francisco also stressed the importance of appropriate textiles—"breathable" clothing—as remaining in a seated position for extended periods every day often results in skin sores and rashes. He would love to see a fabric or material that creates a space between his body and the wheelchair. Francisco seems to be both aware and adapted to the differences in his clothing needs.

Francisco uses social media as a storyteller to share his everyday training and racing.

Francisco Postlethwaite Munos interviewed by Susan Kolko

Discussion: Why might Francisco have chosen a sport with so many wardrobe changes? If you were a designer what do you think would be the most important considerations for a competitive sport that required several wardrobe changes?

Rolland's categories: Three courses of disability

John Rolland has identified three categories of disability that strongly impact identity and are also a factor in the development of adaptivewear: disabilities may be progressive, constant, episodic, or intermittent (Rolland, J., Chronic Illness and the Life Cycle: A Conceptual Framework. Family *Process Journal* 26:203–222, 1987). Understanding the characteristics of each one of these categories is crucial to business planning. To understand adaptive clothing needs, it is important to note that physical, cognitive, and sensory disabilities are the most prevalent in each one of these categories.

1. Progressive disabilities

Rolland describes progressive disabilities as those in which the symptoms, and degrees of disability become more severe with time. These may occur at any time in life, and the degree and rapidity of the progression varies with everyone. Multiple sclerosis, Alzheimer's Disease and dementia, muscular dystrophy, and vision and hearing loss are examples of these disabilities. Progressive disabilities may create stress, as individuals struggle with the varying course of disability progression and their own awareness of the challenges ahead. Clothing needs may require changes with time, as abilities decline, and needs for adaptivewear may increase. An individual's sense of identity may be strongly affected by progressive disabilities, and the role that clothing plays in assisting consumers to address these issues can be an essential contribution to the retention of a positive self-image.

2. Constant disabilities

Some disabilities remain constant throughout life. Although they may occur at different times in the lifespan, and may even be present at birth, once they occur, they remain unchanged. Treatments, careers, personal relationships, and lifestyle changes, and adjustments may need to be addressed if disabilities occur at various stages during the lifespan, but once integrated, conditions remain stable, enabling the possibility of personal adaptation and resulting in stability of both conditions and life circumstances. Constant disabilities include conditions such as hearing loss, blindness, autism, intellectual disability, and heart disease. A person with a constant disability may have an ongoing need for adaptive clothing and depend on adaptivewear to reflect their identity and personal style. A broad range of choices and current styles are especially important for this group.

3. Intermittent, or episodic disabilities

Rolland's third grouping of disabilities includes those whose symptoms and conditions vary with time and conditions. These may be especially challenging because the episodes, their duration, and their severity are often unpredictable, making planning, both short- and long-term, always uncertain. Epilepsy, Crohn's disease, lupus, multiple sclerosis, IBS, rheumatoid arthritis, bipolar disorder, and migraines occur intermittently, and, between episodes, people can function normally. Needs for adaptivewear will also be intermittent, and people with episodic conditions may need fewer special clothing items than those with constant disabilities. Often, this population prefers not to spend money on adaptive clothing: they would rather wait until they can wear their regular clothing, and manage somehow, rather than purchasing a clothing item to use only for limited periods.[19]

Case study: Eightfold Fox

At 21, **Fox** developed a debilitating case of irritable bowel syndrome. This illness is unpredictable and can cause sudden dramatic fluctuations in waist size, with changes of up to 4 inches in one hour. Clothing with set-in waistbands or zippers, any clothing with rigid, fixed sizing that does not allow for expansion becomes incredibly painful if the waist starts to expand. Fox's fluctuation in waist size and the associated pain was a constant source of stress, often causing them to be late for work or miss important formal occasions. At the time that this developed, they were attending graduate school and feeling as though they could not dress professionally because clothing for their disability was not available. They felt unattractive in clothes that were easy to wear, like sweatpants, and uncomfortable in clothes that looked good but couldn't be adjusted for comfort. At the time, Fox was working for a medieval jousting company, and later was a customer for the Connecticut Renaissance Faire. As they began to research clothing and fashion from the medieval time period, they noticed that the lace-up, adjustable style was very conducive to adaptive sizing options. One dress could fit many sizes due to the lacing and ties that were the only fasteners used during that time. Elizabethan and Tudor clothing was designed to be adjustable so that clothing could be passed around and fit through life changes, or even pregnancy. Fox found the concept of expandable waists logical for their situation, and for anyone else with a condition that might experience fluctuations in size.

When the COVID-19 pandemic hit, Fox was working as Director of Speech and Language Pathology at a private clinic in Connecticut, and found themselves working from home for days on end. They started experimenting with fabric from a thrift store and videos on YouTube, and were able to make themselves a pair of overalls. These were extremely comfortable, flattering, and rugged, so they made a few more pairs. They noticed that their outlook and attitude had changed, due to having comfortable and attractive clothing. According to their boss, it became easier to work with them. Fox realized that since they were not in chronic pain from restrictive clothing, they were more available to engage deeply with the world.

Fox now lives in Iowa with their partner, who is a neuroimmunologist. They source primarily secondhand fabric from across the United States, and prioritize ethical, sustainable practices as much as possible. They work from a basement sewing studio, producing original, custom designs created for people with physical differences and disabilities. Currently, they designs independently, but intend to expand when it makes sense. Their primary focus is ethical business practice, and they believe that when the time is right, the business will grow. Fox feels that they want to price items carefully for disabled customers, who often have less disposable income, rather than focusing on bringing in the revenues to grow their business. They feel that it is not right to charge people more for clothing because they have a disability. Their partner, who works as a speech language pathologist, can supplement their income, so they can keep their retail prices low. At the time of this interview, they were working on a fine motor impairment, sensory-friendly adaptive wedding dress for a young woman with early onset Parkinson's syndrome.

Fox is proud of their designs, and feels that what they are doing is quite different from mass-market adaptive clothing lines. Their goal is to create expressive silhouettes that reflect style and character, not just to blend in. They feel pride and ownership in designing for what they call "an invisible illness with an invisible disability". Most of their designs are for GI disorders such as colitis and stomach cancer; however, they have recently expanded into a line of fine motor accessible and ambulatory wheelchair user accessible designs. The positive feedback they have received on social media has made them realize that there really was a need and demand for the clothing they were creating. Fox is extremely committed to ethical standards in the workplace and states that if they were to ever do a collaboration with a mass-market mer-chandiser, such as JC Penney or Target, there would have to be certain sustainability and ethical standards in place.

Fox reflects that it is difficult for their clients to tell them what they want because they have never had the opportunity to make design choices before. They spend time understanding each cli-ent's needs from the moment that they wake up in the morning until they go to sleep at night.

When asked about their company name, Fox responded that in Buddhism the eightfold path is the path to relieve suffering. Their clothing is a tool to help end suffering for disabled peo-ple. In addition, their brand is gender fluid, and they can design and adapt measurements for the trans community. Fox is very eager to share their experiences and has prepared content for speaking to the community and to school about disability, clothing, fashion, and identity.

Fox interviewed by Susan Kolko

Discussion: Why might physical changes in a disability make clothing inaccessible and costly? Fox used their lived experiences to create designs that are affordable, accessible, and adaptable. What might be some other design ideas to accommodate changes in disability?

Summary

Because most adaptivewear is produced for the mass market, it is essential to understand the various groupings of disabilities that define special needs. This chapter has explored several systems that can be considered in developing the adaptivewear market. Although each grouping offers information and strategies, several elements appear universal and should always be considered.

In designing and considering adaptations, it is essential to be aware of whether the disability is physical, cognitive, or sensory. As noted, most adaptivewear is needed by people with physical disabilities, creating a larger market for this population. The severity of the condition is another essential element to consider. Disabilities may be mild, moderate, or severe. People with certain mild disabilities, such as low vision or mild dexterity impairment, may choose not to use adaptivewear, while those with severe disabilities, such as blindness, paralysis, or inability to walk may seek, and welcome, adaptive clothing. A third important consideration is the course of disability, which can be identified using Rolland's three categories: disability may be constant, intermittent, or progressive. Intermittent and progressive disabilities present special challenges to individuals, designers, producers, and marketers.

Learning activities

- Consider the diverse ways of identifying disability. Choose an item of clothing—top, bottom, shoes, etc. Which grouping would be relevant in design and why?
- Consider what grouping an apparel brand might choose to help design the most accessible garments for someone with dexterity challenges.

Why would you make that choice?

- Pick a fashion brand and create an adaptive design concept that can be associated with one of the grouping types.
- Consider the business examples in the chapter. Make a connection between the business and the groups.

Adaptive talk

- John Rolland
- International Paralympic Committee
- World Health Organization
- Progressive, Constant, and Intermittent
- Physical, cognitive, sensory impairment
- Weakening
- Department of Education
- World Health Organization
- Activities of daily living
- SSDI

- SSI
- *Sew Much Comfort*
- Deborah Carabet

Case studies

FFORA – Lucy Jones

DEWEY – Chamiah Dewey

Eightfold Fox – Fox

Buck & Buck – Bill & Julie Buck

Francisco   Postelthwaite Munos

4
Disabilities and clothing adaptation

Introduction

The clothing needs of each person with a disability are unique to that person, and are related to several of the concepts presented in the previous chapter. It is important to consider the nature of the disability, its severity, its onset, course, and expected outcome, as well as the individual's perception of the importance of clothing in reflecting individual personality and lifestyle. It is often psychologically quite challenging for people who have been able to wear mass-marketed clothing until diagnosed with a disability to make the shift to adaptivewear. Both mass market brands and retailers who have extended their product lines to include adaptivewear have been successful, because these enable adaptivewear customers to continue to shop in their chosen stores, and sport familiar products. At times, both brands and retailers have utilized special collaborations with celebrities and as well as appealing brand-name images to encourage and assist this population to explore and accept the shift to adaptive clothing which better meets their personal needs. Understanding that disabilities can be physical, cognitive, or sensory, or a combination of these, can be vital in assisting an apparel business to use textiles and create designs that enhance individual appearance, quality of life, and functionality.

This chapter explores several of the most common needs for clothing adaptations, illustrates both developed and potential adaptations, and considers design, production, and marketing strategies. Because people with mild disabilities often choose not to wear adaptive clothing, the focus will be primarily on moderate to severe challenges to dressing independently in clothing that is both comfortable and fashionable. Some disabling conditions limit self-dressing completely. In those instances, design must also consider the ability of the caregiver to manage the clothing.

Figure 4 Qaysean Williams MANAKIN 'the one hand sewing man'

Learning objectives

- Understand considerations in clothing needs which vary according to disability
- Identify the disabilities that require adaptive clothing

- Understand the reasons why "ease of dressing" is crucial for people with disabilities
- Understand the role access plays in adaptive clothing design
- Categorize the primary considerations for adaptive design
- Consider adaptations primarily according to function, and then to fashion

A. Clothing for people who use wheelchairs

According to the Centers for Disease Control, 12.2 percent of the population in the United States have mobility limitations described as "serious difficulty walking or climbing stairs". The visual image in the report is a wheelchair, and one can assume that a good proportion of this population utilizes wheelchairs for mobility. Wheelchair users tend to remain in a seated position, in their wheelchairs, for extended periods of time daily, and both comfort and attractive appearance are major concerns. Comfortable textures, easy on-off design, ease of access for personal needs, and fit that is comfortable for long hours of minimal movement is essential.

Textures should be smooth, soft, and non-binding.

Although many people who use wheelchairs require assistance with dressing and undressing, many prefer to remain as independent as possible. Clothing styles should be easy to put on or remove, with openings and closures on the sides, rather than on the back, and an extended garment length.

Ease of access for personal needs, such as toileting, is essential for people spending long hours in a seated position, and openings and closures should be positioned to enable fast and easy access.

A specific design need for people who use wheelchairs involves pants proportioning. Sitting tends to pull the waist down in the back, and sitting for long hours can create serious discomfort. Pant proportions can accommodate this by extending farther in the back.

Case study: Rollettes

Conner Lundius is the team captain, choreographer, content creator, and marketing director for the Rollettes, a wheelchair dance group. Based in Los Angeles, the group practices their routines at the Evolution Studios in North Hollywood and the Mihran K Studios in Burbank, and performs all over the country. In 2022, they even performed at the Boston Celtics half-time show! Conner routinely handles all of the Rollettes' social media. She works endlessly, planning, executing, editing, and marketing the group's special mission: to make dance a platform for expression and to encourage others, both individuals and groups, to keep doing what they love, despite any setbacks or challenges they might encounter.

She strongly believes that there is a great deal that is not publicly discussed about disability, dressing, clothing, and fashion by the fashion industry. Though she recognizes that there are advocates attempting to increase and broaden the general awareness, she is very conscious of the fact that the clothing and fashion industry is still not very cognizant of special needs, and how to address them.

Conner also produces both a women's empowerment event for women and girls with disabilities, and a talent highlight for people with disabilities. Her work is highly creative and dance-focused, allowing her to express herself in many ways, with dress as a major component. Her goal in the fashion field is to have fashion and style be attainable for all people. She might wear the same outfit, or the same shoes, many times—she specifically wants others to know that she is a real person, a person with a budget. However, she does not let her budget, or her few items of clothing, control her style: instead, she makes it define her.

Conner began dancing when she was 5 years old, and fashion has always been an essential for her. She feels that her style has built her personal confidence and has helped her to achieve her personal goals. Now 31, she feels that her creative passion and fire, and the confidence that is within her, enables her to use dance to bring both energy and awareness to all people with disabilities.

She has a bachelor's degree in fashion merchandising from Fontbonne University in St. Louis. Upon completing college, she was ready to conquer the world with her passion for fashion, particularly with her interest in trend forecasting and visual merchandising. She loved school, and after graduation, was considering continuing her education with an MBA program and was even considering living in London. However, two weeks after graduation, her life changed forever. She was in a car that went off the road and hit a pole at 60 miles an hour. Only 22 years old at the time, Conner sustained multiple major injuries and was instantly paralyzed for life. She was in the hospital for several months, and then several more months in rehabilitation. She recalls that her major goal through that time was re-attaining her independence. She desperately needed to grasp something that she knew would bring positives into her life and keep her moving. Dance had always given her energy: she put her personal effort into it, and received energy in return. It was this deep love of dance that brought her to discover the Rollettes. She immediately realized that both the strong impact and the positivity that the Rollettes brought to the disability community was impressive, and she wanted to be part of their team. How could she not?

Conner moved to Los Angeles, joined the Rollettes, and has been a part of the team for the past five years. It has been an outlet for expression and change for her, and it has also complemented her love of fashion. She stresses that clothing, the connection one has to one's personal wardrobe, and the ability of fashion to make a person feel complete becomes even more important when life brings unexpected changes and challenges. She shares that the first thing she did after her injury, as soon as she was able, was to go through her entire closet to see what would still work for her. Extreme body changes came with her disability: at one point she had lost 50 lbs., which left her, at 5 feet 8 inches and under 100 lbs., with few clothing items from which to choose. Over time, her proportions changed again, and she learned to accept her new physical self. Conner also has a colostomy bag, and dressing around that is always a challenge. She loves to wear cute crop tops but knows she always must have back-ups for sudden needs. She very much wants to have style, to look cute, to feel good, and to try new fashions, but factoring in her disability makes clothing choices a challenge, because what she wants to wear isn't necessarily going to work for her body.

Both Conner's fashion sense and her education in the field have also made her aware that even if garments are designed specifically for "people with disabilities" they still may not work for everyone easily because of the substantial number of individual variations in proportions and needs. For example, even though special clothing can be designed for the seated body, she feels it is still necessary to make it fit properly on a case-by-case basis. With her fashion background and interests, she embraces this challenge and says she "figure(s) out ways" to make whatever she wants to wear work well for her. She is in a wheelchair but determined that this will not stop her from looking fit and fashionable. She recognizes that style choices for wheelchair users are limited but finds ways to help her friends and fellow dancers select clothes, considering it a "fun challenge", and she eventually would very much like to   return to a career in fashion.

At present, though, she is focused on dance, working closely with the Rollettes founder, Chelsie Hill, and partnering with businesses in the community in an effort to make their products more accessible to people with disabilities. When the Rollettes order apparel for a performance, it often has to be altered by Sewn Adaptive (see Chapter 7), a tailoring company that specializes in adaptive alterations and designs. Conner feels strongly that having models with disabilities is an important part of recognizing these members of the community, and that it is vital for the public to understand that disability is "real", is "here to stay", and that there is a consumer demand for products to meet the needs of this population. Ideally, Conner would like to see Universal Design become more prevalent, but points out that even though an item of clothing might have a broad, customer-based design, it might still need to be reconfigured and adjusted to meet the needs of someone with a specific disability, especially when it comes to buttons, zippers, openings, and pockets. She values fashion, style, and comfort in her clothing. She is not particularly brand loyal, and is willing to consider anything that might work, but does find that Abercrombie's Rebrand works well for her personal needs. She also feels that comfortable undergarments are especially important, and the Rollettes work closely with the loungewear brand Airy, which also specializes in intimates. Conner loves to mix and match her clothes, creating an individual style that both keeps her motivated and inspired, and accentuates her personality.

Conner Lundis, interviewed by Susan Kolko 2024

Discussion: Why might adaptive clothing for Conner Lundis the "dancer" and Conner Lundis the "fashionista" be particularly important for her esteem? Conner mentions Universal Design. In what way might Universal Design apply to people in a wheelchair?

B. Clothing for people with limited dexterity

Limited dexterity can affect everyone at various stages of life—children often have limited dexterity in their early years, and seniors often lose dexterity as they age. In addition, many physical disabilities can limit dexterity. Fingers are most affected, but arm movements may also be more limited. Because so many members of society have difficulties with finger dexterity, many adaptations are familiar, and are more readily available to potential users than some more specialized adaptations.

Clothing that meets dexterity needs is often favored by the general population as well. It enables faster and easier dressing and undressing and has become a commonly used alternative.

As an example, one can hardly turn on the television to watch the evening news without seeing advertisements for Skechers Slip-On shoes. The process of putting on shoes without any manual assistance is shown repeatedly. While shoes that do not require manual assistance may be preferable to all, they provide an excellent alternative to laces and snaps in footwear for people with both mobility and dexterity limitations. There are also several other items that may require specific adaptations for people with dexterity limitations.

1. Jewelry

Jewelry is considered an accessory, and is included as an integral part of the fashion industry. Accessorizing with jewelry is a form of creativity that explores personal tastes and individual choices. Jewelry promotes individuality, and, as a form of decoration, can reflect values, taste, personality, interests, and environment. As an example, one of the most personal pieces of jewelry is a charm bracelet. Each individual charm on a bracelet is a miniature figure and symbol that represents each person's unique individuality, experiences, and fantasies. Jewelry plays a significant role in identity, and there are several brands, businesses, and advocates that are paving the way for adaptive jewelry, as well as other accessories, such as handbags, hair accessories, and men's furnishings, to be included in the adaptive apparel space.

JCK is a consumer trend analysis firm. Karen Dybris has written an article for JCK titled *Disabled + Stylish Collab Highlights Adaptive*

Fine Jewelry and Friendship. The article defines the disability community as potential customers, and explores jewelry options and adaptable solutions that enable the enjoyment of this special accessory. Stephanie Thomas, a stylist for people with disabilities, and an advocate of brands that have developed accessible jewelry for people with disabilities, collaborated with Cut & Clarity to launch a line of accessible, inclusive, and adaptable jewelry. The collection includes bracelets, necklaces, rings, and earrings that are affordable, and that reflect current styles and sustainable design. Molly Wang, a designer who struggles with rheumatoid arthritis, has designed a solution for jewelry accessibility by trying to explore and address her own needs. The "bracelet helper" allows stress-free on/off access for jewelry, with a tool that looks something like an extended small pair of pliers, and costs only three dollars. The jewelry industry as a whole also actively supports the disability community by hiring people with disabilities in sustainable workspaces at the retail and manufacturing level of the industry. In addition, brands creating signature jewelry pieces are donating a percentage of their profits to organizations that support disability. Adaptivewear retailers such as Abilitee and Patty and Ricky carry pieces that incorporate braille, emergency alerts, chewable materials, and sensory designs that integrate smell, have magnetic closures, and feature multi-use styles that can function as a bracelet or necklace.[20]

Jewelry design, purpose, and function vary between and within cultures. Sustainable resources such as ceramics, shells, wood, bone, rocks, gemstones, metals, leathers, string/yarn, and pearls enable creativity in design and function. Young children wear watches that feature their favorite characters, identification bracelets and necklaces with their names, candy necklaces and lollipops. They play dress-up with crowns and wands, and sport character sunglasses. Jewelry and accessories promote fantasy, maturity, and responsibility. Taking care of an important piece of jewelry promotes positive feelings of responsibility as well as ownership. A piece of jewelry might need to be taken on and off throughout the day, depending upon activities and circumstances, and the wearer would then be responsible for ensuring its safety and care. Proof of responsibility often enables the next category or cost of jewelry. For example, responsible Swatch watch care is necessary before Apple watch ownership. Bead necklace wear and careful care, ensuring against breakage, might indicate the ability to care for a gold necklace.[21]

Additionally, individuals become emotionally attached to jewelry because it represents values and experiences, and provides memories. Jewelry also stimulates conversations: it can engender an easy compliment or prompt a question that lightens an uncomfortable moment. Jewelry might also have more than its simple visual effect: it might serve other purposes for the wearer, such as a reminder, a simple tool to focus fidgeting and encourage calmness, or a monitor for both location and health. Lack of dexterity and sensory challenges can make jewelry a struggle for people with disabilities, but with the same personal, social, and cultural experiences as the general population, jewelry is an important accessory.

2. Velcro™

One of the most familiar products that has been developed to address specific dexterity needs is Velcro™. Velcro™ can be utilized to replace buttons, snaps, zippers, and laces. Clothing designed with Velcro™ can "hide" its adaptations easily.

3. Zippers

Zippers offer a fast and easy way to join together parts of clothing, and are most frequently found on jackets, sweaters, and pants. However, decreases in dexterity renders the use of zippers challenging and often impossible. Zippers may be replaced with Velcro™, as noted above, but adaptations that resemble zippers may be more normalizing for some users. Adaptations enable zippers to be utilized comfortably by people with limited dexterity.

Case study: Magzip/Ankhgear

Nancy Peters has been an Occupational Therapist in upstate New York for over 40 years. She recalls being in school when the American with Disabilities Act was in the making. In her opinion, the ADA addressed a lot of critical issues, but missed the piece on dressing. Having watched clients struggle for years, she was determined to contribute to the accessibility of dressing and to the independence this can provide for people with disabilities. Early on she identified that zippers were a source of frustration for her clients with fine motor and mobility challenges.

Her brother suffered from a condition called myotonic dystrophy, which affected his physical ability to manage daily tasks. Nancy's son, Scott, who is an engineer, also wanted to also help figure out a way to make dressing easier for his uncle and others.

Zippers were first invented in the early 1900s, and the basic concept and design had not changed since then, except for fashion styling. Traditional zipper operation requires eight or nine fine motor actions, and two hands. If a person has fine motor challenges, or only one hand, it is almost impossible to operate the zipper independently. Nancy and Scott started to brainstorm. They wanted to get rid of the pin box that locks the bottom of the zipper together, and design a zipper that automatically comes together so that the only thing a wearer would have to do is pull it up using a larger pull. Nancy, Scott, and a friend who is a design engineer, produced a prototype for the idea. It was a long, painstaking process, but the team truly believed in the vision of a better zipper. They created many renditions of the design, and developed prototypes to be tested with Nancy's brother. They finally figured out a functional version of their new zipper design which they named Magzip. They patented Magzip and were on their way to production.

They needed to find a zipper manufacturer but, in the meantime, did some market research to figure out if there was a great enough need for this new universally designed zipper. They found out that there was, indeed, a great need for their zipper. They also placed some videos highlighting Magzip on YouTube, and someone on the Under Armour Team saw their video and contacted them because they had been looking for a better zipper. They were invited to the Under Armour Innovation Challenge, and, after that, the Under Armour company wanted to start putting Magzip in some of their products. Ideal Zipper, a manufacturer, was willing to produce the zipper. They licensed with both UA and Ideal and soon had garments with their zippers available to the public. UA no longer has exclusivity, and Magzip is available in many American and International products. Ankhgear also sells products online, such as hoodies, with Magzip and individual zippers. They can be found online at dnsdesignsllc.com, Ankhgear.com, Magzip-Ideal Fasteners, and Amazon.

Nancy Peters interviewed by Susan Kolko. Case study content provided by Nancy Peters OTR/L

Discussion: Costing for Magzip is much higher than the cost of a regular zipper. How does this impact the consumer? What could be done to decrease the cost of the zipper? How could a brand reduce the impact that the cost of the zipper has on the final retail cost of the product?

C. Clothing for people with access needs

People with disabilities may also need fast and easy access to areas of their bodies which are usually covered with mass-marketed clothing. Access to arms, necks, chest areas, and other parts of bodies may be necessary for ports and intravenous medications and treatments, either constantly or periodically. Access to broader parts of the body requiring treatments may also be necessary. And, of course, access to meet toilet needs quickly and easily is essential.

Openings may be designed to be accessible, and covered by carefully designed draping. Sleeves or pant legs may be designed with openings which extend up the sides. Easy access for toileting needs may be provided using draping over Velcro™ closures. The topic of toileting is particularly sensitive, as there is a risk of public embarrassment, and the realization that body functions are not always controllable.

Case study: Preventa Wear

There are many causes of incontinence, ranging from Alzheimer's disease, dementia, autism, neurological disorders, epilepsy, Parkinson's, significant cognitive and developmental delays, increased age, stroke, surgery, spinal cord injuries, medications, etc. Some people simply have to wear an incontinence brief, but want coverage at all times to hide their incontinence brief. Preventa Wear makes preventive undergarments and bodysuits that are sanitary, provide allover coverage, and are sourced sustainably. Cindi Seifert, the founder of Preventa Wear, created a one-piece body suit for her daughter, who struggles with incontinence. She shares that being a caregiver is hard and often messy work when it comes to toileting: Cindi is a caregiver first and a mom second. Preventa Wear clothing allows her to focus on keeping her daughter Kayla healthy, without spending too much time on washing and cleaning. The brand is recognized worldwide and the business is growing each year.

Cindi Seifert interviewed by Susan Kolko

Discussion: Consider how easy access is important for a caregiver. How might the challenges and emotions of the caregiver differ from the person with the disability? What types of textiles, fabrics, and materials might be used in the construction of Preventa Wear's one-piece body suit?

D. Clothing for amputees, people with braces, and people with varied bone structures

Clothing for amputees and those with shortened or deformed bone structures is designed to minimize the focus on those areas of the body by blending them with other areas. An amputee with an artificial limb may wear pants that cover the limb to the ankle, giving it the appearance of a natural limb. Design may be more challenging for an arm amputee, where draping and folding may be used to minimize focus.

Braces, usually placed on arms or legs, need special clothing adaptations as well, as they add measurably to the width of the limb, and sometimes to its length. Designs may require broader pant legs or sleeves, and a zipper or other device that may be opened to easily slip the clothing item on and off.

Shortened or deformed bones may require that an area of clothing be longer or shorter, larger or smaller, than others. Clothing for amputees and people with varied bone structures may require personal design and fitting and may be challenging for mass-market applications.

Case study: Santa Monica College fashion student

Ridhwan (no last name to protect privacy) was a student in the fashion design and merchandising program at Santa Monica College both before and during COVID. When the COVID-19 pandemic closed academic classes on campus, he and his family moved back to their home in Saudi Arabia. Ridhwan was diagnosed with cancer in high school, and had to spend extended time in the hospital getting chemotherapy treatment. All the medical complications of cancer and its treatment made it difficult for him to be in school. He felt that he needed to be in bed, and remembered being in a very dark state, not knowing how to spend his time awake without feeling lost and depressed. At first, he had regular visitors and felt people wanted to be with him, but after a few months, everything quieted down until there were only very close friends and family visiting regularly, just two or three people. He had a great deal of empty time, felt captive in his bed, and was really at a loss.

As he was yearning for something to inspire his intellect, he began to watch fashion videos and began to draw. He became enamored of Gucci, and watched fashion show after fashion show in which the brand was featured. He wanted to be part of what he saw but was not sure how, or what part, would be best for him. He liked the idea of designing hands-on, and experiencing the fashion industry through drawing, sewing, and creating patterns. He had no experience, and from a hospital bed, with no one to learn from except YouTube and social media, the project seemed very overwhelming.

Ridhwan began to draw, work with color, and experiment with design, and then quickly realized that he needed help. When he was discharged from the hospital, he enrolled in the fashion program at Santa Monica College. He managed all of the complications of attending school on-ground with his disability but still felt very much alone, and the first few months were challenging for him. He didn't know anyone, and felt extremely uncomfortable with the prosthetic leg that was due to his cancer. Slowly, class by class, and professor by professor, Ridhwan found his path, and studying fashion became his recovery. Although he was still making frequent trips to the hospital, and was not able to take more than two classes at a time, his classmates started to connect with him, and his professors inspired him to dig deep into his creative talent. Ridhwan recalls taking a colors class in the evening, and spending time in the sewing lab. His professors, Lorrie Ivas, Jemi Armstrong, Robin Lake, LaTanya Louis, and Susan Kolko, all played a significant role in helping to inspire him, and to encourage his natural talent and interest in learning.

He became aware that the time he was spending in school was making him better and healthier, both mentally and physically, and he no longer felt alone. He recognized that he was very dependent on technology, and that his computer was making everything accessible for him. He wanted to learn more about technology and sustainable business practices, and appreciated every topic he encountered in school.

Ridhwan shared the challenges he was experiencing in wearing pants with his prosthetic leg. He felt that his only option was baggy sweatpants, because he could get them on and off easily. Getting his legs into his pants was a daily challenge, and unless the material was stretchy and allowed for movement, he was unable to manipulate his prosthetic into the pant leg. Soccer pants seemed to work for him, and had a sporty feel with which he could identify. He longed to wear jeans, however, and shared that if he could somehow find denim that would work for his needs, he would want to design a pair of pants.

The support he felt from the fashion department, Ridhwan shared, and from the college, made his education a positive experience. The resources that Santa Monica College provides for students with all types of disabilities were easily accessible to him, and helped to make his experience an incredibly positive one despite the challenges he faced.

Ridhwan interviewed by Susan Kolko

Discussion: Consider Ridhwan as a student. How might other students help Ridhwan to feel a sense of normalcy at school? What could Ridhwan's teachers do to further inspire his interest in education? What might be some of the challenges Ridhwan faces in the apparel industry once he leaves college? Research how life in Saudi differs from life in the United States for a person with a disability.

Case study: Adaptive by Asiya

Asiya Rafiq considers herself a modest fashion designer who creates custom designs for the adaptive clothing market. She is originally from Kashmir, India, where she was educated at Mallinson Girls School. She moved to Mumbai, where she started her own advertising company. She also did modeling assignments and fashion shows as a model. She was always interested in the excitement and creativity of fashion, of taking standard clothing designs and fashioning them into her own styles. Asiya studied psychology in college, and is certified as an Applied Behavioral Analyst. Her passion for understanding how individuals respond to their environment has inspired her to help the disability community. Currently, she resides in Abu Dhabi with her husband and son. Asiya worked closely with the Sedra Foundation, which promotes accessibility and inclusion for the special needs community through services, programs, and events. Her current involvement with drum therapy, her talent for singing and music therapy, and her participation in neurological games has allowed her to contribute to the growth and development of people with disabilities through her art studio Al

Zaid Arts. Jad Ahammad, a young boy with Down Syndrome, has given her the inspiration to do more, because she sees how her work affects children in particular. As a disability advocate, she regularly speaks at local universities and vocational schools, and was the recipient of the "Game Changer of Fashion" award from Amity University in Dubai.

Asiya believes that the fashion industry is moving toward understanding the need for adaptivewear, and that many of the modifications, such as magnets and   Velcro™, can be used for all consumers. She is positive that the apparel industry has become more inclusive, and she hopes to see adaptivewear as a category of clothing. Her work with the Special Olympics opened her eyes to the challenges people with disabilities face in clothing and dressing. Her modest designs provide her clients with fashionable easywear solutions. Asiya regularly attends Dubai's modest fashion week in an effort to learn about the latest trends in design and textiles. Recently, she started using a fabric from Japan that allows for breathability, comfort in texture, and options in color and finish. In addition, she works with a wool fabric to create towel wraps for people with asthma. One of Asiya's most notable contributions to adaptive designs is her creation of the two-piece abaya. An abaya is a loose fitting garment that looks similar to a robe. Muslim women wear abayas to signify religion and modesty. However, non-Muslim women can also wear them. This full body piece of clothing is not practical for someone who uses a wheelchair. However, Asiya has designed an abaya specifically for wheelchair users that allows for easy access, while maintaining the overall aesthetic features of the garment. Adaptive by Asiya provides clothing solutions for people of all ages with varying types of disabilities, and can be found on Instagram and Facebook.

Asiya Rafiq interviewed by Susan Kolko

Discussion: What might be some considerations in abaya designs for people with disabilities who do not use wheelchairs? Asiya is very involved with her local community. How does this help her to better understand her clients?

E. Clothing for people who are visually impaired and/or blind

While blindness and other vision limitations do not require major design adaptation in clothing, there are several important marketing issues which must be addressed to meet this population's needs. According to the Centers for Disease Control, approximately 1 million Americans are legally blind, and an additional 6 million have varying degrees of vision loss. There are more women than men in these groups, and age is also a major contributing factor.[22] In addition, the National Institutes of Health are predicting that the numbers of people with blindness and vision loss will double by 2050.[23]

Inability to see affects many aspects of clothing—from choices of style and design, to ability to perceive how a clothing item looks on one's figure, to coordinating colors and design choices in selecting daily outfits, to shopping for clothing unable to read labels or to view styles and colors in stores, and to the challenges of utilizing more convenient online shopping for clothing. Addressing these presents major challenges to the clothing industry.

In considering one simple issue—labeling—various sources were approached and asked whether labeling in braille might be a possible way to address a concern that routinely affects blind shoppers. The responders noted the high cost of having braille on labels, making this resource unavailable. However, in an article for Perkins School for the Blind, Michela Tavolieri shares that technology has helped bridge to the gap between vision and clothing. Color apps, and The American Printing House (APH) tags, can assist with both wardrobe selection and closet organization. In her research, she shares that the brands "Two Blind Brothers" and "White Cane Label", and the designer Maria Sol Unga specifically cater to visually impaired consumers, offering braille labels for their products.

Jasmin Ambiong is blind and shared her experiences with clothing, fashion, and dressing in a 2022 article she wrote for Billion Strong, a disability organization where she is a development manager. She stressed that fashion is just as important to her as to anyone else. She can understand textiles and fabrics through touch, which allows her to make agreeable purchasing and wearing decisions. She relies on her family and friends to interpret color for coordinating outfits but finds that she tends to stick to neutrals for simplicity. Jasmin has all her garments memorized and her closet organized to make stylish wardrobe selection comfortable. She enjoys shopping for clothes, knowing what is on trends, and choosing her outfits, and wishes that all people with disabilities could experience the thrill that she gets from dressing up.

Differentiating between colors and shades is a challenge for coordinating outfits. More importantly, people who are visually impaired need to be visible to others for safety reasons. Contrasting colors with the colors in the environment, so that moving vehicles and others can see someone who is unable to see for themselves, is an important consideration in dressing.

Case study: Charlie Dorris

Charlie Dorris describes himself as "a low vision person". He recognizes that color, especially color contrast, is a major issue for him and for other low-vision people. He can recognize differences between light and dark colors, and some of the different shades of the same color, but has difficulties distinguishing between blue and black, for example. For clothing, he resolves that challenge by having only navy-blue pants, and not black, and also brown pants in several shades. All his shirts contrast with each other, but work well with both his navy blue and his brown pants. This makes color-coordinating clothing manageable for him.

Charlie is also very aware of the need to "walk defensively and safely" in the streets and prefers light-colored clothing so that he can be seen more easily by drivers, especially at night. During the day, he tries to select colors that contrast with the gray brown of roads and sidewalks. He wants to be clearly visible to pedestrians too, as that makes "running into them" less likely.

From an email on personal clothing challenges by Charlie Dorris

Discussion: Consider color and visual impairments. What could the apparel industry do to make color in clothing more accessible? How could costs of Braille in labeling be minimized? Why does the apparel industry need to consider visual impairments as a serious consideration in design?

F. Clothing for people with developmental disabilities

Clothing for people with developmental disabilities requires ease of dressing and undressing, with simple design and easy fastenings to maximize independence. People may also have specific likes and dislikes in terms of color, but most particularly in terms of texture. Soft, smooth textures tend to be preferred by people with developmental disabilities.

Noise may sometimes be an important factor in clothing use. While Velcro™ may appear to be a logical choice for ease of dressing and undressing, the sound the Velcro™ makes when it is separated may be very upsetting, especially to people with autism. Similarly, the sound of a loud zipper may startle and upset people.

Because all these factors—colors, textures, sounds—and others which may vary by individual conditions, preferences, and habits, it is important to have choices available to meet these special needs.

Case study: Kozie Clothes

Susan Donohoe is the CEO and founder of Kozie Clothes. She is a Pediatric Occupational Therapist, with a Certification in Sensory Integration, Sensory Enrichment Therapy, ADHD Certified Clinical Services Provider, and SIPT testing. She has additional background experience in burn and hand therapy, has a second degree in Physical Education, and is a mother of six children. She is passionate about this project, begun after decades of work as a pediatric Occupational Therapist, with the realization that there were so few options for therapeutically effective, stylish, and well-fitting clothing for kids and babies with special needs. Through many years of working closely with educators, therapists, nursing professionals, manufacturers, and experts in design, she founded Kozie Clothes in 2013 to incorporate neuroscience principles into fashionable, on-trend, adaptive clothing, and products for children with sensory and other medical needs.

Susan has had a lifetime of experience helping people with special needs. Her personal character and career interests have evolved over years of interaction with family, friends, and particularly with children. She is quick to solve problems, and thinking outside of the box comes naturally. Susan's most intimate experience, a guiding light in her business mission, has come from her daughter, who had had an anxiety disorder and a sensory processing disorder. Tags were irritating, and she was ultrasensitive to fabrics. Susan's daughter suffered most with sensory defensiveness in the tactile, auditory, and vestibular fields. She actually was an extremely bright child whose sensory difficulties could be described as anxiety-related, and at times affected her ability to regulate her emotions. There were so many sensory challenges for her daughter, in addition to those related to dressing, that impacted daily functioning and her psyche that, as a mother, Susan went into problem-solving mode. Having worked with traumatic burn therapies, she understood the connection between skin and comfort. As a hand therapist who created splints and manipulated medical resources to adapt to her patients' needs, Susan understood mechanics. And, as an animal lover, she knew what the magic of touch and feel could do for a human. She pinpointed her daughter's consumer needs through her own professional and personal experiences.

Affordability and attractiveness played an important role in the creation of her line of clothing. Considerations of costing and design were key. Most parents/caregivers responsible for the finances associated with raising a child/young adult with special needs have extra expenses due to their child's disability. For example, a two-hundred-dollar adaptive compression top is not realistic for most families, and was the only option on the market at that time. Susan shares that her business sacrifices profitability in favor of providing needed products to an underserved market. Her brand, Kozie Clothes, offers new styles, fabrics, and options with every new collection. Children want to be playful and appear trendy; everyone wants their child to have the resources to feel like they "fit in", and Susan's clothing meets these needs.

Susan currently resides outside of Philadelphia with her husband, enjoying her grandsons, and loving taking care of animals. She had no idea her career in occupational therapy would lead to the apparel industry.

Susan says that Kozie Clothes is committed to serving the unique need for stylish, fun, and therapeutic clothing and products for the Pediatric Special Needs community. "At Kozie Clothes, we believe that all children are unique and deserve to feel comfortable and happy every day. We have a wide range of sensory engineered clothing and solutions for kids of all ages, as well as products designed for toddlers, newborns, and preemies who require ongoing medical care."

Beginning with a compression line, now one of the leading manufacturers of sensory compression clothing, Kozie expanded offerings to include baby bodysuits adapted for ease of care and medical treatments, such as G tubes for feeding and IVs, as well as weighted toys and blankets.

In 2016, after seeing what Kozie Clothes was all about, an RN caring for infants with neonatal abstinence syndrome reached out with a special need: a need for something to support the development of babies born from drug addicted mothers. Susan developed a torso-weighted pad for infants, which she manufactured and provided for a study. After three years of hands-on testing, it was found that the prototype effectively reduced infant heart rates to a healthy range, and decreased overall measures from the Finnegan scale, which assesses the 21 most common signs of neonatal drug withdrawal syndrome. Additionally, the infants slept better, and feeding was improved. She has since continued to address special needs and developed the Patented Kozie Medical Sock as well as G-tube support. Kozie Clothes continues to add to their product line and create content for those seeking a better understanding of the company and its products. In addition to the information provided for each product on their website, the company can be found on Facebook and Instagram. Susan prides herself on Kozie's personal customer service, and often personally connects directly with parents seeking her professional knowledge. She is happy to consult with her customers and to navigate their individual needs.

Susan Donohoe interviewed by Susan Kolko

Discussion: Children often cannot communicate needs because they are not aware of any other options aside from the ones they are experiencing. How does Kozie Clothes advocate for children with disabilities? Why might it be important to inquire about patents for original designs in adaptivewear?

Summary

This chapter has presented some of the special challenges in the design of adaptivewear, with some clothing needs specifically considered. The examples used are accepted designs, addressing needed adaptations commonly utilized by people with specific groupings of disabilities. Several clothing adaptations are more generally needed and used by various disability groupings as well as by the general public. Case studies have further illustrated special needs, adaptive clothing design, production, and businesses.

Clothing in this chapter has included basic adaptivewear, focusing on function, rather than fashion, which will be addressed later.

People with disabilities, like all people, are aware of both their personal self-image and the image of themselves that they present to others, and clothing has always been an important part of this. Understanding the role of adaptivewear and fashion in self-image and the image a person projects is essential in both the design and marketing strategies of adaptive clothing, and these will be addressed in Chapter 5.

Learning activities

- At home, lay out an outfit of clothing—top, bottom, and shoes. With your eyes closed or covered, get dressed. Reflect upon what considerations in dressing might be important for someone who cannot see.

- Try to tie your shoe with one hand. What would make putting shoes on and off easier for someone who only has use of one hand?

- While seated in a chair, put on a pair of pants. Your arms and hands can assist, but your feet and legs cannot move. Explain what you had to do to get the pants on completely.

- Try buttoning a dress shirt with one hand only. How could fashion design make a difference?

Adaptive talk

- Center for Disease Control
- dexterity
- amputee
- Velcro™
- braille

Case studies

Rollettes – Connor Lundis

MIGA swim – Mari Luisa Mendiola

Kozie Clothing – Susan Donohoe

Magzip/Ankgear – Nancy Peters

Santa Monica College – Ridhwan Student

Cindi Seifert – Preventa Wear

Charlie Dorris

Part III
Self-image, public image, disability, and fashion

Introduction

Physical appearance—the way in which people view themselves and others in the context of the broader society provides a vital source of information, essential to all.[24] People tend to understand, to value, to identify with—or not—and sometimes to judge others, as well as themselves, based on physical appearance. While many other factors have important roles to play in a person's understanding of self, and of others, the impression given simply by appearance remains a major one, and appearance thus becomes a major factor in the broader concept of self-image. Appearance as an important part of self-image remains essential even for those with visual impairments, with awareness created by touch and by perceptions expressed or understood by others.

A disability itself can create an immediate personal feeling of difference, and is often an essential issue, addressed not only by individuals but also by family members, colleagues, and friends. For people with visible physical disabilities, appearance can have a major impact on self-image. As noted in previous chapters, clothing is a major determinant of one's appearance, and both fit and style are essential elements. Chapter 5 will explore the concept of self-image, with a focus on people with disabilities, and Chapter 6 will apply this concept to the essential role of clothing and fashion in supporting a positive sense of self-esteem. Appearance as a principal factor in the perception of people with disabilities in society will also be discussed, and the essential role of clothing and fashion design related to appearance explored.

5
Self-image and disability

Introduction

Self-image is the way individuals think and feel about their physical, mental, emotional, and intellectual selves. Self-image affects personal identity, influences choices and decision-making, and may be personally determined by many external factors. Psychologists and sociologists have studied the impact of self-image on individuals' ability to perform life tasks, support meaningful relationships, and maintain positive mental attitudes during challenging times, as well as its impact on individual cultural engagement, community involvement, and contribution to society.

Research studies indicate that clothing and fashion play a significant role in self-image: clothing affects self-confidence, which directly impacts self-image, and fashion is a valuable tool for the development and maintenance of a positive self-image.

Figure 5 So Yes wheelchair trouser with side zippers

Learning objectives

Upon completion of this chapter, readers will be able to:

- Define the characteristics of each of the five levels of Maslow's Hierarchy
- Understand the applicability of the hierarchy to people with disabilities
- Understand the role of self-esteem in determining self-image for people with disabilities
- Define the stages of the life cycle as they apply to people with disabilities.

A. Maslow's Hierarchy of Needs

Maslow's Hierarchy of Needs has long been the model for identifying and compartmentalizing the stages and ranges of human development. **Abraham Maslow** was a psychologist who studied human behavior in the 1940s. One of his most noteworthy contributions to the field of psychology is his development of a pyramid for the categorization of human needs, from the most basic to the most complex and advanced. This pyramid system is termed a "hierarchy" and is used in a wide variety of disciplines, both to determine and to understand issues related to self-image, behavior, and performance. Clothing, fashion, and appearance play a key role in this pyramid, but in order to understand its place and its role in the hierarchy, it is essential to view the hierarchy.

There are five levels of needs within Maslow's hierarchy. Level One is the first, and most basic, and level Five, the most advanced, is the level people strive to achieve, with each person shaping and developing their path to this level in their own unique way. Each level within the system can include varying interpretations of its specific elements, which are utilized, or not, by everyone's personal choice. It is important to note that the theory suggests that each level's needs must be fulfilled before it is possible to advance to the next level.

Level 1**: Physiological Needs –** This level contains the most basic needs necessary for human survival: food, water, and shelter. Healthcare may fall to this level in certain extreme situations.

Level 2: **Safety Needs** – Employment, consistent and equitable government, security, and healthcare exist in an environment that fosters fairness, and allows for predictable outcomes are essential components of this level. For example, a 40-hour work week guarantees 40 hours of wages at a certain rate.

Level 3: **Love and Belonging** – Friendships, family, trust, intimacy, and identification as a member of a group, which may be social, religious, family, professional, community, interest, or other are the elements of this level. A job that guarantees hours and wages and meets the criteria of Level 2, for example, might not necessarily provide for the needs of Level 3, and those needs might be met through relationships with family or friends.

Level 4: **Esteem** – Independence, achievement, status, respect, and a good reputation are the driving forces for Level 4. This level suggests a person can make value-based decisions, based on experience, and can make conscious choices. Using the skills and self-esteem derived from Levels 2 and 3, a Level 4 person might be able to develop their own business, assume an important role in their community, or achieve a highly respected professional position using the skill sets learned in the previous levels.

Level 5: **Self-Actualization** – Achievement and functioning at this level is subject to individual interpretation. Some suggest that individuals like Gandhi and Mother Teresa are the only ones to have reached this level. Other more practical interpretations of self-actualization suggest that it is accessible to any person who has accomplished the first four levels and has the desire and ability to achieve this highest level in the field that most interests, motivates, and enables the application of personal skills and abilities. For example, a researcher who has studied, worked, and given back to the community might create something new, or become aware of a situation where there is the ability to go beyond their immediate setting by taking special resources to other countries, running for a public office, or writing a book.[25]

Maslow's Hierarchy, fashion, and disability

People with or without disabilities work through Maslow's pyramid over their lives. However, the limitations caused by disabling conditions, and, often, the need for assistance, can make progression through the pyramid a more chaotic and unpredictable process for people with disabilities. In the context of Rolland's three categories of disability, it may be possible for people with progressive or intermittent disabilities to experience a greater challenge as they work through the hierarchy, due to the unpredictability created by their disabling conditions, while people with constant but severe disabilities may not have the opportunity to experience life's possibilities fully.

"Clothing" and "apparel" differ from "fashion". "Fashion" is not a necessity, and is generally purchased with discretionary income. In American society, clothes are considered a basic, Level 1 need. People do not "need" fashionable clothing; however, clothing plays an important role in the development and maintenance of self- image, and thus is an important factor in individual's position in Maslow's hierarchy. Image and self-esteem are Level 4 attributes: to reach Level 4, Level 1's basic clothing needs would need to be extended to include the ability to purchase fashionable clothing as a positive reflection of self-image.

Although, as noted above, all people have the same Level 1 basic needs for clothing, achieving Level 4's positive self-image may be much more of a challenge for people with disabilities. Inability to work, lower paying jobs, the higher costs of adaptive clothing, along with the scarcity of adaptive fashions may limit, or even eliminate, the possibility of utilizing fashionable clothing to assist in the development of a Level 4 self-image for people with disabilities.

Maslow's Hierarchy illustrates the inequities in opportunities to develop self-esteem through fashionable clothing experienced by many people with disabilities. Belmont University's fashion program applies Maslow's Hierarchy to help identify consumer needs in fashion design (see Chapter 9).

B. The development of self-esteem and disability

The traditional human life cycle moves through predictable stages.. For people with disabilities, some of the characteristics of the stages may vary, depending on the level of impairment.

Understanding life cycles can help with product planning and development, as well as marketing strategies.

For people with disabilities, life stages can be identified by:

- the age of onset of the disability
- the early years of development,
- the role of education and the developmental stages (which can take place over a lifetime),
- adolescence and young adulthood,
- adulthood,
- aging and changes in independence
- end-of-life decisions

Each phase includes different activities and situations which impact dress and fashion. The early years traditionally focus on adjustment and "fitting in", and the older years are more aware of issues around comfort and cost. Careers, social interaction, physical activities, and finances play major roles in the progression through the stages of the life cycle. Environments that support life changes, and are inclusive of differences, make progression through these stages manageable and agreeable. Fashion plays a key role in each stage, providing a form of expression that promotes self-esteem, and the positive energy that can enable acceptance and positivity in moving toward the stage ahead.

Differences in the type and severity of disabling conditions can create variations within the stages. For example, a person who becomes disabled as an elder would have experienced the life cycle until that point as a non-disabled person. People who become disabled as elders might find their new impairments more challenging to accept, as they are unaccustomed to limitations, and frustrated by the changes in self-image and activities that the disabling condition may engender. People with progressive disabilities may find that they have accepted and become comfortable with their level of functioning and with their life activities at a level of disability that has remained unchanged for many years. Even though they may have been aware of the progressive nature of their condition, a sudden, or severe, change in their ability and level of functioning can trigger frustration, depression, and anger.

Case study: Megami

Jane Fainberg Ivanov is the head of public relations and communications at Megami. Megami, which in Japanese means goddess woman, or female goddess, is a niche fashion brand that provides functional and fashionable undergarment solutions for women who have breast cancer. The brand's focus is on equal rights for women, and it provides a shopping experience that enables women to feel empowered and beautiful.

Jane has 30 years of experience in niche market lingerie. From maternity, to nursing, to breast cancer, she knows what it means for a woman to experience all of the most emotional changes a woman's body can endure. As a business owner, a consultant, and an entrepreneur, Jane has been able to use her experiences and education to help grow a business that resonates with her personal and career goals.

Megami was launched by three friends who went to school together in London. With a combination of firsthand experiences with cancer, design expertise, and a desire to make a difference for women, Megami created a business strategy that could potentially help women worldwide who may need their advice and their products. One in eight women have breast issues, cancer, and/or breast surgery at some point in their lifetime. This large market segment can provide a well-needed service/product and proves to be financially sound.

The brand conducted extensive research, beginning with the way human anatomy is connected to identity, and moved on into the production and design logistics that would be best for their clientele. They learned that breasts, regardless of size, shape or color, are intrinsically associated with being a woman. A negative experience related to one's breasts, beginning at a very young age or at any time throughout a woman's life, can lead to eating disorders, self-mutilation, and extreme vulnerability, while an enlightening experience can manifest itself in a positive change in career, relationship, priorities, and personality traits. Megami found that women were mostly seeking comfort: comfort in who they are, both physically and emotionally. In recent years, the attention to breast cancer awareness has enabled women to share their experiences, and society to understand breast cancer as a topic that can be publicly acknowledged and discussed. Breast differences and challenges, whether genetic or acquired, due to accidents or deformities, have become more openly acknowledged as culture has become more sensitive to the magnitude of the issue. Megami, featured in The Guardian and Vogue, was recognized as a brand that catered to a woman's body and her identity.

Jane stresses that there is no medical research to indicate that wearing the wrong size or style of bra could cause cancer or deformities. However, if one wears the wrong size bra, or a bra that includes features such as wire, the lymph nodes may be impacted, and the drainage that cleans out the body affected, and these may have a negative impact. She has seen women with permanent dents in their shoulders, as well as rashes and irritations from bra straps, and is aware that many women wear the wrong size, all of which might be related to brand identity, cost, and style.

Bras can become very expensive for several reasons. The construction is complicated, and there are multiple pieces and trimmings. The design goal is for the support to come from the band that goes around the back, rather than the straps. Snaps, hooks, wires, elastic, and wicking textiles add to manufacturing costs. Jane refers to the Megami technicians who design the garments as "engineers", because there are so many factors to consider when creating a bra pattern. In addition, prostheses require consideration of the differentiation in weight and volume relative to natural breast tissue.

Jane also stresses the importance of the brand's engagement with the community it represents. Many Megami brand ambassadors are breast cancer survivors. Not only are they the best promoters, those who can best identify with the consumer market, but the ambassadors are also eager to share their stories publicly as part of their own journey. The models used for social media, public relations, and advertisements are women who have been affected by breast cancer and are proud to expose scars and body irregularities. Some women have nipple tattoos in the place where nipples used to be. Others have flowers or inspiring art covering surgery scars. Models with tattoos usually like the artwork to be exposed as an advertisement. Tattoos send a message of acceptance, determination, and beauty, and are something a model wants the world to see.

Megami lingerie can be purchased through over 100 department stores and smaller retail stores worldwide. The brand has extended into swimwear, and design technology, understanding of consumer needs, production abilities, and profitability has allowed it to diversify its product offerings, enabling greater brand exposure. The brands most recent blog shares content that applies to accessibility and affordability for adaptivewear, focusing on insurance coverage for prosthetic bras in Germany. The founder and creative director of Megami is currently focused on laser technology in design, which enables advanced performance in design and aesthetics in function.

Jane Fainberg Ivanov interviewed by Susan Kolko

Discussion: Why was cancer research so important for product development? What design considerations would be different for Megami's swimwear collection? What are important considerations in bra design and why?

Clothing that is fashionable, flexible, and affordable has an important function in each stage of the life cycle. Depending on the lifestyle and the environment, textiles are key components for comfort and style and are often an important consideration in sustainability. The garments worn in each stage vary: people tend to be more active in their younger years, and brands and retailers are key to choices. The fashion industry can help support young people with disabilities by providing trendy clothes that help them "fit in". During the older years, function and style became key. For a person with a disability, independence and independent living shapes identity, and clothing designs and styles which support these offer essential choices and possibilities.

1. Childhood

Childhood years are especially important in the development of a keen sense of self-esteem. Children with disabilities may have the same developmental stages as all children; however, the stages do not necessarily occur within the traditional timeline or manifest themselves in the same manner. Physical and mental development, the ability to be independent, challenges in learning, and an overprotective, or lacking, support environment become key factors in the development of self-esteem. It is essential that children with disabilities have positive role models, a supportive family, educational resources, and positive social experiences. Children with disabilities are often placed in special school programs or academic environments to help ensure positive experiences. However, placement in special programs clearly identifies a child as "different" and may create special difficulties and challenges. Children with disabilities, especially those in special programs, are more likely to be subjected to bullying and stigmas, which drastically affect both self-esteem and mental health.

Mindy Scheier is one of the leading advocates for fashionable clothing for children with disabilities. The struggles of her son Oliver, who has muscular dystrophy, have inspired her to "make a difference" in the lives of children with disabilities. Mindy took her passion for fashion, the concept of easy dressing, and her love for her son, and created Runway of Dreams, a foundation that is a voice for people with disabilities and for the apparel industry. Mindy has shared her story in Chapter 1.

2. Adolescence

Adolescence has many moving parts, and is a time in life when it's often hard to maintain a balance, both for people with disabilities and those without them. These are critical years for socialization and development, and generally "set the stage" for the characteristics one will carry throughout life. Extra-curricular activities at school can play a significant role in supporting a sense of achievement, and in helping to foster positive self-esteem. During adolescence, one becomes more aware of body image, and role models become pivotal in the development of values and goals.

For adolescents with disabilities, the teen years create a heightened sense of awareness of the importance of "fitting in" with friends and peer relationships. Bullying leads to shame and embarrassment, and, as a result, adolescents with disabilities who are bullied, or excluded, by their classmates tend to withdraw from active socialization. Parents and caregivers are more often involved in their daily activities and routines, which can slow down movement toward independence, and unintentionally promote frustration. Considering and planning for future education and careers becomes a challenging priority, and the thought of not achieving personal goals in the future due to a disabling condition can create a feeling of inadequacy, as well as a loss of self-confidence. Having an inclusive environment, fostered by family, mentors, and mental health advisors regularly helps develop confidence and overcome challenges.

Clothing becomes particularly important during adolescence because it defines style, interests, and relationships, and helps to create individuality. Brands, retailers, social media, and other influencers have a direct impact and can create lifelong values and self-image. Adolescents with disabilities might not have clothing that "fits in", and is similar to that of their peers, due to the lack of style choices in adaptivewear appropriate to their age, cost, and their inability to make independent choices in product.

3. Maturity

Many changes come with maturity or midlife: changes in responsibilities, in life circumstances, and in personal identity related to life experiences; in physical appearance, strength, and flexibility; and many others. Self-reflection related to careers, relationships, and societal contributions helps guide individuals through these middle years. Changes in health and family relationships may test resiliency related to self-esteem, while socioeconomic factors, such as financial status and career goals, pave the direction for older age.

For people with disabilities (and for many non-disabled people as well!), the self-reflection process that occurs in midlife may be disappointing: the goals initially set may not have been achieved. In addition, especially with progressive and intermittent or episodic disabilities, the original disabling condition may become more serious and time-consuming. However, dependence on family and community support is more easily accepted, and a positive self-image and ability to embrace disability help ease the change of midlife.

Clothing and fashion, with its ability to influence mental and emotional health, can provide a sense of security and comfort to people with disabilities through brand identity and accessible styles. Some types of disabilities, such as cardiac insufficiency, or Parkinson's Disease, often begin during midlife and can cause a major diversion in life plans. Accepting a new disability can be easier when fashionable and functional clothing is available: it can help ease the painful change in health status. For those who have struggled with lifelong disabilities, there is a familiarity with the availability of clothing and its challenges, but new adaptive fashions that can add life to a very well-used wardrobe have a very positive impact on self-esteem. Fashionable clothing can help ease the pain of a "bad day" for people with intermittent disabilities and make the necessity of accepting impairments more comfortable, both mentally and physically. Universal Design fashions especially enable people with intermittent disabilities to wear the same clothing during episodes of disability they wear when they are fully functional.

4. Older Age

Physical, social, and psychological conditions continue to affect self-esteem, often to a greater degree, in older years. Challenging health conditions tend to become more prominent, increasing both in number and severity, and physical and cognitive health issues can present many difficulties. Medical appointments, lab tests, rehabilitation therapies, and other health-related interventions become part of everyday life, and coping skills become key as medical conditions and physical limitations multiply. The wisdom and experiences acquired during earlier years support motivation and provide a framework for consistency in attitude, beliefs, and functionality. With retirement, socializing and engaging in meaningful activities replace work commitments.

Clothing for elders generally needs to be comfort-oriented, and sizing needs to adapt to changing body shapes and sizes. "Age-appropriate" is a term often utilized by the fashion industry that takes both style and identity into consideration. Current trends suggest that elders value styles, trends, sustainability, and pricing that is reasonable for a restricted budget, as retirement is often accompanied by a change in income. Chico's is an example of an apparel retailer that caters to this market segment, providing affordable fashion that is both comfortable and stylish.

The percentage of people with disabilities drastically increases with older age. Fashion continues to be a form of self-expression, but consumers are more often willing to sacrifice high fashion for comfort, fitness, ease of use, durability, and affordability. Clothing that is versatile and can potentially be used for separate occasions lowers the cost factor and ensures peace of mind, as the user becomes familiar with the look and feel of the garment. Adaptive clothing becomes a necessity, especially due to a decrease in manual dexterity. Zippers may be replaced with Velcro™, and buttons with magnets. The ability of the elderly to dress with fashion and flair encourages respect and admiration, impacting self-esteem.

C. Cultural ableism

People with disabilities often do not speak out, or stand up for themselves, because the environment in which they are living makes both the process of getting attention and being in the attention spotlight uncomfortable. *Ableism* exists when there is a negative prejudice toward people with disabilities. It suggests that people with disabilities are less competent due to their disabling condition and that there is no way that they can live meaningful, productive lives without being a burden to society. Advocates for people with disabilities, and equal rights legislation, have helped to create awareness, ensure accessibility, and hold non-disabled people accountable for their lack of acceptance. Accommodations in residences, workplaces, shopping malls, and community services have created significant changes since the disability rights movement began, and these have minimized the environmental challenges of an ableist society. Physical access, such as larger restroom stalls for accessibility, and communication services, such as talking street crossing signals, are examples of society's attempts to reduce ableism and encourage inclusivity.

Cultural ableism addresses the negative manner some people in a society act, talk, and treat people with disabilities. The manner in which people with disabilities are portrayed in social media can easily sway public opinion, and these portrayals are often based on inaccurate assumptions. Language itself can be one of the most aggressive forms of ableism. The vocabulary and metaphors used to describe people with disabilities are often hurtful, insulting, and currently very inappropriate. As an example, someone with dwarfism, or a little person, who is referred to as a "midget" experiences a degrading form of ableism. Ableism challenges people with disabilities' rights, intelligence, and abilities—in short, their very personhood. As a result of ableism, many people with disabilities succumb to society's prejudices and attempt to lead their lives within the limited context of their personal world: the person with the disability ends up having to "accommodate" non-disabled people by distancing themselves from their presence.

When ableism dominates, people with disabilities may feel rejected, and as though they are a burden to society. They may be fearful of being judged when speaking up for what they need and deserve, and simply accept societal negatives. Depending on the type of individual disability, advocating for equality and accessibility might be difficult due to the disabling condition itself, peer pressure to "fit in", cognitive dissonance, or sheer pressure and difficulty of speaking out for themselves. People with disabilities often do not know their rights, as these are not publicized, or noticeable on an everyday basis. As seen in her case study in Chapter 2, Victoria Jenkins, founder of the brand Unhidden, speaks publicly about the ways society can address ableism.[26]

Case study: Manikin

Qaysean Williams, "The One Hand Sewing Man," has defied the odds as a designer, artist, stylist, and entrepreneur. The world of fashion inspired his creativity, and his natural talent for style led him to a career in the apparel industry. He is considered one of the most eclectic stylists in streetwear and high-fashion glamor today. His services offer personal styling and couture designs and are available to the public through his website. The fashion industry has supported his creativity by exposing his talent worldwide.

Qaysean has Erb's Palsy, a condition that affects the nervous system and muscles in the arms, often as a result of injury occurring during the birth process. His condition was so severe in childhood that the muscles in his shoulder, arm, and fingers deteriorated, and he lost complete function in his left arm. He knew he was never going to be like other kids - and other kids frequently reminded him of that. He felt bullied, and ashamed of his impairments. In most of his childhood photos, he is posed such that his left arm is hidden, so that his condition is not obvious to viewers. He immersed himself in fantasy, in cartoons and comic books to distract himself, and his interests included awareness of costumes and clothing and their role in creating images of people.

This led him to his first fashion show, at the Boys and Girls Club in Trenton, New Jersey, and, from that moment, his yellow brick road was clear. During his youth, he continued his experiences and his successes with fashion show productions. These events sparked his curiosity and his interests and motivated him to learn more about fashion and style, to try things that had never been done, and to turn his disability into an ability. His shows highlighted pop culture, and his style was a sensation, bringing much interest, praise, and popularity to him from his viewers.

As a result of these very positive experiences, Qaysean was convinced that fashion, and the world of design, would give him access to a "normal" life, one focused on his positive accomplishments rather than on his disabling condition. Remaining in his home state, New Jersey, Qaysean put himself through school and graduated from Mercer Community College. He continued to follow his interest in design and taught himself to create patterns, construct, and sew custom designs. His awareness of his disability, and the effect this has had on his own dressing and undressing process, and therefore on his clothing needs, led him to design and create clothing for people with disabilities, as well as for the mainstream market.

It wasn't long before he sold his first design, which gave him more confidence in his chosen path. He realized that he had a lot more to offer as a creative person, and would be able to support himself by continuing to do what he loved. However, he also realized that he was completely on his own, as no one in his familiar world was knowledgeable about fashion or the fashion business. He learned much of what he needed through trial and error, and still today turns every hardship into a learning opportunity.

He continued his education and obtained a Bachelor's Degree from Montclair State University, studying psychology and human behavior. His studies, as well as his personal experiences, helped him to understand how fashion made people feel, and the role of clothing and fashion in affecting behavior—of both the wearer and others. With the ability to design fashion and provide styling ideas, Qaysean had the perfect roadmap for satisfying his clients and building a sustainable business. His brand, which he named Manikin, has been growing exponentially for the past decade. The media has welcomed his talents, and his ability to appeal to a broad market segment makes his designs and personal story easily relatable to others.

Participating in fashion shows and styling celebrities has enabled Qaysean to build his brand, and provides him with creative opportunities to incorporate current trends into his work. As a child, the identity of "The One Hand Sewing Man" would have been an embarrassment and a humiliation. Today, it makes him proud. Qaysean and Manikin collections can be seen on the Netflix series "Next in Fashion", and at red carpet events in a wide variety of industries.

Qaysean Williams interviewed by Susan Kolko

Discussion: Consider Maslow's Hierarchy of needs. What obstacles did Qaysean overcome to move into the next level of the hierarchy? What is the indication of his achievement of self-actualization? How is someone like Qaysean helping to eradicate ablism?

The fashion industry speaks out

Addressing clothing needs is particularly challenging because there are no boundaries or laws that protect or provide for the clothing needs of people with disabilities. The designers, manufacturers, marketers, and merchandisers can develop their own individual business practices related to apparel design. With increasing societal values focused on sustainability, technology, inclusivity, and diversity, the fashion industry, as a leader, an advocate, and a platform for change, is clearly supporting the lawmakers, the advocates, and the disability population by attempting to integrate adaptive fashion designs into mainstream trends and styles. Adaptive clothing is an opportunity for fashion to support, communicate, and normalize disability.

D. Costumes and esteem
1. Children and young adults

American traditions that involve costumes, such as Halloween, often also play a role in defining identity, especially for children and young adults. At Halloween, the issues of self-esteem and ability fade into the background as the Halloween fantasy assumes the front and center spot in schools and at home. In recent years, some schools have opted out of Halloween altogether and have not permitted students to come to school in costume, as educators have advised that Halloween is not holiday appropriate for a school curriculum in response to cultural and religious objections to the relevance of the "holiday" to education.

A Halloween costume creates lasting impressions and judgments about costumes can have a critical impact on a young person's psyche. People with disabilities want to participate in Halloween with their peers and their broader social circles. Expression through a costume enables an individual to assume a chosen identity, portray an interest, and emulate a character or content. The responses and reactions of others to a Halloween costume can build confidence and foster positive relationships. Halloween embraces self-expression and offers the opportunity for creativity in design. However, a negative reaction to a costume from others could also be negative, hurtful, and emotionally damaging. A cute and funny costume, such as a bunny, or a clown, might trigger laughter as a response from peers, but sometimes that laughter is interpreted as "at", rather than "with" with the individual who is wearing the costume. The wearer emotionally defensive, and harmful emotions can cause the wearer to question his or her decision. A scary or "mean" costume, such as a witch or a ghost, might trigger a peer response of fear or aggression that could, potentially, continue long after Halloween. Costumes potentially create longer-term reputations: a homemade costume can not only imply creativity but also a lack of funds. A sloppy costume indicates a lack of time and interest, a princess costume implies fantasy and beauty and a superhero costume implies strength, power, and virtuous deeds. Children and young adults with disabilities both react to others and are affected by the reactions of others at Halloween. A costume that does not fit properly, does not allow for accessibility, or does not highlight strength in differences can make Halloween stressful for people with disabilities, as well as their families, educators, and caregivers.

Children connect to characters in television and film, music, history, and people in the news that are representative of current events. Adaptive Halloween costumes, such as dragons, princesses, unicorns, and robots, can be found on Amazon, and at Target, Disney, and Halloween Express at affordable prices. These costumes are designed for wheelchair use and sensory issues, as well as fit, function, and accessibility. Some of the most common adaptable features include wheelchair compatibility, openings for easy dressing and tube access, interchangeable accessories for comfort and style, fabric that is form-fitting yet stretches and is in style, longer lengths for wheelchair or seated positions, and extra material where needed. However, Etsy, who carried custom costumes, found that time and cost factors related to production must be considered, and their line has been discontinued.

The popular **Disney Adaptive** line of costumes was launched in 2020, featuring Cinderella's Coach and the Incredimobile, specifically designed for wheelchair users. Other popular costumes, such as Buzz Lightyear, are designed to be wheelchair friendly, with special openings and flaps. As a global company, Disney engages children's imaginations and dreams regardless of location or culture. The company has taken worldwide measures to ensure accessible resources for employees and customers.

Veronika Ivanova is a Fulbright scholar and someone who has used a wheelchair her entire life. She is an advocate for the Russian Disability Treaty and has conducted research studies regarding the ways in which culture and environment affect rehabilitation measures. She worked at The Walt Disney Company as their Diversity and Inclusion Leader and helped to create a more inclusive and accessible environment for employees and customers with disabilities. She has also volunteered with the global Disney team to assist athletes with Down syndrome at the World Special Olympics. Veronika understands the power that Disney characters' costumes can deliver and feels that producing and marketing adaptive costumes helps the organization to understand and connect to the disability community. Wonder Woman, Batman, Harry Potter, the Incredibles, Sesame Street, Mickey Mouse, Pikachu, Frozen, T-Rex, Transformers are just a few of the adaptive costumes on the market today.[27]

Veronika Ivanova interviewed by Susan Kolko

Adults

Dressing up in costumes is not exclusive to children. There is also a limited selection of adult adaptive costumes. Many adults with disabilities choose to create their own costumes and gravitate toward spooky, cuddly, or heroesque themes. Adults with disabilities are accustomed to adapting clothing to meet their needs: creating and adapting is not an unusual task. More importantly, as with children and young adults, the costume enables greater freedom of expression, as well as the ability to participate in the fantasy of Halloween, just like everyone else. In addition, planners for extraordinary events, such as West Hollywood's Halloween Carnival, are prioritizing accessibility.

Sara Kim, a freelance writer for the **World Institute on Disability**, analyzes the connection between dressing up for Halloween and disability. She warns that what might appear to be a harmless costume, such as a character with a disfigurement, or strange, awkward behavior, in fact validates the negative perception of people with disabilities: that they are indeed "scary", and that their differences are negative and potentially evil, and should not be brought into mainstream culture. Historically, people with disabilities have been isolated, and often perceived as a burden with nothing of value to contribute to society. When costumes have characteristics perceived as a disability, they can perpetuate the cycle. A costume with a bandage around the head could represent mental issues; a skeleton costume could represent eating disorders; scars, blood, and missing limbs can suggest accidents, indicating deformities that potentially cause direct attacks on the disability community. These also reinforce the notion of disability as something funny, scary, weird, and different, and give a pass for ridicule and contempt. Adults set the example for the younger generation: wearing a costume that could be interpreted as cultural appropriation has consequences that can counter the disability movement and the progress that has been made by and for people with disabilities.[28]

E. Swimwear and body image

Disability or no disability, swimwear is a category of clothing that tends to arouse strong feelings, sensitivities, and physical self-awareness in everyone. The idea of wearing something that exposes one's body in ways that everyday clothing covers up can be stressful, embarrassing, and sometimes confusing. The swimsuit is a category of clothing that has, over time, become more form-fitting, and skimpier. As water sports have become more popular, and women's rights have emphasized all forms of free expression, including clothing choices, revealing swimsuits became increasingly popular. As adaptive clothing is explored and developed, awareness and sensitivity to this category's special challenges require careful consideration. Adaptive apparel aims to make dressing accessible and comfortable, styles current, pricing affordable, and marketing effective but also, very importantly, to make the adaptations non-obtrusive and minimally obvious. Swimwear exposes everything—it is as if one is wearing their underwear in public. A person with toileting issues, differences in body shapes and sizes, challenges with dexterity, and mental health challenges such as anxiety and depression may find choosing and purchasing a swimsuit, usually with few choice options available, an exceedingly difficult task, and may choose to opt out of this clothing item altogether.

Swim brands that address the needs and challenges of people with disabilities understand the complexity of providing a solution that is accessible, affordable, and attractive. Nancy DeValut reviews the most important components of adaptive swimwear and the brands that are available, and offers suggestions: a tankini, a swim top that covers the abdomen, allows for easy access and trendy fashion; a long-sleeve, one-piece swimsuit is ideal for someone with skin issues, such as eczema, psoriasis, or skin cancer; and bottoms with a reusable swim diaper for children and adults provides protection from accidents, is sustainable. There is a variety of prints and styles from which to choose. Style options include crop tops and adjustable swim skirts, magnetic technology, chlorine-resistant fabric, mastectomy tops, sensory-friendly fabrics, built-in suit-floatation devices, and UVA-proof one-piece bodysuits. Selections in adaptive swimwear may be found on Amazon, MIGA Swimwear, Target, Patti&Ricky, WowEase, Lands' End, Kohl's, and H2owear.

Case study: MIGA Swimwear

To create community among women, **Maria Luisa Mendiola** created and founded MIGA Swimwear. At the age of 13, she found that she had a genetic condition called Jeune Syndrome. This condition is extremely rare, affecting an estimated 1 in 100,000 to 130,000 babies per year. As a result, she has Brachymetatarsia, which causes one of the five long bones of the foot to be abnormally short, resulting in a shortened toe. Growing up in Costa

Rica, she became very self-conscious about her feet, as the climate is warm and humid, and people usually wear open-toed shoes. She quickly found that wearing bright-color swimsuits was a way to distract people from looking at her feet, hence her love for swimwear.

Her condition is not considered a disability by law, but has had drastic effects on her self-image and mental health. Maria Luisa's undergraduate degree, from Georgetown University, is in Economics. Reflecting on an econometrics class she took, she recalls having to look at the different variables which must be considered in planning a business model. The takeaways from that course have helped her to plan her current production and marketing strategy. She applies the garments she is producing to a community that is marginalized and tries to account for all the moving parts throughout the supply chain, from understanding exchange rates, to sourcing materials, and to the marketing challenges. All these factors play in the ultimate goal of satisfying a special target market.

Upon graduating from Georgetown, Maria Luisa set off for London to work in finance, only to discover that she really wanted to tap into her creative side. During her graduate work at Central Saint Martin's, U.K., she continued her interest in swimwear and began to develop designs that encouraged women to love and accept their bodies. Her program, called Applied Imagination in the Creative Industries, is the equivalent to a design thinking course in the United States. In her course, students write journals to reflect on individual experiences that can be applied to the real world.

Maria Luisa gravitated to body image, and to exploring how her disfigurement affected self-image and esteem. She found an organization, Changing Faces U.K., that advocates for people who have disfigurements, and that put her in touch with people who were looking for garments that would empower them to feel more comfortable in their bodies. One of her first clients was a burn survivor, who had been asking her doctor if she knew of swimsuit brands that are able to protect her burn scars, but had learned that there were none. When she reached out to the doctor and client, Maria Luisa's career was born. Her business and creative skills, combined with her desire to make the world more accessible, manifested itself in the development of swimwear for the disability community. Very aware of women's needs with swimsuits, she quickly realized that she could create designs that would build a community where women could embrace their differences. Maria Luisa started her brand as an extension of her senior thesis.

It was not long before she realized there was a vocabulary, a "politically correct" vocabulary, in the world of disability. In the United Kingdom, the term "disfigurement" does not have the same negative connotation it has in the United States. Maria Luisa defines herself as a woman living with disfigurement. She passionately believes that the word "disfigurement" describes her condition, yet recognizes that, for some people, the stigma attached to this word is debilitating. When she launched her collection, inspired by women's stories with disfigurements, it was well received. However, knowing her brand was going to be global, and marketed in the United States, she recognized that the term "disfigurement" needed to be reconsidered, as it takes a lot of finesse and positioning of the brand's language and marketing to attract its primary customers. Maria Luisa found it difficult to determine the best vocabulary to use in describing her products, to refer to her customers with disabling conditions, and to communicate with them. She also knew that non-disabled women could benefit from swimwear that is easy on/off, uses comfortable materials, and includes adaptations to address limited mobility.

Maria Luisa believes that language is one of the biggest challenges in the disability community. Her goal is to create community, and she feels that language seems to divide, rather than to unite, groups of people. Although she writes articles as an advocate for disability, she has been judged, because her disfigurement is not considered a disability by law. Some critics have even suggested that she should not be spearheading MIGA, but she believes that people can experience disability and feel the inaccessibility of this world without being in a wheelchair. It is this passion for inclusivity that drives MIGA Swimwear, and Maria Luisa's commitment to social justice and representation for marginalized communities are the center of the MIGA mission.

Swimwear, she says, hits the body image full force, with so many presumed ideas about what one should and should not wear related to physical features. As an example, bikinis are considered appropriate to a certain age and shape of body. Maria Luisa wants to get rid of the rules and to promote the idea of feeling comfortable in your own body, because acceptance and the embracing of differences leads to a positive self-image. She says that pain, suffering, feeling inadequate, and feeling as though one doesn't belong is a universal feeling and is not particular to the disability community. The broader community, she says, can benefit in many ways from hearing the voices of members of the disability community. Products should be designed more universally, with mindful adaptations to traditional design that are able to accommodate everyone. MIGA has worked with over 400 plus women to produce functional yet beautiful designs.

Maria Luisa has had several challenges with social media. MIGA Swimwear was "flagged" on social media as posting discriminating content. Facebook and Google's algorithm noticed trigger words that identify with disability and chronic illnesses, and the MIGA ads were pulled. MIGA received notices that the ads were flagged, with no explanation given. The social media agency with which MIGA was affiliated at the time suggested re-launching the ad, and removing the term 'ulcerative colitis is from the product page. The new ad was approved. Facebook had claimed that the ad was discriminating against people with ulcerative colitis, even though the ad's goal was to connect with people who have ulcerative colitis.

Maria Luisa also plays an instrumental role in the development of the Coalition for Adaptive Designers. She stresses the importance of consumer perceptions and reverse discrimination. Through her experiences with Google and Facebook, she learned that although a business' goal is closing the societal gap for an underrepresented population, the approach, communications, and positioning of the business needs to reach the mass market to be profitable. Thus, she created the Ally Collection - swimsuits that appealed to a mass market, while also raising awareness about the importance of everyone joining together in making this world a more accessible place. Having a disability and a strong mission to create products that satisfy others in the same situation is not sufficient in creating a successful business: it also takes a strong business plan, and the ability to "navigate uncharted waters." MIGA Swimwear has moved away from the "adaptive" stigma toward a concept of universal accessibility. She regularly collaborates with other entrepreneurs in the adaptive clothing market to help her make the most realistic and profitable next move.

Maria Luisa Mendiola interviewed by Susan Kolko

Discussion: Why is social media so important for people with disabilities and adaptive brands? Why is swimwear a particularly sensitive category of clothing when it comes to disability?

Summary

This chapter has explored the ways in which self-image is guided by stages in the life cycle and the special challenges and interests of each stage. Maslow's Hierarchy of Needs was explored and applied to each stage, guiding the reader toward an understanding of the unique characteristics and experiences of each individual. In addition, some of the special concerns and challenges that may be encountered by people with disabilities at each stage have illustrated the variation in the needs for adaptive clothing, and the value and importance of fashion in supporting a positive self-image and a sense of self-esteem. The impact of costumes on reinforcing both negative and positive behavior, particularly at Halloween, and their effect on self-esteem was explored through specific character examples. The effect of ableism is addressed as a contributing factor to how people with disabilities perceive themselves. The next chapter will build upon this information to further consider the essential role of clothing and fashion in supporting self-esteem.

Learning activities

- Consider the levels in Maslow's hierarchy. Where do you see yourself today? What is preventing you from getting to the next level?
- Give examples of how clothing could play a role in each level of the hierarchy. Consider how clothing could help or hinder the ability to move up the hierarchy.
- Recall your Halloween costumes over the years. If possible, create a timeline of costumes. Consider how each costume made you feel before you left home, while you were out, and how you felt the next day and weeks after.
- Think about a time when you felt like you needed help or deserved help and did not ask for it because you did not want to draw attention to your needs.

Adaptive talk

- Abraham Maslow
- physiological
- self-esteem
- inequity
- self-actualization
- age-appropriate
- adolescence

- maturity
- ableism
- dwarfism
- Disney Adaptive
- Veronika Ivanova

Case studies

Megami – Jane Fainberg Ivanov

Manikin – Qaysean Williams

MIGA Swimwear – Maria Lousia Mendiola

6
Inspiring confidence, communication, and connection: Apparel for enhancing self-esteem

Introduction

The previous chapter has explored the concept of self-image and its vital role in self-perception and self-esteem. Appearance—the way in which we see ourselves, and the way in which others see us—guides much of society's understanding of each individual member. Based on appearance, society can include, or exclude, individuals as well as groups. This concept can be seen broadly throughout all societies, throughout history, and has often focused on visible characteristics, such as race, physical attributes, and religion, which are often clearly defined by specific clothing choices. Disabilities, especially visible disabilities, have traditionally been another group whose position in society has been strongly affected by physical appearance, and ill-fitting clothing, poorly adapted to meet the needs of individual conditions, has been an essential element in the determination of the role and position of individuals. This perception and judgment of people with disabilities by others in their society, in turn, plays an essential role in individual self-image and self-perception. This chapter will consider several characteristics of both individuals and the broader society, and the roles of each of these in creating and developing images of people with disabilities based on assumptions created by appearance. The role of adaptivewear in mitigating negativity both on a personal and on a societal level will be explored.

As has been discussed, at every age and stage of life, fashionable clothing increases self-esteem. For people with disabilities, finding accessible, functional, and affordable fashion is often a challenge. Today's world values inclusivity and diversity more than ever, and laws and practices encourage societal awareness of the rights and needs of people with disabilities. They are designed to diminish the disparity between people with disabilities and the general population and create equal opportunities for all. Adaptive clothing plays an essential role, as it enables people with disabilities to have equal access to fashion.

Adaptive clothing fosters inclusivity and promotes the development of a positive self-image, leading to positive self- esteem, and fuller integration in the broader society.

Figure 6 Aaron Fotheringham "Wheelz"

Learning objectives

- Understand the role of health and fitness
- Relate to the effects of social media on self-image
- Define how global awareness influences adaptive clothing
- Be aware of the names of major adaptivewear brands
- Be cognizant of the work of fashion industry advocates
- Understand the difference between Universal Design and adaptive design

A. Self-Image, Disability, and Fashion

Feeling comfortable, being able to express one's individual style, and feeling included is empowering, and has a direct, positive effect on mental health. Fashion helps to express identity by creating a positive body image and by encouraging social connections.

Self-image, personal values, and the image individuals wish to project of themselves to family, friends, colleagues, and the broader society, are all reflected in personal choices. Ethics, culture, and personal style are major driving forces in consumer behavior. People with disabilities may encounter barriers and limitations in society which can impact individual physical, emotional, and mental well-being. Clothing, a major contributor to the development and maintenance of a positive self-image, as well as to society's perception of an individual, is clearly an essential element to consider. National brands such as Zappos Adaptive, Disney Adaptive, and Tommy Hilfiger Adaptive, all presented in previous chapters, are major brands helping to pave the way for new standards in the prioritization of adaptivewear. Individuals, such as Marta Elena, who have created their own fashion brands, are also an important part of creating awareness.

Case Study: Abilitee

From a very young age, **Marta Elena Cortez-Neavel** was very creative and enjoyed the arts. Drawing, fashion, and decorating came naturally to her. She was a bright student with solid grades, despite her challenges with ADHD, anxiety, and depression, called "invisible disabilities", as they are not obvious from a physical perspective: she was not in a wheelchair, did not have difficulties with fine motor skills, nor did she require any specific adaptive clothing. However, Marta Elena says that she could empathize with people with disabilities, because she felt "the uncomfortableness inside that others felt on the outside". Originally from Austin, Texas, Marta Elena was very familiar with the medical world, as both of her parents were practicing physicians. Their intention was for her to follow in their footsteps and go to medical school, a very heavy weight as she was growing up.

She actually became personally connected to the medical world, though from a different perspective. As a child, she went to day camp with other children who had a wide range of disabling conditions. Some were similar to hers, while others were much more severe, such as an inability to speak, or requiring feeding tubes and 24-hour care. At one point, she attended a sleep-away camp for children with disabilities, where her parents were the physicians, for a week. At the camp, she was able to have one-on-one attention from counselors and began to really understand some of the ways both to address her own personal disability and to actualize her ability to do whatever she dreamed possible. She learned about neurodiversity disabilities to better understand herself, while continuing to feel a real connection with other campers struggling with different conditions. At that time, there was no concept of an actual "disability culture" as there is today, with the changes in laws, social media, resources, and advocates for people with disabilities raising awareness and responsiveness in the general population and culture.

During her youth, Marta Elena's neighborhood was very conservative, at times seeming very segregated, and she was not aware of any neighbors with disabilities. She felt different, in an uncomfortable way, and clothing and fashion became an outlet for both her creativity and her happiness. In middle school, and in high school, Maria Elena sewed her own clothes "for the fun of it", imagining she was the fashion designer she wanted to be in the future. Coming from their own academic and scientific world, her parents were not enamored with the idea of fashion design as a career for their daughter. Marta Elena was accepted to the University of Southern California and, while studying there, convinced herself that medical school was the logical route for her future, as her parents wanted, while also realizing that she was suppressing something important in her identity. She was close to her brother, who was coming into his own identity as well, and the two of them listened to each other, understood each other, and helped each other as they searched for their personal meaning of life.

Marta Elena was accepted into several prestigious medical schools, and began her studies, but she became distracted by her passion for design and started a company with a pediatric surgeon, catering to the disability market, called **Abilitee**. She has since branched off on her own and is determined to use her design talent and her business savvy to ensure the integration of fashion in her products. She is inspired by others in the disability and fashion movement and finds that the community they have all built together is working well as a whole and creating change. Victoria Jenkins and her company, **Unhidden**, presented in Chapter 1, serves as a special role model for inclusivity and accessibility. Marta Elena believes that education plays a key role in change,and that if students were learning about adaptive fashions and disability in school, instead of seeing only tall, white, skinny women as fashion models, the stigma attached to disability would dissolve, and the world would have a more accurate representation of reality.

When she refers to "inclusivity", Marta Elena is not only referring to the disability market but is identifying this concept as essential to race, gender, and size as well. She feels that "inclusive clothing" is about having *functional* clothing, clothing that speaks to everyone's identity and needs—people with disabilities as well as athletes, non-binary people, people with different skin tones, and all other groups. Inclusive clothing should therefore be guided by brands that can support a wide range of needs. She does not feel that a brand addressing the needs of one group alone is inclusive, because it excludes others. Her company focuses a bit more on medical concerns, but the products she is bringing to the market are items like insulin pump belts and ostomy bag covers that are fashionable, things to which a person can feel connected well beyond their specific medical functions.

Working with other creative designers like Helya Mohammadian and Lucy Jones in tight community, Marta Elena believes that there are many possibilities for adaptations for people with disabilities, and that designers have many options, not only in design but also in marketing. As an example, she describes a cyclist's needs for specific cycling outfits—outfits that cannot be found in large department stores, while specialty stores can provide choices and styles, and can meet needs for special functions and various uses.

Marta Elena feels that designers should design more inclusively in general, and make accessibility an attainable goal for all brands. Teaching existing brands how to include adaptive clothing and other items without changing their brand identity, she feels, will come only with the next generation of designers, who will bring awareness of special needs into their patterns and construction concepts. "Disability," she says, "does not need to be in a box in a hospital gown, and does not need to make current brands look medical." She believes that the changes and adaptations are simple, but that they require a re-thinking of design. She also notes that the apparel industry continues to manufacture overseas, even though the focus is on sustainability, and there is a need to move toward local sourcing to support the country, state, and city. She notes that buying locally from businesses that are making efforts toward inclusivity is the "only way our world will progress".

In the United Kingdom, Marta Elena is also a part of an adaptive fashion network. The network's goal is to serve as a governing body for clothing that meets the needs of people with disabilities. It is composed of representatives from the fashion industry and medical fields. The group feels strongly that large companies, those with more than 1,500 employees, should be obligated to offer adaptive lines.

In terms of design, she believes that comfort comes with streetwear and that this is the most realistic option for people with disabilities. An example, she suggests, is Diane Von Furstenberg's wrap dress, which can meet the needs of someone who is unable to get their top on and off easily, yet wants to look fashionable. Sizing, colors, and the creation of categories for clothing, she feels, would appeal to a wide range of consumer ages. She is brainstorming with like-minded designers, such as Victoria Jenkins and Alexandra Herold, in an effort to build community and create standards for inclusivity. She shares that Etsy has been a profitable source for launching her business, and is much more financially realistic than some other possibilities. She feels that developing Google search terms is also very helpful and that technology has a major role to play in the future of adaptivewear design and marketing.

Marta Elena Cortez-Neavel interviewed by Susan Kolko

Discussion: Consider invisible disabilities. In recent years, mental health has become a normalized disability. Historically, it was shunned and society did what it could to hide people with invisible disabilities. How has Marta Elena Cortez-Neavel helped to redefine the needs of this undeserved market and create awareness for invisible disabilities and clothing?

B. Global awareness, disability, and fashion

Global awareness related to fashion and disability is a major and ever-growing trend. Adaptivewear for people with disabilities increases inclusivity, promotes accessibility, and has an impact on societies worldwide. Due to global awareness of the importance of fashion for people with disabilities, advocates have initiated social change and created opportunities for this formerly underserved market segment. Brands, retailers, and designers aware of the movement toward inclusivity have created niche product lines that address core business values and promote current societal trends in diversity acceptance.

International fashion events are an influential platform for exposure and place design adaptivewear initiatives front and center. They create public awareness of the concept that people with disabilities both desire and deserve to be an integral part of society, with the same access to fashion, thereby increasing the possibilities for this becoming a reality.

However, the major financial challenge created by adaptivewear remains an obstacle that must be addressed. Budgeting, and the return on investment for adaptive clothing, does not manifest as high profit margins: adaptivewear garments are more costly to produce. Therefore, national brands and retailers are better able to support adaptivewear on a large scale and to have the most influence in creating change. They are also the businesses that can afford lower profit margins this specialized clothing creates.

In addition to designers and brands in the United States, brands in other countries are helping to make adaptive clothing a growing category. Several brands have taken the initiative to develop adaptivewear styles. IZ Adaptive, discussed in Chapter 1, and Alter Ur Ego are two Canadian sportswear brands that offer accessible, functional adaptivewear without jeopardizing style, and Able2Wear, from the United Kingdom, offers adaptivewear for children and adults. In addition to these Canadian and British brands, Japan is known for both quality and contemporary adaptivewear designs, Australia for the practicality and function of their designs, and the Netherlands for its sustainable practices for sportswear production.

In Israel, Palta is a company that provides people with disabilities opportunities in the fashion industry. In 2021, Palta designed the uniforms for the Israeli team for the Paralympics in Tokyo. They collaborate with the community on projects that support inclusive and accessible work and learning in all aspects of fashion design, merchandise development, and marketing efforts.

Chava Kuchar wrote an article about Palta for Wrapt Magazine. She reports that the fashion design house and fashion brand consultancy strives to bring inclusiveness and societal change for people with disabilities. The company is led by Shay Senior, an IDF soldier who suffered an injury, and Netanel Yehuda Halevi, a wheelchair user born with muscular dystrophy. The Palta team has conducted extensive research related to clothing, fashion, and disability. Based on their research findings, the brand's inclusive designs use braille tags, digital labels, a chatbot service, 3D printed braille catalog, smart fabrics, inclusive size ranges, and produce multifunctional clothes at an affordable price point.

These nations and products are at the forefront in the manufacturing, production, and marketing of adaptive clothing, reflecting national cultural values focused on inclusivity, legislative and government policies that support diversity, and the financial means that make production a reality.

Case study: Alter Ur Ego

In 2007 **Heidi Mc Kenzie** was in a car accident that left her a paraplegic. At the time she was in college studying fashion merchandising. She sustained a Spinal Cord Injury and is unable to walk, using s a wheelchair for mobility. After the accident and rehab, she moved in with her father, who was able to take time off from his work to help Heidi in her recovery process and adjustment to her new life. She graduated from Morehead State University with a Bachelor's Degree in Business. Despite her disability, Heidi has maintained her love of the fashion world. She was voted Miss Wheelchair Kentucky 2012, and from there competed in Miss Wheelchair America. Although, she did not win, her participation in the wheelchair competitions enabled her first exposure to others in wheelchairs, opened her eyes to the many places people with disabilities come from, and some of the experiences they have endured. She realized that a career as a fashion buyer was not going to be realistic with her disability, but she still wanted to be a part of the fashion industry. Not only did she want to work in fashion, she wanted to make a difference for others struggling with disabilities and dressing issues these can create.

Heidi explored other possibilities for a fashion career, and landed herself in clothing for those, like her, who used wheelchairs. Jeans, one of the most basic, all-American, fashions were no longer an option for her. And if they were not an option for her, they were not an option for other wheelchair users as well. Heidi signed herself up for an online accelerator program called Factory 45 which caters to business entrepreneurs in the fashion industry. The program helped Heidi learn how to create a kick-starter campaign and put together a crowdfunding platform with the goal of reaching her financial goal in 30 days. Her design concept was well received, and she was able to go into production. However, the majority of her investors were able-bodied people. Her business was not reaching the disability consumer market, and soon it became obvious that she was not going to provide a return on investment if she were to continue to produce large quantities of jeans.

Heidi has closed her website due to low demand. She is very involved with her community as a mentor for other spinal cord injury patients, works for SpinLife, an online medical equipment company, and loves to share her experiences and insight at guest speaking events. As disappointing as her adaptive jeans business was, she regards it as an emotional success. Her energy, using learning from her studies at Factory 45, creating a kick-starter business, and having the business not go in the direction she had anticipated was time well spent. Heidi's motto "Keep rolling forward" is what she continues to do everyday.

Heidi McKenzie interviewed by Susan Kolko

Discussion: What do you think the biggest obstacles were for Heidi McKenzie and her kick-starter business? Why might denim be more challenging when designing for a seated position? How did Heidi McKenzie use fashion as a tool for her recovery process?

C. Social media, disability, and fashion

Social media influences all aspects of our lives, creating awareness, influencing opinions, and normalizing uncomfortable and inaccurate perceptions. The media can promote or denounce current trends, economic policy, and cultural behaviors. Adaptive clothing brands use social media to gain exposure and support. Both Instagram and Pinterest use photographs to share adaptive-wear designs and experiences. In an effort to create awareness, both Tik-Tok and YouTube also share video content that features adaptivewear clothing trends, styling tips, and disability-related topics. Twitter enables conversations and discussions on fashion for people with disabilities. Fashion influencers use social media to educate the general population about disability misconceptions. Social media helps to create awareness and is an informal activist for change.

Collaborations in fashion are more popular today than in the past. Brand and product collaborations can increase sales and expand market acceptance for both fashions and styles. Younger people with disabilities rely on social media, and on celebrities, for personal styling ideas, and this technology has enabled easy access for everyone. More importantly, celebrities in social media have become both role models and mentors for a specific segment of the population—people with disabilities—who have emotionally essential wants and needs to support both self-esteem and mental health.

Notable adaptivewear collaborations:

J.C. Penney – James Perry
Isaac Mizhari and BILLY Footwear – Selma Blair
Tommy Hilfiger – Jeremy Cambell
Nike – Tatyana McFadden
Zappos – Mindy Scheier
Victoria's Secret – Victoria Jirau

Ali Stroker, the first actor on Broadway in a wheelchair, is just one of the few examples of celebrities with whom people with disabilities can identify, who create disability awareness for the public, and who help to close the gap between mass-market fashion and adaptive clothing.

Ali Stoker is a Tony award-winning actress. When she was only 2 years old, she met with a car accident that left her paralyzed. She has spent her entire life using a wheelchair. Over the years, the entertainment industry has embraced her talent, and her disability has not prevented her from award-winning theatrical performances. Her motto, "turning limitations into opportunities" is reflected in her costumes and elegant formalwear.[29]

Keisha Greaves was studying fashion design and merchandising when she was diagnosed with muscular dystrophy. She used her acquired disability as an inspiration to explore adaptive clothing. Her brand, *Girls Chronically Rock*, was named as a reference to people with chronic illnesses. She is developing adaptive fashion styles, visiting schools to teach about adaptive fashion, and doing community outreach to share her mission of creativity, inspiration, motivation, and style.

Using technology and social media, Keisha began to understand the magnitude of the disability consumer market, and that everyone was struggling with the same issues as herself. This both motivated and inspired her. As a design student who continued her education to receive an MBA, Keisha has applied her knowledge, her interests, and her personal experience to the world of fashion and disability to create her own special brand.

D. Health and fitness, disability, and fashion

Individual health and fitness have a direct effect on self-esteem and can also influence the perceptions of the broader society. Proper nutrition, medical care, daily exercise, and positive social interaction with others have both mental and physical benefits. "Fashion" and "fitness" have become almost synonymous terms in the minds of the public. Brands like Nike, Adidas, and Under Armour market their athleticwear as sportswear. These brands also have adaptive lines, which enable them to provide a needed product to an underserved population. Able2Wear carries a line of fitness clothing specifically designed for people in wheelchairs and others with more limited physical mobility.

Achieving and maintaining fitness can be more of a challenge for people with disabilities, as access to resources may be limited due to location, limited personal resources, inaccessible equipment design and program development, and personal limitations. Fitness activities promote personal achievement, social awareness, and enhanced control over the physical body. For a person with a disability, these benefits directly affect mental health and contribute strongly to self-esteem. Tatyana McFadden, a wheelchair racer, and Jessica Long, a para-swimmer, are advocates for people with disabilities and help to raise general awareness of special needs. They are also inspiring to the general population, creating respect and inclusivity for people with disabilities in sports.

Fitness clothing enhances the sports experience by providing style, function, individuality, and comfort. Adaptive fitness clothing is an especially essential element in supporting the performance of people with disabilities who enjoy competition. Going to the gym, taking an exercise class, participating in a competition, and training for an event requires cognitive and physical energy and focused attention, and appropriate clothing provides essential support for athletes with disabilities. Designing, producing, and marketing adaptive clothing for sports enables access to this experience for all. Adaptive fitness clothing has multiple uses, which can justify the cost for the consumer.

Chelsea Hill, founder of Rollettes, the team of women who use wheelchairs and encourage fitness and athleticism, presented in Chapter 4, is an advocate for people with disabilities. For the women on the team, the experience itself creates an environment that supports both self-expression and athletic achievement. The

Rollettes have a solid group of followers, and perform their dance routines all over the country. Chelsea is a motivational speaker, a master of social media, and a creative designer.

Kayna Hobbs left the NYC high-fashion design world to focus on people with disabilities. She learned that sportswear, in general, does not seem to exist for the "non-average consumer"— which includes anyone who does not fit into standardized sizing, or whose needs cannot be met within the limitations of standard design. Through spending an extensive amount of time in Colorado Springs with a paralympic shooting athlete, Kayna learned the challenges related to adaptive design. She has developed a five-step process to assist the apparel industry to better serve the "non-average" consumer and to make the industry itself more aware and inclusive. The five steps shared in her Tedx Talk are:

1. Build a relationship of trust and communication, taking the time to get to know the consumer on both a personal and a professional level.

2. Understand consumers' needs and wants. Clothing for non-average consumers needs to be comfortable, but consumers also want it to be stylish. Learning about the lifestyle, values, and interests of potential consumers can assist in style development.

3. Understand consumer shapes and sizes, and the adaptations these require.

4. Follow up with frequent updates and ask for feedback, especially regarding performance and usage.

5. Ensuring that changes made will build customer loyalty by addressing and fixing any problems expressed.[30]

E. Universality, disability, and fashion

Universality, a broad and inclusive term, can be found in science, culture, language, philosophy, and design, as well as in many other fields. With clothing, the term "universality" applies to an aspect of design. *Universal Design* refers to the specific design of a product that can be used by all. This includes both the population with disabilities and the general population. For example, Nike's FlyEase athletic shoes serve a broad market. The line focuses on footwear fashions for a larger consumer segment, rather than shoes designed for specific athletic performance. Nike's FlyEase's collection serves many people with disabilities. It is not designed to serve a specific disability: it is designed to serve all: its Universal Design promotes inclusivity and supports the need for people with disabilities to have equal access to clothing.

It is important to note the difference between Universal Design and adaptive design. *Adaptive clothing* is designed to meet the needs of people with a specific disability. *Universal Design* is a general term, used to describe fashion that encompasses a broader market segment, potentially serving all members of a population. The designs consider cultural and practical norms, and preferences, develop styles that are timeless rather than trendy, and are consistent with global fashion trends. For people with disabilities, Universal Design promotes inclusivity, and produces clothing and accessories that can be used by all, rather than a specific population grouping. If the disabling condition is severe or requires unique features and special adaptations in design, adaptive clothing more effectively meets these needs. MagnaReady, Zappos, Silverts, Patti & Ricky, and Unhidden

Clothing are examples of clothing brands that promote Universal Design in their fashions.

Universality allows everyone to "fit in". Products, fashions, and styles that can be used by all emphasize similarities rather than differences among people, promote inclusivity and acceptance of all members of society, and support a positive self-image for people with disabilities.

While Universal Design is ideal in promoting acceptance and inclusiveness for all, it cannot accommodate *all* disabling conditions, and the special needs of a number of these fall beyond what has been achievable through Universal Design. As an example, a universally designed pair of pants may have an elastic waist, more leg space, pockets, and openings, and high-tech material that is water-wicking, but still be unable to accommodate someone in a wheelchair, because the proportions and design pattern are not functional for daily wheelchair use.

Sinead Burke is an activist for people with disabilities. She is of Irish descent, is a member of Ireland's Council of State, and regularly speaks at events that focus on disability and design. Burke has become well known in the fashion industry for her appearances at the Met Gala, the White House, British Vogue, and, most recently, in modeling for Gucci. Her TED talk stresses the importance of design in **everything** related to apparel, from engineering to pattern making. Burke is a little person, who has had challenges with her dwarfism and with the inherent design of the world around her since birth. Her talk provides insights into her world, and into the changes that would enable her full integration into the broader society.[31]

Case Study: PLAE

Ryan Ringholz founded a footwear company that grounds its business model on technology-based customization. What first began as a lifestyle brand that catered to children has expanded into gender-neutral styles, with options for all ages. Within ten years, PLAE has expanded from a top-selling shoe for Nordstroms to global collaboration and markets.

One of the key elements in the brand's success is their customer return rate, which is a direct result of their ability to cater to a niche market. Ryan was the Lead Designer at Puma, and played an integral role in reinventing Puma's image in the early 2000s. He also played a pivotal role in launching Diesel's footwear line and served as a consultant for Ugg. PLAE footwear, with its customizable special features, can accommodate a very broad spectrum of activity, fashion, comfort, and performance needs. Children and play were the initial inspirations for the brand, which suggested that it was geared toward free-spirited, uninhibited, and naturally active users.

"If you can design for the most complicated needs", Ryan notes, "then you can design for everybody." His design theory is rooted in Stanford University Professor David Kelly's design thinking, a methodology focused heavily on creativity and new ideas. For the category of footwear, and for PLAE specifically, it was important for the brand to begin at the beginning: the anatomy of the foot. Everything from bone structure and development to cultural norms was researched and studied to develop the brand. With his background in footwear, and his focus on children, Ryan knew there was a market for shoes that allowed for freedom, and could adapt to change and activity for children, and that this market was currently not addressed. Ryan's career experience enabled the successful launch of a new brand that set PLAE apart from other "shrink and pink" footwear brands. ("Shrink and pink" is a phrase coined by the apparel industry and is based on the concept of taking something that has been successful for adults and creating a smaller version in catchy colors and artwork for children.)

The challenge that "shrink and pink" presents, however, is that it does not take into consideration anatomical changes in the foot. Ryan explained that the bones in the feet are not fully fused until around the age of 18. This means that whatever footwear is being worn is not only shaping the foot, but the shoes themselves are also a mold that sets up the rest of the body, particularly for the knees and hips. Traditional footwear does not allow for freedom of movement, resulting in the bones shaping and accommodating to whatever standard sizing and design is being worn. If the foot is not allowed to develop the way it was intended to naturally, everything that is supported by the foot is affected. PLAE designed their business model considering the more complicated and unique needs of what he calls the "outlier", the person who is not a match for the options that are available.

Another analogy Ryan considers is a comparison between teeth and feet. Youth and young adults have the ability to shape and mold teeth with the use of braces, because teeth adapt to movement until the bearer is close to 20 years of age. Similarly, if a child's foot is not developing correctly, which could have adverse effects later, there are options of AFOs (ankle foot orthotics) that can be designed from 3-D printing and allow PLAE shoes to be customized for the wearer.

The brand contracts with sustainable factories overseas that have the capability of producing customized, durable designs. Overseas manufacturing enables PLAE to keep costs within reason for the customer. With their average shoe pricing at under $70, PLAE's customized, high-quality, fashionable shoes are very reasonably priced. However, manufacturing costs have risen since the COVID pandemic, and keeping the shoes at this price point is a challenge for profit margin goals.

PLAE engages users, and has even had contests for kids to create the design concepts and characters for their brand. PLAE believes that children's uninhibited creativity allows for originality and an openness to change, because their eyes are not yet "tainted by the world they live in". The shoes are designed for maximum flexibility, with protection and comfort in mind. PLAE's gender-neutral concept allows for no distinctions, from style, to function, to fit. PLAE has the ability to design for everyone through customization, thus relating to the Universal Design concept. Should there be a need for extreme adaptations, the brand has the technology to create for specific needs and disabilities, but PLAE does not classify its products as adaptivewear, as they feel that the designation can create boundaries for marketing efforts.

Ryan is an example of a fashion industry designer who has built a business from years of experience working and consulting for national brands. He has studied both the psychology and physiology of the anatomical area involved in his product. His business strategy was carefully designed and is supported by a methodology that had a proven track record for success. People with disabilities gravitate toward PLAE shoes because they allow customization, and carry a fashionable brand identity. Ryan's focus on children, their physical and mental development, and the creation of a product to satisfy a child's need place the brand in mainstream consumer markets as well as the disability market.

Ryan Ringholz interviewed by Susan Kolko

Discussion: Consider why it was so important for Ryan Ringholz to factor in medical research in creating his designs. How has that benefited the brand? What might you do if you don't have access to medical research in designing for people with disabilities?

F. Global, social media, health and fitness, adaptive and Universal Design at the 2024 Paralympics

People with disabilities have participated formally in sports for over 100 years when sports were introduced to help injured war veterans in their rehabilitation process. Research, initiated by Dr Ludwig Guttmann, indicated that sports could be a key component in recovery success, and the implementation of organized, recreational sports for people with impairments became standard in rehabilitation facilities. The Stoke Mandeville Hospital, in Great Britain, moved from recreational sports to competitive sports for its patients, and in 1948, Dr Guttmann led 16 veterans and civilians with disabilities through an archery competition. The Stoke Mandeville Games changed their name to Paralympics in Rome, Italy, during the 1960 summer Olympic games, and in 1972, the first winter Paralympics were held in Sweden. Since the late 1900s, the Paralympics have been held side by side, in the same city, and at the same venues, as the Olympic games, hence the word *Para*lympics, "para" meaning alongside. The International Paralympic Committee was established in 1989 and serves as the Paralympic movement's governing body.

The Paralympic movement developed side-by-side with the more general disability movement. Disability advocacy spurred the movement toward equal treatment and opportunities for Paralympic games and athletes. Athletic apparel has always been a niche category, with classifications and subclassifications covering a wide span of sports and teams. Attention to the uniforms that represent each country is a high priority, and has become synonymous with brand loyalty, marketing, technology, and sustainability. Paralympic athletes' uniforms require more time and money to produce, and the challenges in the design and production of adaptive athletic uniforms are intensified by the magnitude of this global event. Ralph Lauren was the official outfitter for the 2024 Olympics, designing all the opening and closing ceremony outfits for Team USA.

The word "uniform" means "the same". The purpose of uniforms is to identify a cohesive group of members, who stand for the same values, interests, and skills, and may also share a common nation, state, or city. Uniforms standardize likenesses and similarities. If a designer or a brand values inclusivity, the needs and comfort of the wearer must be carefully considered, and modifications developed to support accessibility for all team members. The mascot for 2024 was itself a symbol of French culture, representing both freedom and energy. The Paralympic Phryge is a red figure with a prosthetic blade, which promotes positivity, strength, and awareness for people with disabilities.[32]

Adidas, one of the brand sponsors for the 2024 Olympics and Paralympics, spent more than two years researching and designing adaptive training gear and competition uniforms. New to Addias, the research revealed the necessity of design adaptations for athletes in a seated or wheelchair position. Adidas also noted and addressed the needs of athletes, both with and without disabilities, for adaptations to standard sizing, features, or design. Universal Design is key to Adidas' mission, and their products are intended to meet the needs of all athletes. The brand has made major efforts in its research for the adaptive market, to ensure inclusivity and performance standards: they have conducted studies, created samples, and tested uniform kits in the design process. Considerations in seam placement, colors, iconography, trimmings, and sizing differences were some of the more obvious adaptations developed. Jacqueline King, Design Director for Adidas, stresses the brand's priorities: to create sportswear that enables parity for all Olympic and Paralympic competitors. She also recognizes the importance of the disability community as a resource for research and learning. Australian designers for the Paralympic team created uniforms that included elastic waists that allowed for fluctuations in size, zip-up sneakers for improved efficiency, and magnetic fasteners for ease of dressing. The nation of Australia is one of the leading innovators for adaptive clothing, and both the culture and the government have set a standard for inclusivity, and for the treatment of disability as a government responsibility.

Additional designers and brands who have designed for the 2024 Paralympic Games include:

1. Lululemon

Lululemon is well known for its yoga, running, and athleisure wear. The brand chose to include parathletes themselves in the design process, in order to ensure that adaptive concepts were top priority for the team kits that they produced. Three-time Paralympian Zak Madell, who was involved in the wheelchair kit design, found that being part of the process itself, and not only being the end user, was an enlightening experience that allowed him to witness firsthand the research, attention, and care that the brand was willing to devote to Paralympian comfort and success.

The results of their efforts were designs that included magnetic-close zippers, braille labeling, access loops, technology-driven fabric, and no back pockets—all considerations and applications that can enable an athlete in a seated position to have mobility and accessibility with style and comfort. Lululemon Team Canada Creative Director, Audrey Reilly, felt strongly that unpredictable weather needed to be accounted for as well, and designed an adaptive rain poncho for the athletes.[33]

Lululemon's *Future Legacy Program* donates 10 percent of sales from all Future Legacy items to the Paralympic Foundation of Canada, and to the Canadian Olympic Foundation. The brand's use of focus groups and testing teams allows for accuracy in design and demand.

2. Skims

Skims, a specialty brand known for comfort, technology, and inclusivity, partnered with Team USA to develop a collection of undergarments and loungewear for athletes and fans that was meant to be worn both on and off the field. Men's swimwear adaptive styles were also introduced for the 2024 Olympic and Paralympic games. Robes, nightshirts, swimsuits, mini dresses, boxers, and tank tops in Paralympic style were part of the limited-edition TEAM USA 2024 collection. Skims has a reputation for designing underwear and loungewear to fit every body type and size. The brand embraces diversity, which is clear in their ability to satisfy a large market segment, as well as providing options and solutions for smaller segments that have been historically neglected.[34]

3. UNIQLO

UNIQLO produces LifeWear, high-quality everyday clothing that places quality, innovation, and sustainability front and center in both design and production. The brand has been designing for Team Sweden for five years. Designers and merchandisers work closely with athletes to create solutions that will enhance performance, from training to competition. UNIQLO not only designs for people with disabilities but is also committed to hiring employees with disabilities. In Japan, UNIQLO employs the highest percentage of people with disabilities, higher than any other large corporation, with the goal of at least one person with a disability in every store. The brand feels that employees with disabilities enhance customer service and communication. In addition to the 2024 Paralympics, UNIQLO is also a sponsor of the Special Olympics.[35]

4. Holyland Civilians

Paralympic Team Israel's Holyland Civilians is a fashion brand that prides itself in intertwining the history and the traditions from the Mediterranean. Founded by Anat Meshulam and Dor Chen, graduates from Shenkar College of Design & Engineering, the brand ensures that sustainability is a high priority in sourcing, manufacturing, and production, and that its aesthetics are designed with a utilitarian purpose in mind. Holyland Civilians incorporates Israeli symbolism into their designs to enhance strength and pride in the 2024 Olympic teams. An exclusive capsule collection of uniforms, created specifically for the Israeli Paralympic team, was carefully and thoughtfully designed, with accessibility, comfort, and function as a high priority. El Al, the official airline for the Paris 2024 Olympics and Paralympics, hosted a ceremony to introduce the uniforms designed by Holy Civilians.[36]

5. Ralph Lauren

Ralph Lauren, the official outfitter for the 2024 Olympics and Paralympics, designed the opening and closing ceremony uniforms. Their Team USA retail fan collection consists of both Olympic and Paralympic signature items.

6. Nike

Team USA was given a Nike athlete goodie bag with adaptive apparel. The brand provided clothing not only for competition but also for social and professional needs. Nike's EasyOn footwear continues to be the foundational product for their adaptive brand. Using magnetic zippers and illuminating laces, ties, buttons, and traditional zippers gives the Nike "Just do It" marketing strategy a whole new avenue of business opportunities, in providing products for an underserved and growing population.[37]

Summary

The place of each person in society is determined by many things, and an essential, basic component of this is appearance. Appearance strongly influences self-image and the perception of the individual by others in society, from the most intimate relationships to broad global awareness and perceptions. Clothing and fashion play a key role in both creating and supporting personal self-image, and in the wider perception of an individual with disabilities by the broader society. Increasing global awareness and social media play a pivotal role in shaping personal, individual, and societal perceptions of people with disabilities, and clothing, along with the advertising, promoting, and availability of fashions has always played an essential role in supporting inclusivity and acceptance. This chapter has explored fashion's important role and shared some of the stories of designers and brands who have brought attractive and comfortable adaptivewear to the market and thus to the public. The concept of Universal Design, clothing designed for all, has also been presented as one of the fashion strategies addressing the needs of people with disabilities.

Learning activities

- Make a list of things that you think contributed to the development of your self-image.
- What specific resources outside of your family or caregivers were most helpful? For example, school, after-school activities, sports, religion, community, scouting, music, arts, etc.

- Consider clothing. How did clothing play a role?
- How did clothing make you feel at school?
- How did clothing make you feel if you had to wear a uniform or dress in a particular way?
- Review your list and imagine you had a disabling condition

- How might clothing make life complicated and frustrating?
- How might this affect you socially?
- How might this directly affect your self-esteem?

Adaptive talk

- Universal Design
- universality
- social media
- global awareness
- ableism
- Paralympics
- Neurodivergent
- Palta

Case studies

Abilitee – Marta Elena Cortez-Neavel

Alter Ur Ego – Heidi McKenzie

PLAE – Ryan Ringholz

Sinead Burke

Kayna Hobbs

Chelsea Hill

Ali Stroker

Addias, Lululemon, Skims, UNIQLO, Nike, Holyland Civilians

Part IV
Marketing program development

In addition to considering disability from the individual perspective, it is essential to be able to utilize that information to create a viable marketing plan, a plan which is accessible, cost-effective, and supports the personal needs of individuals with disabilities. People with disabilities are unique individuals, members of families and social groups, colleagues, and an integral part of society. Each of these—the individual, the immediate social circle, and the wider society—has a key role in the development of marketing strategies that can specifically engage people with disabilities. However, it is also necessary to consider some of the special needs, limitations, and concerns of this segment of the population.

Chapter 7 will explore the social world and some of the models used to define this special population. Specific challenges to marketing will be defined and considered so that, in Chapter 8, strategies can be explored, and potential marketing plans be developed. Chapter 9, the final chapter, will illustrate the issues, concerns, reasoning, and planning of people with disabilities and disability advocates in a variety of fields, as well as some educational resources for further exploration and study in the field of adaptive fashions.

7

"Fashioning" the social model of disability

Introduction

"Fashioning" the Social Model explores people with disabilities' own understanding of their position in the society in which they live. As discussed in the previous chapter, the manner in which disability is defined by society affects not only one's personal self-image, but also social relationships, educational and career opportunities, and the potential for personal fulfillment. Shifting from the "medical model" to the "social model" of disability broadens perspectives and understanding of disabling conditions, and offers a model that includes people with disabilities in the broader social community. Clothing and fashion can play an essential role in enabling, or hindering, a positive life experience for people with disabilities of any age. However, there are several specific challenges to be considered by the fashion industry in designing and marketing for special needs in clothing.

Figure 7 Blind music artist LACHI wearing Asthma stole - Adaptive by Asiya

Learning objectives

- Upon completing this chapter, readers will be able to:
- Define the differences between the medical and the social models of disability
- Use vocabulary associated with adaptive clothing and social disabilities
- Understand the difference between impairments and disabilities, and how this might affect clothing design
- Apply fashion theory to both the medical and social models of disability.

A. The social model of disability

We are all participants in the social world of home and community, and well aware of the importance of positive interactions and relationships. People with disabilities are often especially sensitive to these, due to their awareness of the personal differences inherent in their disabling condition. As we have seen, the medical model has been the dominant way in which both individuals with disabilities and the broader society have traditionally understood disabling conditions. The medical model continues to be essential in terms of potential treatments and interventions, as well as in facilitating access to government programs and support. However, this model often has a negative connotation, as it tends to "label" individuals according to their medical conditions alone. These often become so dominant that other personal characteristics fade into the background, and are not recognized by the individual or by others. For this reason, it has been essential to develop an alternative, more positive, model of disability—one which has been formalized as the "Social Model".

The Social Model of Disability suggests that if full environmental and cultural choices were accessible to all people, including those who may be physically or mentally challenged, this special population would not view themselves, and their place in the social world, differently from others. The model focuses on the role of society in defining and framing disability, and in integrating everyone with a disability within the whole, rather than viewing the person only in the context of medical conditions and the labels associated with them. Thus, the goal of the social model is the development of an inclusive, welcoming society, where people with disabilities can participate fully in all the activities of life in their communities, including familial, social, athletic, career-oriented, travel, community-centered, and other activities and interests.

1. Terminology: "disability" versus "impairment"

This model also challenges us to understand and consider the differences between impairments and disabilities. While we often use these two terms interchangeably, their meanings are quite different, and this difference is essential to our understanding of the way a person with a disability may be integrated into the broader society. An *impairment* is a person's physical or mental limitation, such as the inability to walk independently, to see, to hear, to speak clearly, to reason logically, or to coordinate fingers and hands. A *disability* is a condition that is caused by an environment that does not provide equal treatment for all, including people with impairments, such as crosswalks without sound indicators or ramps, narrow and irregular sidewalks, phone messages which require verbal responses, and elevators that do not verbally indicate floors. Apparel, and the apparel industry, also play vital roles in the social model of disability, and can be essential in assisting people with impairments to function fully and comfortably in their social world.

2. "Fitting in"

Appearance, as we have seen, is the first thing we notice about people. It creates first impressions, and often lasting ones. Dress can communicate many things, such as taste, colors preferences, culture, interests, and style—but also position, status, and financial resources. Everyone wants to communicate a positive image of themselves, and clothing is an extremely powerful communicator. Interest in fashion varies with age, personality, financial status, social relationships, culture, and environment. People are very much aware of the image that clothing communicates, and, to a greater or lesser extent, there is a general desire to "fit in" to the social world around us and to project a positive image. On an individual level, this involves having clothing with features, colors, and styles, that in some way "blend in" with the clothing of others. The range of choices available to people as they shop for clothing enables these kinds of choices. At any given moment, available selections tend to be "in fashion" and similar in a basic manner, though many details may vary. Many people enjoy adding something distinctive, or something original—but these additions are choices that we make individually.

In most circumstances, people with disabilities have a much more limited choice of clothing available to them. Styles, colors, materials, and designs may differ from fashion trends, and may not "fit in" with current styles. In addition, they may be uncomfortable to wear, and may not fully meet special individual needs. The sense of difference that individuals experience due to a disability may be increased by the awareness of additional differences, communicated through clothing.

B. The fashion industry's challenge

The manufacture and production of apparel is one of the largest industries in the world. It supports economies through the jobs it provides, the products it produces, and the revenues it generates. Clothing is a basic everyday need for everyone and is also a natural communicator of identity. The development, and the

normalization, of adaptive clothing as a fashion category enables meaningful progress toward the creation of a society that
is welcoming and inclusive for all. If a person who is blind could
coordinate an outfit by using a special tagging system, dress
with ease using touch indicators for direction, shop in a store
that is merchandised in a logical format for all, and have access to
a sales staff that has been educated to assist shoppers with disabilities, he or she would have equal access to the act of shopping,
to the coordination of dressing, and to the positive experience
of independence. Similarly, wheelchair ramps, wide shopping
aisles, accessible clothing racks, large fitting rooms, and clothing
that is conducive to comfort in the seated position help to normalize the shopping experience and selection of clothing for all.

However, developing both a shopping experience and clothing
with adaptive features remains a major challenge for the fashion industry. Although the data, statistics, and analytics we have
seen in Chapter 2 indicate the extensive size of the disability
community, the major changes involved are costly, and revenues
might not compensate rapidly for the initial investment. There
is a clear need for both community and government support
for small businesses, as they seek to normalize and mainstream
this social model and provide fashionable adaptive clothing to
meet all needs.

One of the major challenges for the fashion industry involves the
words used to describe adaptive clothing lines. Fashion-focused
brands do not want to be labeled as "medical" to the public, as
the word "medical" implies some sort of special need or necessary
accommodation due to a disabling condition. The use of a medical term might negatively affect sales, as the brand or the retailer

might be viewed as serving a limited number of people rather than a general population. Retailers such as Zappos and Kohl's, and brands such as Disney and Tommy Hilfiger have striven to normalize adaptivewear, and want their specialized brands to be marketed and accepted as mainstream fashion products, without the "medical label".

C. The three "A"'s

The three A's merchandising theory was developed by Dr Juliet Rothman, a former UC Berkeley professor specializing in disability, and this book's author, Susan Kolko. They suggest that there are three essential considerations in merchandising and marketing for people with disabilities. Introducing a new brand, or a new line of clothing, is challenging regardless of merchandising category, and these three A's should always be considered in both the design and the marketing of clothing for people with disabilities.

1. Adaptable – Is the design adapted for the specific impairment? If the design is an adapted version drawn from a preexisting collection, it is essential that the adaptation maintains the intended aesthetics and characteristics of the original design, and thus remains strongly associated with it. For example, Disney-adaptive costumes need to maintain the same character vision, while incorporating adaptive features.

2. Accessible – Is the design accessible for fit, purchase, and customer service? Consideration should always prioritize size and fit. For example, will the item use the standard international sizing charts, or an individual chart based on the modifications made? It is also important that the items be accessible for purchase—where can the customer purchase them? Is the design made to order individually, or is it part of a mass merchandise collection? Is there someone able to assist with decisions and transactions? What is the return policy if the item does not fit? Which retail platforms are most appropriate?

3. Affordable – Is the design affordable to the population for whom it has been designed and produced? It is important to be aware that, according to the Department of Labor and Statistics and the Census Bureau, people with disabilities often have lower incomes than the general population. In addition, adaptive designs tend to be more costly to produce. It is extremely important to carefully consider cost, pricing strategy, and inventory, and to allow for deep fluctuations in profit margins depending on the stage of the product life cycle.

Case study: So Yes

Jessie Provoost and **Sofie Ternest** are occupational therapists who worked together in a rehabilitation facility. Their patients' struggles with dressing and undressing, and the lack of functionality of their clothing inspired them to launch **So Yes,** a brand that carries clothing for all types of disabilities. Their clothing for wheelchair users provides stylish, functional options to meet the needs of their patients. The unique part of Jessie and Sofie's design journey has been their ongoing contact with the end users of their products. Sofie still works in the rehabilitation center as head of the neurorehabilitation team, and Jessie often stays connected with the target group through appointments with clients, models, and rehabilitation centers.

Their patients and customers can share their opinions, assist in altering designs, and serve as models for fit. Although Jessie and Sofie do not have a disability, they work so closely with the consumer market of people with disabilities that they can create products to serve them with accuracy and care. So Yes is constantly testing the marketplace for product designs that will be profitable, as are other adaptive brands.

They contemplated a line of labels in braille so that blind shoppers would know size, color, fabric qualities, and other features of clothing as they shopped. The concept was realistic, and the designs were production-worthy. However, as is often the case with problem-solving products for people with disabilities, research proved that the marketability and affordability of Braille labels was not reasonable: they are simply not affordable for the average consumer on a disability budget. So Yes uses their test market to ensure adaptable, accessible, and affordable products.

Jessie Provost and Sofie Ternest interviewed by Susan Kolko

Discussion: How does So Yes increase value through client relations? What are some factors that could bring the cost of Braille labels down?

D. Two essential considerations

With an understanding of the goals and perspective of the social model, and the role of self-image with the need to "fit in", as well as some of the essential considerations of merchandising theory, it is also essential to consider traditional business and merchandising factors.

1. "Labeling"

As we have seen, disabilities have historically been defined by physicians using the medical model. Disabling conditions generally carry medical "labels", which often play a major role in the development of self- image, and in the person's integration into society. However, it is important to be aware that the medical model also plays a vital role in access to clothing for special needs.

Research related to marketing adaptivewear has noted the complexities involved in the practice of labeling some clothing items as "medical". If an item is labeled "medical", it may be eligible for reimbursement from insurance companies, thus making it affordable to a broader range of the population with disabilities. However, this presents a challenge for the fashion industry: brands do not want apparel and accessories they have designed and marketed to be labeled "medical", as this would potentially affect the brand's image, and thus general consumer interest in purchasing their products. Due to this important consideration, businesses strongly prefer marketing-adaptive items similarly to mainstream fashion items. However, eliminating the medical label might not be realistic in terms of reimbursement from insurance companies, and, as many people with disabilities are challenged by restricted incomes, reimbursement is an essential consideration in purchasing clothing. Eliminating the medical label might impact sales.

2. Cost

In addition to the image-related issues engendered by medical labels, most adaptive fashions are higher priced, as they require more labor in manufacturing and greater consideration of the fabrics and materials. During the process of design and merchandising, it is essential to recognize an important consideration related to marketing: every business must have products that provide a profit margin.

However, some businesses carry products that provide a lower profit margin, or serve as loss leaders to provide a full range of consumer options and support a moral value or a trend. Adaptivewear might very well fall into the lower profit margin category, and potentially create a loss of return on investment. However, it may support important values, such as inclusiveness for all. In considering the development of a line of adaptivewear, it is important to analyze both the long- and short-term budgeting goals to develop a realistic merchandising plan. These two essential considerations must be carefully integrated into both design and marketing development to produce a product that is not only adaptive and attractive, but also easily integrated into a company's overall business plan.

E. Addressing adaptivewear costs: Government assistance and insurance policies

As we have seen, adaptive clothing costs and the limited income of many people with disabilities are major factors for both businesses and consumers. Insurance might alleviate the cost issues for consumers, but the medical labels required for reimbursement may also negatively affect brands. It is important to consider current policies and how these may affect business decisions.

1. Insurance policies and coverage

Generally, adaptive clothing in the United States is not covered or reimbursed by insurance at this time, unless the item is considered medically necessary, and is prescribed by a physician. People with disabilities often have limited financial resources, and, like all people, need a positive self-image to "fit in" socially. Meeting these positive self-image needs helps to support both mental health and socialization, and clothing serves as a vehicle for communication in many aspects of life.

Currently, insurance companies are reimbursing for adaptations that need to be made in the physical environment, such as the installation of wheelchair ramps, and in the technology that can assist with hearing and vision impairments. However, the only categories of clothing that are even remotely considered for reimbursement are shoes that have certain orthopedic requirements. Footwear companies BILLY Shoes and Friendly Shoes, regularly face challenges with insurance coordination. If the disability is the result of a work injury, worker compensation might provide an allowance for benefits related to adaptive clothing expenses.

2. Government programs

The U.S. Department of Veterans Affairs provides a VA clothing allowance. Under this assistance program, clothing that has been damaged related to a disability may be replaced at government expense. The service-connected condition must be a result of an injury related to military service. This program, called the "annual clothing allowance", enables the individual to determine and make choices regarding items to be purchased.

Harry Thal provides advisory services for people seeking Social Security and Medicaid benefits. In a recent interview, he stressed that Supplemental Security Income (SSI) for individuals under the age of 18 can help to address some of the expense issues related to clothing, toys, food supplements, learning materials, and other essentials. SSI can provide monthly funding for youth. While this assistance is temporary (until the youth reaches 18 years of age), it may assist in addressing young people's need for fashionable adaptive clothing, rather than restricting youth with a disability to the most basic items. As an example, a medically necessary undergarment might automatically be covered or reimbursed by insurance, while a more fashionable boutique brand that specializes in the same accommodations, such as Slick Chicks or Liberare, might not be reimbursable. SSI payments, however, he suggests, might be used to support purchases that are deemed not only medically necessary but also socially relevant.[38]

F. Three nations' adaptivewear policies: A comparison

1. United States

As we have seen, insurance plans in the United States do not cover the costs of adaptivewear. There are no government subsidies, except limited coverage for veterans, and, potentially, SSI coverage for youth under 18 years of age. This leaves most people with a disability responsible for meeting the cost of their own personal clothing needs, which may be higher than the costs for the general public.

2. Australia

In contrast, Australia provides funding through a program called The National Disability Insurance Scheme (NDIS). Under this government program, a person with a disability is provided funding for adaptive clothing, as it is considered assistive technology neccessary for everyday activities. Funding varies for participants. Australian brands and retailers, such as Every Human and Christain Stephans, specifically coordinate with the NDIS and can fill adaptive clothing orders using combinations of insurance and private consumer funds.[39]

3. Canada

In Canada, adaptive clothing is called a "zero-rated supply" and is therefore taxed at 0 percent if a medical practitioner prescribes or approves the need. Canada's adaptive clothing is also known as "specially designed clothing" and is listed as a medical and assistive device.[40]

Adaptive Clothing – Insurance	United States	Canada	Australia
Allowances for spending	**VA program** **SSI for under age 18**	Varied amounts depending on disability for all citizens	**NDIS – varied amounts depending on disability for all citizens**
Tax incentives	**Tax free with perscription**	**Zero tax**	GTS free(no tax)

As can be seen in the chart above, the United States has not addressed this important issue effectively, thus limiting the assistance needed to effectively enable all people with disabilities to purchase and utilize adaptivewear. Advocacy, in general but particularly from the world of fashion, could enable fuller access to adaptivewear for those needing this important accommodation.

Case study: Sewn Adaptive

Alexander Andronescu and **Lynn Brannelly** have worked together in the clothing manufacturing industry for many years. Lynn is a costume designer for film and television, and met Alex while they were working on Cirque du Soleil costumes for the company's New York shows. Soon after, Alex received a call asking if he was interested in tailoring for Runway of Dreams, the runway show featuring disability fashion that was presented in Chapter 1. Neither Alex nor Lynn were familiar with the world of adaptive fashion, but, in less than 48 hours, they found themselves totally immersed in the process of tailoring and producing 200 alterations to existing styles of clothing, in order to enable models with disabilities to show the styles on the runway. It was a demanding undertaking, but they were both up for the challenge!

Most of the show's models had never had clothes that fit comfortably and attractively, and the existing adaptive options that Alexander and Lynn found, the Runway models shared, were not really clothing items that "spoke" to them. Many of the models said they had never had clothes that fit them properly and that the available adaptive clothing options really did not work well for them. "They were retail options," Alex shared, "that were being showcased, and we had to adapt them in order to make them suitable for the particular disabilities of the models, which made it really tough for them to feel, I think, inspired about."

When their job with Runway of Dreams was completed, Alex and Lynn "walked away feeling like (they) wanted to do more". The emotions they had seen in the models that had had to wear name-brand clothing that didn't fit either attractively or comfortably, and that did not make them feel positively about their appearance, cried out to them—and they knew that they had the ability to satisfy this underserved market demand. They both felt that this work had made meaningful use of their talents and realized that they very much wanted to be part of the future of adaptive fashion. They brainstormed ideas and business concepts that could provide a solution to what they perceived was a gap in the consumer marketplace. Lynn shared that she herself is neurodivergent, and severely dyslexic. She attended fashion design school with disability accommodations. She found this to be very different from the educational experience of her younger years, and had a deep appreciation for the resources available to her through the school. She also developed a strong connection to the disability community, and wanted to "make a difference" for them in her own field.

Alex and Lynn believe that stately design does not have to disappear in the presence of an adaptive element. However, they understand that it is a challenge for big brands to invest in the adaptivewear market, even though more than 25 percent of the population potentially has special needs in clothing. Adaptive clothing, they feel, doesn't need to be strictly a medical necessity, or something that needs to be concealed. People with disabilities deserve to have clothing choices like those of the rest of the population, and should be able to create their own aesthetic through their personal choices, rather than having to choose within an extremely limited pool of options. "Everyone has to get dressed," they say, "but people with disabilities are not really excited about it."

The result: a tailoring shop, Sewn Adaptive, that would cater specifically to people with disabilities. Lynn had 40 years' experience in sewing, and had been a costume designer for almost 30 years. She and Alex had worked together in production, and understood what it meant to work with specific needs, timelines, and sometimes stressful situations. The alteration shop Lynn and Alex developed is equipped with a full fitting room and a tailoring shop, and everything, of course, is fully accessible. They are also able to do virtual video appointments for alterations for long-distance clients, and have clients all over the country. Very simple and objective alterations, that don't require measuring, are common adaptations, such as adding zippers to pants, or a small opening to a sleeve. Gowns and suits tend to be the most challenging to design and adapt, but Alex and Lynn find them manageable. They also often find that brands of adaptivewear need further adaptation to fit a specific individual—for example, Tommy Hilfiger Adaptive often still needs to be adjusted for that perfect personal fit! Sewn Adaptive has worked with amputees, limb difference, people with spina bifida, wheelchair users, MS, ALS, and many other disabling conditions. They are able to adapt, develop, and produce every category of clothing, from shoes, to undergarments, to formal clothing.

Currently, they are in the process of designing new costumes for the Rollettes, the team of wheelchair dancers presented in Chapter 4. Designs for wheelchair dancers must take into consideration the choreography as well as the group's need to move in unison. Costumes also need to coordinate well from dancer to dancer, and to flow easily in the eyes of the audience. Rollette designs need to be cohesive, from head to toe, to waist, to top of knee, to ankle. Chelsie Hill, the founder of Rollettes, has also been immensely helpful to Alex and Lynn in getting the word out, and in marketing Sewn Adaptive.

Lynn has also created designs licensed with the "big five" pattern companies (McCall's, Vogue, Butterick, Simplicity, & Know Me), and she is hopeful that this success will lead toward the standardization of design and the mainstreaming of manufacturing efforts. She has designed a special denim pattern for wheelchair users that has been remarkably successful with their clients. Sewn Adaptive currently has two adaptive sewing patterns under their trademark with Simplicity: one for an adaptive SHACKET, and the other for a pair of jeans sold in the adaptive category, the first of its kind. Alex has also worked specifically with clients of short stature. One of his adaptivewear clients was in a film at the Sundance Film Festival, and Alexander's custom tailoring has given several of their clients with dwarfism and wheelchair users suits that have proper fit and proportion for the first time, for them.

Alex and Lynn say that they have a very "yin and yang" business model. They are also finding that they have become technical advisors. As the entertainment industry has become increasingly inclusive, they have found a meaningful market niche that is in high demand. Entertainment productions have many moving parts behind the scenes, but what audiences primarily see and relate to are the actors. The role of the costume designer is not only the provision of a wardrobe that supports the character roles and the specific scenes, but, perhaps more importantly, making the actor comfortable enough, and confident enough, to play the role well. To achieve this goal, actors also must be comfortable enough to talk to the stylist and the costume designer about their adaptive needs and challenges.

To raise public awareness of options and needs, as well as possible personal preferences, Lynn and Alex try to go to as many events as possible, such as the Abilities Expo. For example - a magnetic zipper: an able-bodied person might think, "Why would anyone need or want that?" whereas people with a dexterity challenge might think, "Wow, you mean that's an option?" Interestingly, however, Alex and Lynn have found that many times people who do not have special needs still might prefer the magnetic zipper. It is faster and easier to use for everyone!

Alex also mentions that Mindy Schierer, president of Runway of Dreams, has been a leader in the field, and has been in the forefront of adaptivewear advocacy, consulting with companies to minimize costs and maximize marketing and production efforts. He notes that Victoria's Secret has researched products that have led to innovative adaptive designs. One of the biggest challenges, he notes, is change itself. Change in consumer perspective, change in marketing strategy, and change in production costs takes careful analysis and strategy, and not all businesses are interested in making the changes and adjustments that are necessary to achieve a potentially insignificant increase in margin, if any at all.

Sewn Adaptive also works with brands to provide a service in altering their regular merchandise to meet specific individual consumer needs. The main challenge with this business model is that it does not adequately account for merchandise return, as merchandise cannot be returned and re-sold once it is altered, and the return rate impacts margin. With the growth of online shopping, and with Amazon paving the way for ease of merchandise return, consumers expect a return poliy as a part of normal customer service.

A challenge for the apparel industry, Alex believes, is that it must not only market to the adaptive consumer but must follow up the marketing with both merchandise and service. He understands the special challenges of the adaptivewear market, related to population size, marketing reach, and advertising. On paper, the numbers look small, compared to those of the general population. In addition, manufacturing and production in smaller quantities is more expensive, most excess merchandise cannot be sold to the general market segment, and businesses often need to create entire new departments to manage the adaptive category of clothing.

Both Alex and Lynn are passionate about their work, and about addressing the needs of consumers with disabilities. They believe that education about adaptivewear needs, design, and markets are essential in meeting these needs. They would very much like to teach a course, lead a seminar, or participate in an event that would help to foster awareness and create interest.

Alexander Andronescu and Lynn Brannelly interviewed by Susan Kolko

Discussion: If Sewn Adaptive continues to grow, what business planning considerations might Alex and Lynn face? How might sustainability play a role in business decisions? Sewn Adaptive's return policy is a challenge. How might the business be able to take returns and preserve profit margin?

Case study: Myself Belts

Belting challenges are an important consideration in dressing for people with disabilities. Many people have difficulty with threading, fastening, and manipulating their way through the dressing and undressing process. Challenges with fine motor skills, coordination, intellectual or mental disability, and other problems make performing this essential function particularly challenging, or even impossible. Myself Belts has developed a line of belts which address these problems, which are marketed online through the designer's website, as well as through major retailer platforms, such as Amazon and Zappos.

The company was founded in St Louis, Missouri by two sisters, Talia Goldfarb and Danielle Eason. Talia is a mom and a social worker, and Danielle is a mom and a retail veteran. Talia had a young child who had difficulty manipulating a belt, which then impacted toilet-training. When Talia shared her struggles with her sister Danielle, the engineering concept of Myself Belts was created. Myself Belts is an example of a business that was born through an experience, and a subsequent recognition of an unmet need in the apparel industry. Their belt design is innovative, patented, and can effectively serve a universal population.

The business took front and center on Shark Tank, a television program where entrepreneurs can pitch their business concepts to potential investors. Myself Belts was a success, and continues to grow every year.

Myself Belts has developed a product. However, due to the absence of adaptive apparel in the mainstream fashion market, the company finds that there is a need to raise awareness of this market need, rather than simply entering or expanding it. Several major decisions may need to be made, such as marketing methods, target market specifications, and potential collaborations.

Talia Goldfarb interviewed by Susan Kolko

Discussion: What other products might effectively complement Myself Belts' current product offering? Why do Talia and Danielle feel that a Universal Design is more marketable than a medical design?

Summary

There are several considerations that have been found to be essential in planning the production and marketing of adaptive-wear fashions. An essential, challenging issue to consider is terminology: the use of a medical label versus a more inclusive social description of adaptivewear. While the social, inclusive terminology is preferable, any reimbursement, by insurance or by government programs, appears to require medical terminology. This becomes a particularly difficult choice due to the higher costs of adaptivewear and the potentially lower incomes of customers. Planning also requires attention to the three "A"'s: adaptability, accessibility, and affordability, each of which must be carefully considered. In comparing the United States' policies related to costs and reimbursements, it was seen that both Australia and Canada have plans which offer greater cost coverage for clothing for people with disabilities. The Case Studies accompanying this chapter have focused on marketing to illustrate some of the challenges and potential resolutions chosen by the businesses.

Learning activities

- Research designers and brands in the adaptive space that support the desire to "fit in". How do the businesses' marketing missions and business strategies attempt to close the gap between ability and disability?

- In terms of government, write a law or policy that would help to subsidize clothing costs for people with disabilities. Provide the rationale related to cost of living, employment, and accessibility.

- In the United States, footwear is usually the only item of clothing that is potentially reimbursed by insurance. What other category of clothing do you think should be considered for reimbursement and why?

- Research other countries, besides the United States, Canada, and Australia, to learn more about insurance coverage and reimbursement policies.

Adaptive talk

- medical model
- social model
- impairment
- three A's

- VA clothing allowance
- National Disability Insurance Scheme NDIS (Australia)
- Zero-rated supply (Canada)

Case studies

So Yes – Jessie Provoost and Sofie Ternest

Sewn Adaptive – Alexander Andronescu and Lynn Brannelly

Myself Belts – Talia Goldfarb

8
Business development, marketing, outreach, and access

Introduction

Previous chapters have introduced disability and adaptivewear, addressed some of the special issues and concerns shared by people with disabilities, provided some examples of adaptivewear, shared the stories of designers, businesses, and adaptive wear consumers, and presented some of the challenges inherent in this segment of the fashion industry. This last chapter explores some of the issues in the development of a business model that is inclusive of the special needs of people with disabilities, and presents a successful model, with disability as an added dimension, for consideration. Three case studies illustrate successful marketing models and suggestions for further resources are offered.

Figure 8 Dewey Clothing and Selfridges Collaboration

Learning objectives

Upon completion of this chapter, readers should be able to:

- Identify the elements of an adaptivewear business plan
- Understand the power that words have in normalizing disability

- Relate fashion and disability to the TRACOM model
- Understand the challenges of outreach to the disability community
- Develop a plan to maximize access to products, both online and in stores

A. Elements of a successful business model inclusive of people with disabilities

In addition to traditional business plans, there are several topics that must be closely examined and considered when launching an adaptive clothing business with a goal of moving away from the medical model and normalizing the social model. Difficulties that can occur when these are not carefully considered and specifically integrated into planning can create challenges for businesses, as we shall see in the case presented below.

The essential elements of an effective business model include:

1. **Executive Summary** – The executive summary states the business mission, goals, and objectives, based on the 3 A's of Universal Design and adaptivewear design. The summary should be culturally sensitive, and cognizant of the need for updated standards related to accessibility and clothing. A mood board, a collage of images, colors, text, and other materials that sum up the concept in a visual presentation is helpful.

2. **Company History** – The story/background of the company brand, especially related to the merchandising concepts, focused on experiences that have prompted the desire to advance adaptive design and merchandising. A personal experience, a business goal, or other relevant subject matter

that inspired the mission may be included. These elements may be important in the development of the company's image and may also influence customers.

3. **Market Analysis** – An analysis of the quantitative and qualitative consumer disability market segment, the resource market related to design and manufacturing, competition, and potential legal challenges. The use of diagrams and graphs is helpful in visualizing this essential information.

4. **Products and Services** – Sketches, designs, and samples, along with cost and spec sheets are essential elements in the development of plans for design and production. Related technology, fabric considerations, and textile development should accompany these, and the role and accessibility of customer service, the location of leased / franchise departments, and consultants should also be included.

5. **Strategy and Implementation** – Specific marketing goals should include the communication of image and positioning, as reflective of the business mission. Advertising and promotion plans may be focused on the challenges presented by a fashion paradigm shift. Budgeting and costing methods, and long- and short-term financial goals must be considered, along with a current interpretation of both the product life cycle and the fashion life cycle.

6. **Sustainability Plan** – Environmental awareness, labor standards, recycling and upcycling options, globalization, technology, and philanthropic interests are essential elements of a business plan. In addition, it is necessary to include ADA laws and cross-reference ethics related to sustainability, as well as an appropriate Code of Ethics, with accessibility as a central theme.

7. **Website** – In designing a website, awareness of the special needs of the target population must be considered, and special formats, such as adjustable font size, verbal descriptions and access, customer support, and other technologies that support accessibility must be included. Omni-channel formats, aesthetics, purchasing policies, and other support services must be integrated into website design.

8. **Key Financial Reports** – Traditional financials requiring content relevant to the market segment, such as sales reports, inventory reports, profit/loss, mark-up, turnover, stock-to-sales ratios, and merchandising plans, including open-to-buy should be included. Most importantly, justifying the potential for a low profit margin, and specifying the measures in place for long-term sustainability are essential to the business plan as well.

9. **Reflection** – The plan should justify and quantify the risks associated with the business mission. How could the risk of financial failure, and/or the changing of brand's images link to the goals and objectives of the mission?

B. Changing terms, changing images

Normalizing adaptivewear can play an essential role in ensuring the success of the shift from the medical to the social model of disability. As we have seen, clothing, and the image it communicates, is essential both to the development of a positive personal self-image and to the first impression everyone makes in the social world. In designing a business plan which is inclusive and normalizes the use of adaptivewear, it is important to consider associated language and images, and the way that these communicate both to the individual with a disability and to the public.

1. Words make a difference

One of the first steps toward effective change and the general acceptance of the social model is the creation of a vocabulary that feels comfortable and desirable, one that promotes positive integration into society rather than the victimhood often associated with the vocabulary of the medical model. Re-defining language is the first step toward normalizing something that might otherwise be described as foreign, unusual, strange, or undesirable. Medical terminology suggests that "disability" implies a physical or mental inability to function under "normal" conditions: the challenge is to re-imagine and redefine "normal".

For many people with disabilities, it is not the physical or mental challenge engendered by the disability itself that is the major challenge—it is the way society perceives, addresses, and accommodates differences in physical and mental abilities and functioning. Words such as accessible, adaptive, universal, functional, comfortable, and inclusive have an important role in acceptance and can be used in advertising, marketing, and describing adaptivewear.

2. The ADA and the handicapped icon

As has been described in the first chapter of this book, the Americans with Disabilities Act of 1990 was the first step toward the acknowledgement of, and support for, the disability community. The ADA has created both a standard and an expectation of full inclusiveness. Incentives are given to businesses and communities that have implemented programs and developed environments that support people with disabilities living and working in their communities.

The blue and white icon known in the United States as the "handicapped" or "wheelchair" symbol for disability was originally created in 1968 by Danish graphic artist Susanne Koefoed. The icon was developed to serve as the universal symbol of accessibility. Over the years, there has been controversy related to the need to "humanize" the original headless stick figure, an icon that seemed to imply disability instead of accessibility. Today we see a change: the original icon now has a head attached to the figure. There may still be negative connotations associated with the icon, however, which must be considered in advertising and marketing, online websites, and adaptivewear retail areas.

C. Social style: A behavioral preference model for communications

Social style theory was first developed in the 1950s by psychologists David Merrill and Roger Reid. The theory suggests that people have preferred forms of communication which are dependent on their personal character and natural style.[41] TRACOM provides Social Intelligence assessments and training, including their flagship SOCIAL STYLE Model™. SOCIAL STYLE™ is used by organizations worldwide to improve communications, culture, and performance. SOCIAL STYLE is a model for understanding one's own behavioral preferences and those of others. This is compared to Myers Briggs which is a typology for personality. The TRACOM SOCIAL STYLE Model™ can be applied to fashion design, to disability, and to adaptivewear needs requiring the attention of the fashion industry. There are four unique SOCIAL STYLES: Driving, Expressive, Amiable, and Analytical. Each Style describes personal preferences regarding how people in each group act with others, how they use their time, and how they make decisions.[42]

Personal style can be a natural bridge to understanding the ways in which styles in clothing and the social model of disability connect. The goal of social style analysis is to assist individuals, communities, and businesses in understanding the characteristics of individual personal behavior and preferences. These personal environments may either enhance or limit people from being able to respond physically, mentally, emotionally, and/or socially, to meaningful and appropriate personal goals. The SOCIAL STYLE Model™ may be utilized to support the attainment of self-actualization within Maslow's Needs hierarchy, addressed in an earlier chapter. TRACOM's research shows that having a full understanding of style, personality, and character enables an individual to both set and fulfill life goals, with an introspective understanding of themselves and others.

According to TRACOM™ the STYLES are distributed evenly within a population. However, certain STYLES might cluster in industries that are naturally conducive to the behaviors and characteristics of a particular Style.

Applications of the SOCIAL STYLE TRACOM MODEL™ can be seen in sales and customer service, leadership and management, healthcare, education and training, technology and engineering, finance and consulting, human resources and recruitment, marketing and advertising, government and public sectors, and manufacturing.[43] Clothing for people with disabilities is a component of the adaptive space that has not yet been explored, nor endorsed by TRACOM™ SOCIAL STYLES™. Their application to the fashion industry, in the context of this book, are conclusions based on the author's research and have not been assessed nor confirmed by TRACOM™.

Considering the characteristics of the four individual styles and their application to fashion and adaptivewear in the context of the social model can be helpful in the development of marketing strategies. Understanding SOCIAL STYLE™ can assist apparel businesses in offering goods and services that will best meet industry needs. In addition to accurate product development and merchandising, services, shopping platforms, payment policies, employment opportunities, training programs, and technology in the multiple levels of the industry throughout the channel of distribution might be better served by understanding SOCIAL STYLE™. A consideration of each model is presented below from the perspective of clothing and disability.

1. "Driving" style with a disability

Driving style individuals are fast-paced, decisive, and like to have control. Clothing choices for people with driving style are directly impacted by the tasks at hand, and clothing can enable them to successfully accomplish what they have determined that they need and desire. Clothing must adhere to certain specific criteria: a business suit in court, sports shorts at the gym, a stylish wedding gown, and practical, easy-to-care-for uniforms are all driving style apparel. There is a goal, and a desired result, linked to the adoption of one of these fashion styles: winning a court case, winning a basketball game, getting married, and feeling confident at work are all related to driving style.

This style could be very frustrating for a person with a disability and financial limitations, who might feel that without the proper and appropriate clothing, the task at hand may not be achievable. When a person encounters a challenge, it is quite easy to feel intimidated by competition, by the time frame, by specific features, or by the task itself. As we have seen, appearance related to clothing tends to be the first thing that others observe, especially if they do not know the person, and may also strongly affect self-image and self-confidence. How can a person with a disability have an equal chance, if that first impression is weak? A fashionable power suit or wedding gown should be attainable for everyone.

2. "Expressive" style with a disability

"Expressive" individuals are enthusiastic and emotional, and they are guided by their feelings and passions, either spontaneous or logically premeditated. People who identify with the expressive style tend to embrace the individuality and uniqueness of their own world, regardless of criticism or speculation by others. They may enjoy clothing that stands out in color and style, and that represents their feelings, passions, and interests. At times, this population might seem self-centered and eclectic, because their expressions may not fit into the traditional societal mold. This market gravitates toward "prophetic" styles, usually found in the introductory phase of the fashion life cycle—"prophetic" because they often have features that become part of later trends.

For people with disabilities, the expressive style of clothing may offer a positive, alternative way to stand out, superseding disability in gathering the attention of others. Alternatively, the expressive person may choose to blend in with a specific group or culture, cultivating group membership, even though their personal style craves originality. Expressive styles are also representative of culture, such as the bright colors worn by people of color, and religious clothing with specifications regarding habit and custom. Outfits representing hippie, goth, and preppy subcultures are all forms of expressive style and should be available to all.

3. "Amiable" style with a disability

"Amiable" people are friendly, supportive of others, and relationship-driven. This market segment is very conscientious, and always aware of the needs and concerns of others. Amiable people are team players, with interpersonal skills that encourage coordination of efforts, as opposed to needing to win or to prove themselves individually. They are very agreeable and able to make changes on short notice.

The amiable style embraces a laissez-faire attitude and tends to be open to a broad spectrum of personalities. Sportswear in general would fall into this category, as well as clothing styles that can be worn for multiple occasions, and that blend in with surroundings and tasks in the moment. For people with disabilities and the broader general population, the amiable style is agreeable and comfortable in materials used and price.

4. "Analytical" style with a disability

Thoughtful, slow-paced, and reserved best describes members of the "Analytical" style group. Derived from the word "analytics", this style is driven by consumers who are cautious decision-makers, and who carefully consider all probabilities and risks before making decisions or taking actions. They tend to keep their opinions to themselves, unless expressing them aloud would benefit "the greater good". This market segment is focused on fit and sizing and on current design trends.

Analytical style individuals with disabilities are constantly searching for new and improved ways of doing things, including modifying clothing. Whether it is jerry-rigging a pair of pants, or altering a dress, this market segment embraces innovation and creativity. They may, indeed, be the most well-fitted people with disabilities, who are *not* using adaptivewear, but also welcome the comfort and convenience adaptivewear can offer.

5. SOCIAL STYLE™ and Fashion Summary

The interpretations of SOCIAL STYLE™ can be helpful in defining the character types that tend to guide the choices people make in dress, the ways they want to be viewed, and how they internalize an understanding of the projection of personal image. People with disabilities can also be identified utilizing these styles, and thus providing marketers with information that can assist in assessing conditions, planning designs, and developing the means to address the adaptations in clothing that might be needed.

SOCIAL STYLE™ is a registered trademark of The TRACOM Group. The SOCIAL STYLE Model™ is a trademark of the TRACOM Group. Learn more about SOCIAL STYLE™ and TRACOM at Tracom.com.

D. Case studies for thought and discussion

The three case studies presented here illustrate several aspects of the world of disability and fashion. Each highlights the career of the individual creator, and the concept that she or he developed. Each innovator was aware of a special need and developed a range of products to meet that need for the adaptive market. Each is grounded in the social model of disability, considers the importance of self-image, the role of society, and the possibility of furthering the inclusion of people with disabilities into the broader fabric of culture and society.

Case study: BILLY Shoes

A business story of Universal Design, BILLY Footwear, is the brainchild of two Seattle locals: **Darin Donaldson** and **Billy Price**. After breaking his neck from a three-story fall in October of 1996, co-founder Billy became paralyzed from the chest down, losing the ability to move much of his body, including his fingers. Not only did he suddenly face mobility challenges, but also daily tasks that he had always taken for granted, such as dressing himself, became more difficult. Over the years, he taught himself tricks for dressing more easily, but the one piece of clothing that always eluded him in his efforts to be independent was shoes. Billy was never able to find a pair of shoes that were both attractive and able to be put on independently.

Fast forward half a lifetime, and the solution was born at last. With Billy's propensity for problem-solving and Darin's spark for business innovation, the two friends created a prototype that fulfilled Billy's personal needs. But then, the solution Billy had been seeking for his own challenges grew into something bigger—it became Billy and Darin's mission to create shoes that were functional, fashionable, and inclusive, usable by everyone, and that could be marketed in the fashion mainstream.

Merging fashion with function, BILLY footwear incorporates zippers that go along the sides of the shoes and around the toes, allowing the upper part of each shoe to open and fold over completely so that the wearer can place his or her foot onto the shoe footbed unobstructed. Then, with a tug on the zipper-pull, the shoe can be closed and secured over the top of the user's foot. It is simple! It is easy! There are also slip-on shoes, easily accessible for users with mobility impairments.

In developing his shoes, Billy considered the term "Universal Design", frequently used in the construction of homes and city buildings and indicating environments that accommodate all parties. Universal Design has even appeared "right under our noses", with the advancements and popularity of smartphones which incorporate features that are not only convenient for the masses but also allow individuals with vision, hearing, and mobility impairments to access the same information. "The designs of these structures and gadgets are universal," the BILLY website notes, "so why not apply the same term to fashion?"

Although other designers have noted that Universal Design is a very broad term, meant to accommodate all users, but that, in reality, cannot accommodate some of the complex and singular disabilities people may experience. BILLY Shoes appears to come very close, and features designs for children and adults in several widths, from dress to sports to sandals, in many colors and styles—there are even designs for amputees!

Billy's website includes a BILLY logo, with the statement "Fashion Meets Function: Inclusion for All", and features a wide variety of shoes with their innovative zippered tops and slip-on styles. They are available online at Amazon, Zappos, Scheels, and other sites, and are also available at Target, Kohl's, Nordstrom Rack, and DSW.

Billy Price, interviewed by Susan Kolko, and BILLY Footwear's website[44]

billyfootwear.com

Discussion: Footwear is one of the most common challenges for people with disabilities. What are some of the ways BILLY Footwear has set itself apart from the competition? How does Billy's relationship with disability allow him to be both business savory and consumer sensitive?

Case study: Liberare

Emma Butler is the founder and CEO of Liberare, which markets functional and fashionable lingerie for people with disabilities. Her mother was diagnosed with chronic illnesses and was struggling specifically with bra hook challenges. Emma watched her mother, living with chronic pain, and struggling with limited hand dexterity. The only clothing her mother was able to find that could be used with her disabilities was medical grade and unattractive, and this depressed her. At the time, Emma was at

Brown University studying visual arts, and became friends with some young women with the same disability as her mother. She witnessed their everyday struggles with clothing, including their frustration with their appearance when going out in the evenings.

Emma comments that shoulder and hand dexterity are challenged when one attempts to put on a bra *without* a disability and, of course, become extremely challenging with limited dexterity and shoulder mobility. Emma envisioned a solution that would not only satisfy an underserved market but would also provide a nice profit if the business strategy were organized properly, as 600 million women struggle with this problem on a daily basis.

She was determined to combine her love for fashion design with her desire to make a difference and solve the problem of adaptive undergarments for people with disabilities. Her challenge, however, was that she did not have any background or education in business and had no idea where to start. She read books, conducted interviews, built a website, created a business plan, and reached out to investors. Emma researched other brands that were producing something similar to what she was hoping to create. The adaptive apparel community is exceedingly small, and many of the designers and business owners know each other. They also know that there is plenty of room in the adaptive space, and that the more they learn and understand each other, the better they can differentiate from one another.

Emma hired a designer, and is working with patented technologies around fasteners and loop grips. She has maintained her connections with her colleagues at Brown, which has served as a huge support system for her business growth. Intimately. co recently launched side-opening panties, front-closing magnetic bras, and period panties. The brand continues to innovate through research and technology, and has recently raised $1 million in funding, secured by Venrex and the British Fashion Council. *Vogue Business* predicts that the adaptive apparel market will be worth $400 billion (about $1,200 per person in the US) by 2026.

Emma stresses the importance of vocabulary and descriptions that will allow people with disabilities to find what they are looking for. Often, people know that they have a problem, but do not know what, if anything is available to address their difficulties, even though most of the adaptive brand websites provide product descriptions with unbelievably detailed specifications to enable potential customers to consider their needs and select helpful products.

She feels that the word "adaptive" is not in the mainstream clothing vocabulary and is often not used to search for what is needed. Unless you or someone you know is directly affected by disability, she says, adaptiveness does not come up in conversation. She also considers that people with acquired illnesses and disabilities must first spend their available funds on medical care and equipment, often a huge and unanticipated expense. Clothing and fashion "take a back seat to other priorities", and the person with the disability relies on the medical team to make recommendations for clothing brands. Fashion brands, as discussed, do not want to be lumped in with medical-grade garments, but the medical field can be an important part of an adaptive brand's business strategy.

Emma believes that education plays a key role in normalizing adaptive clothing. She seeks out designers who understand the adaptivewear customer and have the skill set to provide solutions. She also believes in providing employment for people with disabilities. Her content creator met with a car accident, is paralyzed, and will be in a wheelchair for the rest of her life. She witnesses daily what her co-worker endures, and can incorporate some of her customer's needs from this first-hand experience. She stresses that working with the population that you serve is the only way to ensure your products meet their needs and specifications.

Liberare easy-on bras are loved by women of all ages, with disabilities, chronic pain, arthritis, rotator cuff injuries, pre- and post-surgery, and women who just want an easier bra to use. The brand carefully and thoughtfully creates designs to include the disability community and, as a result, they create inclusive designs for all. The website includes selections of attractive undergarments and advertises that shipping is free, and that "returns are always free".

Emma Butler interviewed by Susan Kolko

Discussion: Consider why it would be advantageous to work directly with the market segment that you are serving? Why is a bra such a complicated garment to design? What are the considerations that need to be made for people with disabilities?

E. The disability market: Three essential elements

Outreach, access and education are essential considerations specific to this special market that address several of the challenges presented in this book. Design issues and concerns that must be considered in meeting the needs of people with disabilities have been addressed in earlier chapters. In this concluding chapter, it is important to integrate these three additional strategies to implement a successful business strategy. Each of these is specifically illustrated in the two case studies above but may also be seen in the other case studies presented in this book.

1. Outreach to the adaptivewear market

An essential consideration in adaptivewear business and marketing strategy involves the development of strategies to reach out to the market—people with disabilities, their caregivers, and their families. The disability itself, but also age, limited resources, location, and other factors may limit the ability of an individual to familiarize her or himself with available adaptivewear resources. A helpful, attractive, desirable product can be developed and produced—but also needs to reach its market.

It is important to be aware of the potential limitations created by disabling conditions that limit access to information: people who are blind, or who have limited vision, are unable to easily read newspapers and magazines, or see images on television or on the web. People with mobility impairments may not frequent shopping malls and may be unable to see clothing shown in shop windows. Those with dexterity limitations may not be able to easily type to access websites, and others may be unaware that comfortable, fashionable clothing that is adapted to their personal needs exists.

While direct outreach to the individual is preferable, outreach to healthcare providers offers an alternative route for the provision of information related to product design and availability. Emma Butler suggests that many people seek the advice of healthcare providers and follow their suggestions regarding brands and types of clothing to meet their needs. In addition, if the person meets one of the admittedly limited criteria for government reimbursement of special needs clothing, costs may be reimbursed if deemed medically necessary.

In addition to healthcare providers, outreach to families, friends, and caregivers may serve as a valuable resource for reaching people with disabilities who might not be able to be reached directly. Because there is often a need for assistance, people with disabilities tend to have frequent contact with others, and each of these individuals can be a source of information about resources, special products, and adaptivewear as well.

People with disabilities, family members, and caregivers also often belong to community groups that may be specific to conditions and disabilities. The Multiple Sclerosis Society, The ARC, which serves people with intellectual and developmental disabilities, the Lighthouse for the Blind, United Cerebral Palsy, Association of the Deaf are examples of these organizations. There are also organizations that offer a broad range of services, such as Centers for Independent Living (CIL), the National Disability Rights Network, The American Association of People with Disabilities, the World Institute on Disability (WID), and many others. Outreach to these organizations will reach a number of people with disabilities, families, and caregivers. Billy Price's choice of Universal Design, rather than adaptivewear, offers additional possibilities for outreach. The term "universal" itself is inclusive of all people, and Universal Design clothing is meant to be usable for all people, not specifically or only for people with disabilities. This enables a much broader outreach approach.

Case study: Cur8able

Stephanie Thomas is the visionary Founder and CEO of Cur8able: A Fashion Tech Company, dedicated to transforming the online shopping experience for people with disabilities. Born with a disability herself, Stephanie has spent over two decades advocating for inclusivity and accessibility in the fashion industry. Through Cur8able, she harnesses cutting-edge technology to create personalized fashion solutions that address the unique needs and preferences of individuals with disabilities, eliminating the guesswork from finding suitable clothing and products. As a renowned disability advocate and fashion stylist, Stephanie's expertise has garnered attention from over thirty prestigious publications, including People, Forbes, Vogue India, The New Yorker, Vogue Business, and InStyle. Her thought leadership extends to her impactful TEDx Talk "Fashion Styling for People with Disabilities", her role as anthology editor for "Fitting In: The Social Implications of Fashion and Ableism", and her participation in a groundbreaking SXSW panel on inclusive design. Under Stephanie's leadership, Cur8able has been recognized as a trusted member of The Valuable 500 Directory of disability-related companies, providing invaluable guidance to Fortune 500 companies worldwide. Her induction into the esteemed Business of Fashion #BOF500 underscores her commitment to driving meaningful change within the fashion industry. Central to Cur8able's innovative approach is Stephanie's proprietary Stephanie Thomas Styling Method™, which she integrates into advanced algorithms to revolutionize online fashion shopping for people with disabilities.

By translating her extensive experience styling disabled actors and public figures into scalable technological solutions, she ensures that individuals with disabilities can navigate the digital fashion landscape with unprecedented ease and confidence. Cur8able offers a pioneering Omni-channel framework for fashion brands and retailers looking to enter the disability market.

The "INCLUDE" framework guides executives through the customer journey: I - Inventory Selection, N – Navigation & Access, C – Customer Service, L – Look & Feel, U – User Experience, D – Data & Feedback, and E – Evaluate & Adapt. This comprehensive framework addresses crucial aspects of inclusive fashion retail, from product curation and enhanced accessibility to inclusive marketing and continuous strategy refinement. Stephanie's multidisciplinary approach is grounded in her academic background, with advanced degrees in Communication and Fashion Journalism. She also serves as a corporate DEI&A council member for Comcast/NBC Universal, ensuring that diversity, equity, inclusion, and accessibility remain at the forefront of industry conversations. Through Cur8able's groundbreaking work in fashion technology, Stephanie is challenging deep-seated societal norms. Her unwavering dedication to advocacy is paving the way for a future where everyone, regardless of ability, can confidently express their unique style and identity. With Cur8able, Stephanie is spearheading a paradigm shift, ushering in an era of unparalleled inclusivity and empowerment in the fashion industry.

Discussion: Stephanie Thomas is on the cutting edge of technology and marketing for business-to-business solutions. What might some of her challenges be with her business mission? What will make it possible for the aging population of business owners to connect with Cur8able? What might be the consequences of a fashion business that is not aware of the disability market?

2. Education and the disability market

Successful outreach regarding clothing fashions for people with disabilities is the first necessary step in marketing to this population. Another essential element involves education—education about adaptivewear and fashion specific to people with special clothing needs. People with disabilities, family members, friends, and caregivers are often unaware of the specific clothing adaptation available to meet a special need. Direct outreach to individuals, marketing by mail and internet, and providing speakers for organizational events and meetings are helpful strategies for providing both general and specific information. Many organizations have monthly support group meetings that would warmly welcome speakers sharing information about specific products.

An essential element of education for individuals is the provision of information regarding specific items, and how to address sizing needs and specific adaptive features. Availability of clothing to meet a specific need is one consideration. Another is education in special sizing features, and how to measure and select the garment that best meets an individual's need. Specifics may be presented individually or at community meetings and available on information sheets, booklets, and online.

Emma Butler, and Liberare, her brand of undergarments, believes that education plays a essential role in successful marketing, at several different levels. She recognizes the importance of raising awareness about product availability and specific designs for people with disability and their families and caregivers, but also feels that education offers a strong path toward the "normalization" of both people with disabilities and adaptive clothing. Her focus on education takes another consideration too: she believes her designers also need education about disabilities and the needs of the population she serves.

Communities in the United States often have several community organizations that offer support groups, recreational activities, resources, and assistance to people with disabilities. How would a business locate these? What might be some effective strategies in reaching out to them?

3. Access and the disability market

Creating advertising and reaching out to the disability community, their healthcare providers, friends, family, and caregivers is the first, necessary step in marketing fashion and adaptivewear to people with disabilities, and education is also essential in providing the information to motivate customers. However, these two elements are often not sufficient. People can know about an adaptivewear product and want to buy it—but access to purchasing it is also a consideration in business planning.

Websites are the easiest way for people with disabilities, and indeed, for everyone, to access, view, order, and purchase products. Both BILLY Footwear and Liberare have extensive, colorful, well-designed websites, with product and ordering details that are clearly written and specific to the item described.

Websites for people with disabilities need to include easily accessed and viewed clothing details; descriptive and complete sizing charts; access to staff members for consultation; special details, alterations, and accommodations; and policies regarding payments and returns.

Adaptivewear is also available in retail stores, both small businesses and big box stores. Access to clothing must be carefully considered: it needs to be accessible, on a wide aisle that can accommodate wheelchairs, easily reachable, and available in varied sizes, colors, and styles. Dressing rooms need to be accessible, with seating, and staff members available to assist and to answer any questions or concerns. Clothing adjustments are often needed, even with adaptivewear, and access to alterations is essential for people with disabilities.

Locating adaptivewear in a retail setting can be a complex and challenging issue. Inclusiveness and normalization suggest that adaptivewear for women should be in the women's department, for men in the men's department, and for children in the children's department. Just as there are petite, plus, and tall size clothing racks—there can be adaptivewear clothing racks as well. However, creating an adaptivewear section or department allows for specially trained salespeople, and easier access to the very often needed alterations department. How might these needs be prioritized, or reconciled?

The National Football League was the first professional sports league to introduce adaptive apparel in their fan collections. The clothing is intended for both people with disabilities and those without disabilities who cannot find either comfort or appropriate fit in standard clothing. The adaptivewear designs accommodate a diverse population of fans and provide accessible clothing for fans of all thirty-two teams. The collection includes t-shirts and sweatshirts with magnetic closures and zippers, wider openings, extended pullers, and bungee cords. Children often become attached to teams at an incredibly young age, families and friends experience game days together, players become heroes, and some fans go on to play the game in local leagues, and in school. Football has become notorious for head injuries, and, in recent years, innovations in protective gear, as well as changes in game rules, have helped to ensure a safer playing field. Youth play flag football and/or participate in junior leagues where the team names are the same as the NFL teams, which encourages an even stronger attachment and identity with the sport. Team logos can be seen everywhere, from cereal boxes to bedroom decor, and to school clothing. Young people identify with the strength and character of the game, which is why standards for sportsmanship and character for players are so important. In considering the rapidly growing number of people with disabilities, including the aging population, NFL-adaptive apparel not only clearly satisfies a consumer need but also has the possibility of becoming a profitable category of merchandise.[45]

One of the key issues in adaptivewear is that it often does need to be altered and, once altered, cannot be returned if the owner is unhappy with the item, if it does not fit well, or if it does not perform as advertised. Adaptivewear is often a marginal profit item already, and returns would create additional strains on profits. What are your thoughts, relative to business and marketing, about alterations and returns?

Summary

In this chapter, elements of a business model are presented and related to the development and marketing of adaptivewear. Focusing on the social model of disability, the TRACOM SOCIAL STYLES MODEL™ is interpreted and applied by the author to consider the effect of personality styles and needs related to clothing and disability.

Two case studies illustrate the process of business development: the awareness of a need, the commitment to addressing it, the development of a product, and the planning of business and marketing considerations. Using the case studies as examples and models, considerations of outreach, education, and access are explored, and thoughts for discussion are included to engage the reader in further business planning considerations.

Learning activities

- Consider why some cultures and nations might favor, and choose to follow, the medical model or the social model of disability.
- Research impairments that require considerations in design for the social model.

- Search social media for supporting evidence of the social model of disability.
- Select and expand upon your own personal style using the TRACOM style model.
- Research your personal health insurance policy's options for adaptivewear coverage.
- Consider the ways the government can provide support for retailers carrying adaptive clothing such as incentives or rebates that might help to offset the low profit margins.

Adaptive talk

- market analysis
- sustainability plan
- executive summary
- normal
- TRACOM
- Social Style
- driving style
- expressive style
- amiable style
- analytical style

Susan Koefoed

Case studies

BILLY Footwear
Liberare
Cur8able Stephanie Thomas

9
Supplementary information: Notable figures and educational resources

Introduction

This text has presented the information needed for the consideration of adaptivewear and fashion in several dimensions: first, through an understanding of the history and characteristics of people with disability, and their clothing and fashion needs, then through examples of adaptive clothing, with an understanding of the importance of positive self-image and the essential role of appearance in creating and maintaining self-esteem. A discussion of the importance of fashion as an element in appearance, business planning, and marketing to this special segment of the general population has been considered.

This last chapter will illustrate the issues, concerns, reasoning, and planning of people with disabilities themselves, as well as disability advocates in a variety of fields, focusing on fashion and the special clothing needs that disability can engender, to assist readers in personalizing and identifying some of the processes described. It is hoped that these stories will assist readers to more fully understand the motivations and processes of people who relate positively to the goals envisioned here, and inspire their own creativity and interest in this developing field of fashion. Educational resources are included to help interested readers explore and engage with this developing field of fashion.

Figure 9 Stephanie Thomas Founder Cur8able and the Disability Fashion Stylist Podcast

Learning objectives

- Identify public figures with disabilities.
- Understand how athletes, celebrities, politicians, and artists help close the gap between ability and disability.

- Explain the role of business leaders in creating platforms to communicate and educate communities about disabilities and impairments.
- Identify the learning institutions that are making adaptive clothing a priority in fashion, design, and business programs.

A. Public figures, fashion, and disability

People who are in the "public eye" are recognizable and familiar, and their personal appearance, beliefs, attitudes, and behaviors often have a disproportionately strong impact upon the general population. Public figures, such as athletes, musicians, politicians, and artists, can be role models and advocates for many causes, including disability rights. As we have seen, appearance, and clothing, can engender respect and support. Several people with disabilities and disability advocates, noted here, have helped to integrate people with disabilities into the fabric of society.

1. Athletics

As has been seen in Chapter 5, appearance plays an important role in creating a positive self-image, and fashionable clothing, well-styled and fitted, plays an essential role in the development of self-esteem and self-confidence. These, in turn, can contribute to a competitive attitude in sports and foster an able-bodied personal attitude, enabling success in athletics.

Tatyana McFadden is an American icon, known for her style and athletic achievements as a wheelchair racer in the Paralympics. She has advocated for inclusivity, freedom of expression, and accessibility in sports, and has been pivotal in the paraplegic movement. She is the recipient of dozens of awards, from Forbes'

2017 *Best Female Athlete of the Year to* achieving a first place in the The Boston, NYC, Chicago, and London marathons. Tatyana is featured in social media and magazines like Esquire and Marie Claire. On *Project Runway*, Tatyana's designer, Nancy Volpe-Beringer, designed a ball gown with a long train for her, and she is an inspiration to adaptive designers. Other para-athlete role models **Robyn Lambird** and **Kanya Sesser** regularly appear in competitions, promote fashionable, accessible sportswear, and are featured in social media as well.

Aaron Fotheringham, motocross athlete, races in a wheelchair. "Wheelz", as he is known, has developed a cult-like following, which is based not only on his raw athletic talent but also on his flair for catchy fashion that appeals to young people.

Alexander McQueen and para-athlete **Aimee Mullins** paved the way for inclusivity over twenty years ago when McQueen designed a pair of wooden legs for Aimee to wear on the runway for his show. This was a revolutionary moment in fashion history, where disability met design on the catwalk. McQueen, who is known for his dark, shocking designs and face coverings, fully captured the power of the connection between disability and fashion. This collaboration initiated the movement of disability and design.

Fashion brands like **Palta**, who designed the uniforms for Israel's Paralympic athletes, are also committed to social change and stress the importance of closing the gap between mainstream fashion and the fashion needs of people with disabilities. Competitive athletes are continuously in the public eye as they engage in their sport, setting trends for activewear design across many consumer markets. Athletes with disabilities communicate an immensely powerful image in competitions and use that attention to embrace their disability as an inspiration for others. Sporting a logo creates an identity and, in current times, can be associated with a brand that fosters social change and accessibility. The New School's Parsons School of Design partnered with the Special Olympics to pave the way for the next generation of fashion designers. As a result, a collaboration of designers created fashions that helped to spark awareness of adaptive fashions in an academic learning environment. Their efforts received public recognition and helped to inspire new business standards for the apparel industry.[46]

The **National Football League** was established to support equity in talent, pay, and cost for both teams and individual athletes. There are NFL players with mental health challenges, such as autism, learning disabilities, bipolar disorder, depression, and anxiety. The League launched a program called *Total Wellness* to help players with access to resources and support for mental health issues. Some of the most recognizable NFL players have physical disabilities that require adaptive uniforms, practice gear, and clothing.

Noteworthy players with physical disabilities include **Samari Rolle**/Oilers and Ravens, who has epilepsy, **Rocky Bleier**/Steelers with a foot and leg injury from Vietnam war, R**om Dempsey**/Saints who has a deformed kicking foot and needs to wear a special boot, and **Shaquem Griffin,** whose amniotic band syndrome affected his right hand, which eventually was amputated. As an organization, the NFL also supports people with physical and mental disabilities by assuring compensation for disability due to playing injuries. In addition, they provide the most positive fan experience possible for all and offer a wide variety of adaptive apparel for fans.

2. Actors and models

Selma Blair, an actor known for her roles in *"Legally Blonde"* and *"Cruel Intentions"*, recently collaborated with Isaac Mizrachi to create her own adaptive clothing line, currently offered on QVC. In 2018, she was diagnosed with Multiple Sclerosis. After intensive healthcare, including chemotherapy, her MS went into remission. Currently, she has Meige Syndrome, which creates involuntary movements in her face on a daily basis. With her positive energy and her comedic character, she has become a relatable disability advocate for the American people. She was recently invited to visit the White House to celebrate the "Americans with Disabilities Act" and spoke of the need for more legislation to ensure jobs for people with disabilities. Blair is always stylish and can be seen regularly at red carpet awards, talk show events, and interviews.

RJ Mitt, an actor on the TV series *"Breaking Bad"*, has lived a lifetime with Cerebral Palsy. Footwear has always been a challenge due to its leg braces and all the physical and environmental limitations that accompany crutches and braces. He was recently the spokesperson for Runway of Dreams, and is an activist for people with disabilities and an advocate for adaptive clothing. He loves working with children and minors and seeks to inspire them toward a bright future as they grow and develop. RJ has also been a model for The Gap clothing, a spokesperson for the

Paralympic games, and has walked on the catwalk for Vivian Westwood.

Lauren Wasser, (back cover) has been a model and athlete from an early age, and lost her legs to Toxic Shock Syndrome. She continues to model and is known for her outspoken feelings about disability rights, inclusivity, and accessibility. The fashion industry has named her the "*Girl with the Golden Legs*" and, instead of shutting her out, has embraced her strength and poise. Lauren models, participates in sports, and can be seen regularly both at top designer shows, such as Louis Vuitton, and as a star in fashion campaigns, such as Lacoste, Furls, and Shiseido. She believes the advances in technology have been key to her advocacy, and have helped her communicate the realities people with disabilities face every day to the general public. Rather than having people feel sorry for her, and finding her disability disturbing, there is an aura of inspiration and beauty that, through social media, normalizes differences.

Wasser along with Aimee Mullins and Jilian Mercado are top models with disabilities, constantly trying to break perception barriers and move through glass ceilings to advance rights and treatment for all people with disabilities.

3. Politicians

Politicians address policy and engage in decision-making on a large scale and can create change through legislation. When a politician is viewed as stylish, or on trend, with classics in mind, the population perceives an image of integrity and that engenders trust in policymaking. Fashion does not make politics a popularity contest, but it helps create impressions, and politicians can use it as a form of communication and identity.

However, it is important to note that, in general, there are few people with disabilities holding positions in political offices. Currently, activists like **Senator Bob Casey** are trying to pass legislation that will enable more people with disabilities to run for elected offices. A likely reason that there are so few is that the campaign itself creates a roadblock, instead of an opportunity: being engaged in politics can mean losing access to healthcare, as the Social Security Administration might consider them ineligible, even if they are volunteers on a campaign. The Social Security Administration's disability requirements for benefits stipulate that the disability must prevent the individual from gainful activity: if one cannot work, one cannot participate in other activities, such as community service or running for elected office. Currently, disability advocates and policymakers are making efforts to amend the requirements.[47]

There are a growing number of young people with disabilities running for offices nationwide, such as **Yuh-Line Niou** from New York and **Lydia X.Z. Brown** from Maryland, but their chances of reaching an elected seat are currently strong. As disability is still stigmatized, and associated with *in*ability, people would rather vote for a less qualified candidate than one with a disability. People with disabilities are very much needed in public office, however, because they represent, and express, points of view and experiences that are important.

Tammy Duckworth, one of the most notable politicians with a disability, is the US Senator from Illinois. She served as a lieutenant in the National Guard, lost both of her legs in the war in Iraq. She is the first female double amputee in the national Senate, and the first in Congress. She is a disability rights advocate, with a keen sense of fashion and style. As a professional, she wears custom-made suits and has been known to wear skirts, which defy the accepted standards for wheelchair attire. Her public appearances have helped to break boundaries for disability and fashion.

FDR, Franklin Delano Roosevelt, the 33rd president of the United States had polio, and is still considered one of the best-dressed presidents of all time. He was always seen in stylish tailored suits in his wheelchair. He wore unique jackets and suits, his favorite being the Norfolk jacket, and was even seen wearing a cap on several occasions. Neckties, bow ties, pocket squares—he loved them all and used them to create a sense of style. His clothing set his identity apart from others and created a presidential image of confidence and trust.

Politicians are not in the public eye to bring us entertainment, in the way of musicians, artists, and athletes. Rather, they represent policy and decision-making on a large scale and can create change through legislation. When a politician is seen as stylish, or on trend, with classics in mind, the population perceives an image of integrity and trust in policy making. Fashion does not make politics a popularity contest, but it does help to create impressions, and prompt identity connections to the public. Politicians with disabilities can use clothing as a form of communication, as all others do.

4. Musicians

The music industry has always been open and welcoming to people with disabilities. Music provides a platform for communication that is not bound by the usual physical and mental boundaries.

Stevie Wonder and **Ray Charles**, two of the most popular American musicians, are blind. They both connect strongly to American pop culture with their musical talent, promoting acceptance. They defy traditional boundaries through the music they create, and the result is an image of self-worth, which is validated with style. Both artists have a style that encourages freedom of expression and promotes a unique and personal fashion style. Stevie Wonder, with his hats and colorful clothes, and Ray Charles, with his classic, but trendy, suits both use fashion to define character and values.

Rick Allen, the Def Leppard group's drummer, lost his arm in a car accident. Technology has enabled him to use his foot to replace his arm on the drum kit. Also known as "thunder god" for his heavy metal drumming, Allen is a philanthropist as well as an artist. He is currently launching a unisex handbag, under the name BonSac.[48] As a vegan, he ensures that his bags are all made with sustainable vegan textile products. **Toni Iommi**, of Black Sabbath is missing fingertips due to a work accident in a factory. Iommi is known for his biker leather jackets with fringes, his silk shirts, and his necklaces with crosses. **Jerry Garcia** lost one of his fingers in a wood-chopping accident when he was a child, but has spent his lifetime as a guitarist. As the lead singer and guitarist for *The Grateful Dead,* Jerry paved the way for hippie culture with his tie-dye designs, bell-bottom jeans, big buckle leather belts, flowing dresses, and flowers.

Music itself is a powerful platform for communication. Jazz, funk, bluegrass, hip-hop, rock, country, folk, indie, pop, R&B, metal, and classical music appeal to a wide variety of followers, promoting freedom of speech and communication. Music education in school plays a significant role in intellectual and social development. In addition, listening to and playing music does not require vision, is available to people with mobility impairments, and can often be adapted for people with dexterity challenges as well. Music enables people with disabilities to express themselves, and listeners to engage, without knowledge of who the artist is, or what his or her disabilities may be.

Henry Duarte, leather and denim artisan and legendary fashion designer for the rock world, stresses the importance of movement in clothing for music performers. He calculates carefully when creating his designs, considering not only for the artist but also considering design from the audience's view, as perspectives are different. He wants the artists to feel confident in what they are wearing while at the same time pleased with how they look from a camera angle on the side, below, or on top. When asked about musicians, fashion, and disability, he shared that his designs are all custom made. Each piece is uniquely designed for the artist, to ensure aesthetics and function. Buckles, snaps, buttons, and closures are all designed with ease of dressing considerations. In addition, jewelry, belts, shoes, and hats are designed to the performer's specifications not only in measurements, but in relation to movement that would not impact the viewers' performance perception. Fabrics and textiles are carefully selected and custom-finished. Each performer needs clothing and costume tailored to their needs, disability or no disability. Duarte considers that some performers struggle with strain injuries caused by repetitive movements that musicians make while playing. The construction of the garment and the choice of fabric are intended to support and energize allowing the performer to focus on playing.

5. Artists

The imagery that artists portray can have a significant role to play in the understanding of viewers, and their personal stories are often reflected in their art. Artists with disabilities can portray their own unique perceptions of the world around them, and communicate their understandings to viewers through their images. Through the years, there have been, and are, many artists with disabling conditions. A small sample is included below.

Riva Lehrer is an American painter and writer who was born with spina bifida. In her early childhood, she was fortunate to attend one of the first schools with a program for students with disabilities. In her younger years, she had many surgeries and took medications to help minimize her condition. Her paintings depict how bodies are understood within society, and especially how they are defined by culture. In her series of artwork titled The Circle Stories, she interviewed and spent time with other artists with disabilities to create her art with accuracy and perception. Her artwork is featured in museums all across the United States, and in 2017, she received the Society for Disability Studies' Presidential Award. She is an adjunct professor at the School of Art Institute in Chicago.

During the last fifteen years of his life, **Henri Matisse** had cancer and continued his art from a wheelchair. His years with a disability allowed him to reconsider the things that meant the most to him in his art, and, although always identified with fauvism, shifted to working with paper and scissors. His "cutouts", made of colorful paper, are one of his most notable contributions to modern art.

Paul Klee, a surrealist artist, and an accomplished musician, suffered from scleroderma in his later years. He continued his artwork with his disability, focusing on spirituality and, at the time of his death in 1940, had produced over 9,000 pieces of art.

Yinka Shonibare has also spent most of his life in a wheelchair, due to a rare infection in his spinal cord. He is paralyzed on one side of his body but dedicated to his art and has assistants to create his art under his direction. His artwork focuses on cultural identity, globalization, and the link between Africa and Europe. He works in painting, sculpture, photography, and film, and his clearly identifiable Ankara fabrics.

Frida Kahlo was one of the most well-known artists of the twentieth century with a disability. Of Mexican descent, her fashions, styles, bright colors, flowers, and lace are clearly connected with Mexican culture. She was born with multiple disabilities and acquired others later in life. She suffered both physical pain, and pain in addressing her personal identity. She found herself fragmented by her disabilities and had to think outside of the box to create fashions that were functional for her. She always wore long skirts to hide disfigurement due to polio. Most of her clothes were made of breathable textiles, such as cotton and silk, to allow for comfort, and she devised creative ways to sew her clothing into finely fitted pieces, to draw attention to her face and her head, rather than to her body. Her art reflected her struggles with identity and political views, and her wardrobe was a manifestation of her physical self. She used clothing to express herself and to hide herself, both at the same time. Interestingly, her artwork communicates openly about her disabilities.

Kahlo had an extensive wardrobe that her husband, Diego Rivera, kept private for many years after her death. In recent years, her wardrobe has been made public, and viewers, both in person and virtually, can learn about Kahlo's struggles with identity through her art and clothing design. Her life and her work are valued by sociologists, artists, fashion designers, and political figures, and children learn about her art and disability in school. She has become a relatable, and not a "scary" figure, and therefore serves as a model for disability that can help young people relate to a disabled world that might seem unattractive and unhealthy in appearance. Adolescents and young adults study Kahlo in more advanced classes and explore and consider the psychological challenges related to identity with a disability. Adults consider Kahlo an inspiration for creativity, a distinct way of understanding suffering, and to explore the possible influences of politics on identity. Fashion design classes learn the history of Kahlo's designs, as well as the Mexican and European influences in her styles and fabrics, while becoming more aware and sensitive to the world of adaptive clothing.

B. Activists, fashion, and disability

Many activists who advocate for people with disabilities have been presented in the case studies throughout this book. Three additional activists are included here, as their contributions have been singular, and especially important to the disability community.

Liz Jackson struggles with idiopathic neuropathy. Her first cane, given to her by the hospital, was first seen as an emblem of disability and dependency and was quickly replaced with a stylish purple cane that became a source of inspiration and ability. Liz created and initiated "The Disabled List", a group of designers, businesses, and consumers, that advocate for people with disabilities by providing both employment and mentorship opportunities. One of her major missions is advocacy for people with disabilities' employment by larger companies that call themselves sustainable, and claim to be accessible, yet do not have people with disabilities working as creators. Her website and her many articles share her personal insights into the world of disability and fashion and point out the gaps that need to be filled.[49]

After being rejected from over 100 jobs by the age of 16, **Dr Shani Dhanda** is today an award-winning disability activist and influencer in the United Kingdom. Dr Dhanda is of Asian descent and is a well-known Asian activist with a disability and an inclusion specialist, shattering business, government, and community boundaries limiting people with disabilities. Dr Dhanda has created the Asian Disability Network, an organization that provides a supportive platform for people of all cultures and ethnicities experiencing stigmas attached to disability. She is also the founder of Diversability, a financial resource for people with disabilities, and believes that it is "not fair" for people with disabilities, with low-income levels, to pay full retail prices for energy bills, or for the equipment they need to survive. Applicants need to qualify for assistance, and there is still a wait-list, but Dr Dandra's proactive efforts to help reduce the cost of daily living for people with disabilities is the most notable contribution to disability financial assistance in Asia. Dr Dhanda regularly speaks at events promoting the need for change and openly shares her experience with employment, disability, and the job search. She stresses that no one with a disability should feel that they should remove their disability condition from a job application. Dr Dhanda's Tedx London talk expands on her position and describes efforts to reduce and end disability stigmas.[50]

Dr Janina Urussowa spearheaded the Bezgraniz Couture project that proposed a new outlook on disability in Russia through fashion and art. She is a consultant in disability inclusion, a creative producer, and a speaker on the subject of disability. Bez Graniz (Russian for "Without Borders") is an organization that is considered a leader in the integration of disability that uses art and fashion as a platform for change in perception of ability.

Dr Urussowa interviewed by Susan Kolko

bezgranizcouture.org

Since 2010 Bezgraniz Couture has been an active voice for disability organizing conferences and focus groups that highlight the creation of clothing for people with disabilities. The organization coordinates efforts with local and international education and fashion events and is a reliable source data and statistics that quantify the disability population on a global scale. Dr.Urussowa is passionate about her mission and is eager to connect with others in the adaptivewear space.

C. Education, fashion and disability

Education about disability, and for people with disabilities, has had an early history of exclusion and non-responsiveness to special needs. However, today, both traditional and innovative educational environments, inclusive and diversity-sensitive instruction, advocacy, the increased possibilities for participation and comfort offered by adaptivewear, and the disability community itself have created resources which have enabled instruction and stimulated the interest of program participants.

Currently, specific education regarding adaptive clothing is communicated through marketing media platforms, and can be integrated into design and marketing curricula, as well as into other majors in the form of special projects or lesson plans. The goal is to not only provide education regarding this necessary resource for all, but also the inclusion of people with disabilities as teachers, mentors, and learners.

Dr Juliet Rothman is a professor in the Social of Social Welfare at the University of California, Berkeley, and one of her areas of expertise is disability studies. She has been an advocate for disability rights, both in her career and in her personal life through education and community service. She has published many books on social work topics such as bereavement, disability, and diversity. During the COVID-19 pandemic, she presented to a group of this author's fashion students at Santa Monica College on the special clothing and fashion needs of people with disabilities. After her presentation, the students were divided into groups, and each group was assigned a disability condition that would require clothing adaptations. Still new to the field of fashion design, and new to the concept of adaptive design, they sketched their group designs for adaptivewear. Students were enthused and shared their appreciation for learning something new about clothing, something that could change lives, something that had a purpose and a meaning that could both include and broaden their concept of aesthetics and the traditional definition of fashion.

It is essential to consider the ways in which adaptive fashion can be taught to students interested in design, marketing, and the apparel business. The listings below include some of the schools, programs, events, and leaders who include education on the topic of adaptive apparel both in their traditional academic environments and through unique events, seminars, periodicals, and journal news, as well as social media. Education includes creating and promoting awareness, teaching specific skills, and providing feedback and resources for learning. Approaches may vary among institutions, programs, and educators, but the value and importance of education in this field are unquestionable.

1. Businesses as educators

Open Style Lab is a nonprofit organization that coordinates design efforts between educators, brands, technology, and the medical community. It is a design resource that breaks barriers and makes inclusivity a reality by providing tools to enhance accessibility. It plays a vital role in traditional education and coordinating learning efforts and research between community and business. Each year, a theme is selected to enable learners to focus on one specific aspect of design and to integrate tactics that apply to all channels of distribution. OSL programs elevate design information and education beyond the simple function of the clothing by offering equal opportunities for employment to people with disabilities, who are then involved with the design process to ensure accuracy in function as well as aesthetics in style. OSL coordinates its efforts with The New School, which is affiliated with the Parsons School of Design, making both courses and fellowships available for students.

One of their most notable contributions to adaptive apparel is **Ryan's Jacket**, a rain jacket with adaptive features. As we have seen in a previous chapter the jacket was originally designed for Ryan DeRoche, a competitive cyclist with a spinal cord injury. OSL soon realized there were multiple uses for the jacket and expanded ideas and design concepts for more adaptive garments.[51]

Tracy Vollbrecht is an adaptive fashion and Universal Design expert, with experience building adaptive fashion brands. She founded **Vollbrecht Adaptive Consulting** to partner with industry leaders and educators to transform the fashion industry, tapping into the value and market potential of authentic disability inclusion. Recognizing the lack of education for the adaptive fashion segment of the fashion industry, Tracy developed a comprehensive ten-part curriculum that addresses the entire adaptive fashion lifecycle—history, customer, market, design, merchandising, and marketing. Her curriculum is available through Udemy, an online learning platform for professionals and students, and through the University of Fashion, an online resource for educational institutions.

Inspiration for Tracy's work was drawn from her experience with using Universal Design principles to help her father mitigate the clothing-related challenges from his Multiple Sclerosis (MS). Tracy's experience with working alongside the disability community continually reinforces her belief that simple yet effective updates, growth-oriented brands, inclusion-driven educators and students, and innovative fashion professionals can make clothing functional and fashionable for all.[52]

2. Educational programs

a. Belmont University Design School Project: Designing adaptivewear using Maslow's Hierarchy

At Belmont University, Professor Laura Horner incorporates adaptive apparel into her junior year curriculum with the Junior Design Studio project, where students create collections and apply Maslow's Hierarchy to identify designs and consumer needs.[53]

b. Brenau University: Combining studies in fashion and healthcare

Brenau University in Gainesville, GA, offers fashion students the opportunity to work with medical professionals to create adaptive designs for wheelchair users. The Director of the fashion program and a Professor of Occupational Therapy coordinated their efforts to offer fashion students the opportunity to learn from the residents of Champion's Place, an independent living facility for young adults with disabilities and then to create designs for consumers with special needs based on wheelchair-user priorities in designs and styles. Interdisciplinary courses that integrate community advocates and people with disabilities offer opportunities to create student designs and collections that reflect consumer demand and realistic design concepts.[54]

c. Drexel University: Integrating adaptive clothing design and merchandising

Drexel's curriculum for design and marketing students accommodates student interests and trends. The program is designed to enable students to work on adaptive design and merchandising considerations. Dr Ali Howell Abolo, Associate Professor and Program Director of fashion design, has created a learning space that is open to a wide variety of student interests. The program connects with local apparel businesses that support the needs of people with disabilities and is focused on apparel challenges and opportunities. The program is growing due to the opportunities it offers students for exploring their interests.[55]

d. Fashion Institute of Technology: Final Capstone project option

Professor Deborah Beard is Associate Professor and Chairperson of technical design and pattern making. For their capstone projects, Beard's students created designs for cancer patients and people who are blind. FIT also hosted various programs, and coordinated collaborations with students from various disciplines, to learn about the characteristics of the broad number of individuals who "live and breathe everyday adaptive fashion". The Adaptive Design Series project is intended to integrate channels of learning distribution, as educators, professionals, students, and consumers work toward making equity, diversity, and inclusion of high priority for the fashion industry.[56]

e. *Iowa State University: Book Publishers—Adaptive Apparel*

Iowa State Digital Press published a book centered on adaptive apparel. The book titled *Adaptive Apparel,* by Professor Ellen McKinney and Assistant Professor Rachel Eike, outlines a step-by-step design and merchandising plan for the category of adaptive clothing. Dr McKinney, Chair of the Department of Clothing, Textiles, and Interior Design, at the University of Alabama, embraced the research and challenge of apparel design. The co-author, Dr Eike, focuses her research on function and design. She is part of the Apparel, Events, and Hospitality Management Program at Iowa State University and aims to advance product designs that focus on quality-of-life improvement. McKinney and Eike collaborated on efforts to publish a practical resource for learning.[57]

f. *London College of Fashion*

The London College of Fashion collaborates with the Global Disability Innovation Hub to develop and maintain current research and education. Students can engage in research, take courses, and become engaged with community service that enhances awareness and offers solutions to apparel-based challenges in design. The coordination between technology and disability innovation enables research students to focus on an aspect of design that satisfies the needs of the disability market.

The program offers courses and coordinates team research, between University College London, Loughborough University, London, and the London College of Fashion.[58,59]

g. Milwaukee Institute of Apparel Design: Capstone projects in adaptive clothing design

The Milwaukee Institute focused on specific target markets, including the adaptive clothing market, and Capstone projects of seniors in the Apparel Design program have included adaptive luxury and formal wear, and adaptive knitwear. In the pattern making and construction course, students learn special designs for size inclusivity, non-binary customers, and adaptive clothing.[60]

h. North Carolina State University: Wilson College students design for spinal cord injured patients

North Carolina State University and the North Carolina Spinal Cord Injury Association collaborated on a fashion show of Mary Grace Wilder and Sabrina Martin's "Sonder" Collection, which was inspired by Frieda Kahlo. The designs were intended to promote accessibility by utilizing Universal Design principles. The College and students coordinated their efforts with Belk Department Stores to create a video that offered tips for consumers on shopping for adaptive apparel. The project incorporated insights and information from several sources: from Associate Professor Kate Annette-Hitchcock, a specialist in inclusive design, to Wilson College students, to the broader medical community, and, finally, to fashion retail. Wilson College also specifically developed and coordinated efforts to raise awareness and promote acceptance.[61]

i. Parsons School of Design: Dedicated courses for adaptive design

In the United States, Parsons School of Design had historically both set the example and taken the lead in design education, often producing creatives like Tom Ford. Parsons hosts lectures and initiates partnerships with groups like the Special Olympics and Open Style Lab to create team uniforms. The school also has courses in which students are paired with a person from the disability community to co-design an adaptive garment. The latest course "Fashion and Disability Justice" suggests that fashion needs are not a simple problem that needs to be solved: they can offer a valuable, desirable experience. Parsons engages people with disabilities to become active in the process of clothing design.

Dr Ben Barry, Dean of the Parsons School of Fashion, and Sinead Burke, an Irish disability activist, have together developed academic accommodations for people with disabilities, to enable them to obtain degrees and to have careers in the fashion industry. Their mission focuses on disability inclusion, and reflects the need for more people with disabilities to be a part of the adaptive apparel space. The program's goal is to utilize fashion design as a special means of changing the way disability is viewed. Parsons believes that disability is not a problem that needs to be solved. It is a "quality and characteristic" that helps the world to understand differences. Scholarship funding from H&M has made the program a reality and has encouraged and motivated other brands to get involved. The Ford Foundation also assists with academic programing by following the experiences of fashion students with disabilities.[62]

j. University of Alabama and University of North Carolina, Greensborough: Integrating adaptive design into preexisting courses

These two universities collaborated to create a project that is part of a special grant to both. The project seeks to integrate adaptive apparel and design education into preexisting courses as new modules or projects. The research related to student learning and experience with this project's grant includes design students who create adaptivewear solutions for student athletes with special needs. The project aims to develop a Certificate program, whose focus would be adaptive design in apparel. This would be the first program of its kind in the United States.[63]

k. University of Missouri: Accessibility of adaptivewear research

Li Zhao is Assistant Professor in the Department of Textile and Apparel Management. Zhao and her team conducted research to examine how retailers were addressing the adaptive clothing space. She reviewed customer comments from Amazon on Silvers and IZ Adaptive offerings, and concluded that product availability was insufficient, and not always helpful to customers trying to address special needs. Her study also concluded that apparel for people with disabilities was often difficult to locate online, as e-commerce navigation is not user-friendly in general, and especially challenging for people with disabilities.[64]

Dr McBee-Black has been instrumental in the textile and apparel program securing grants, mentoring students, and conducting research on the topic of Universal Design and adaptive apparel. Her work has been in scholarly publications, exhibitions, and multiple media platforms. She is considered an authority on the topic of fashion and its relationship with inclusivity and diversity.[65]

3. High Schoolers

a. *PennMar Fashion Show: Designs both made and worn by students with disabilities*

At Maryland's Penn-Mar Fashion Show, Advanced Placement Art students feature adaptivewear using models with intellectual disabilities. Penn-Mar is a nonprofit organization that is a resource for people with developmental disabilities. The designers attended The Jemicy School, a special school that caters to students with dyslexia and language-based learning differences, and the models, who were part of Penn-Mar programming, set the stage. Students were assigned three models for each collection, and researched design concepts that would directly reflect their models' special needs. They learned the importance of gathering information and getting to know clients to ensure meeting consumer needs appropriately. In addition, students felt that the show fostered their personal creativity, and they became motivated by the subject matter of adaptivewear itself. This fashion show is an example of ways in which the disability community is able to coordinate among themselves to bring adaptive fashion concepts to a runway show—designs made and worn by people with disabilities.[66]

b. *Beverly Hills High School: An art and fashion design assignment*

Beverly Hills High School offers a fashion pathway that can begin with classes in ninth grade. The goal of the program is to gain skills in order to prepare for a career in fashion. Frida Kahlo, the historical artist with multiple disabilities and creative fashion designer, was the inspiration for the 2022 end-of-year fashion show. Students included colors, patterns, and modern-day styles that were reflective of Kahlo's personal values and favorite designs. They learned about Kahlo's life and the many challenges she faced in her struggles with disability, self-image, and society.

Summary

This concluding chapter has presented the stories of a broad variety of people, all of whom have a connection to both the field of disability and to fashion. Athletes, celebrities, politicians, musicians, artists, and educators share their experiences, along with people in the fields of fashion and disability, integrating the various concepts and issues addressed in earlier chapters to illustrate how these may be applied and developed personally by advocates, designers, businesses, marketers, and—of course—consumers.

In addition, a list of resources for further education about this new and developing field has been included for readers interested in exploring adaptive design in fashion and business in greater depth.

Learning activities

- If you were instructing students about challenges and needs in the adaptive space what would be some topics you would address?

- How could a learning institution that does not have a fashion program educate students about adaptivewear? Where might it fit into a general studies curriculum? Why?
- If you were an artist or a musician, how might your work be inspired by your disability?
- If you were a politician with a disability, what obstacles might you face?
- If you were an athlete, how would clothing play a key role in performance?
- If you were a designer or merchandiser that did not carry adaptive specific clothing and was not planning on caring adaptive specific clothing, what could your business do help address some of challenges people with disabilities face in the fashion industry

Adaptive talk

Vollbrecht Consulting

Ryan's Jacket

Tatyana McFadden

Aaron Fotheringham

Alexander McQueen

Aimee Mullins

Palta

NFL

Selma Blair

RJ Mitt

Lauren Wasser

Jillian Mercado

Yuh-Line Niou

Lydia X.Z. Brown

Senator Bob Casey

Tammy Duckworth

Franklin Delano Roosevelt

Stevie Wonder

Ray Charles

Rick Allen

Jerry Garcia

Toni Iommi

Riva Lehrer

Henri Matisse

Yinka Shonibare

Frida Kahlo

Janina Urussowa

Bezgrahiz Couture Project

Paul Klee

Dr Shani Dhanda

Liz Jackson

Henry Duarte

Asian Disability Network

The Disabled List

So Yes

Open Style Lab

Dr Juliet Rothman

Vollbrecht Consulting

Figure 10 Runway of Dreams-singer Ollie Gabriel, founder Mindy Scheier and Mindy's son Oliver

(i)

(ii)

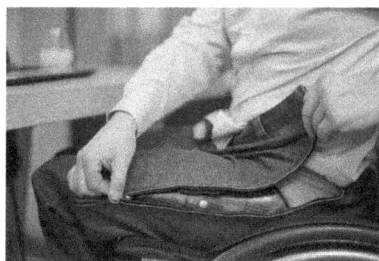

(iii)

(iv)

Figure 11 i. Kozie clothes – sensory weighted vest, ii. PLAE – adaptive footwear, iii. So Yes – zip jeans, iv. Magzip / ANGEAR – magnetic zipper

(i)

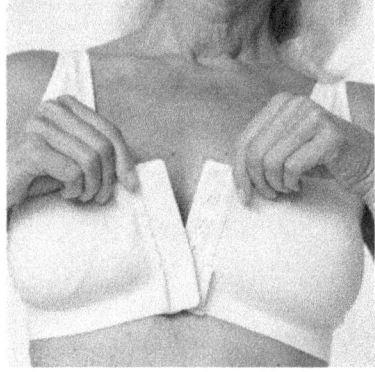

(ii)

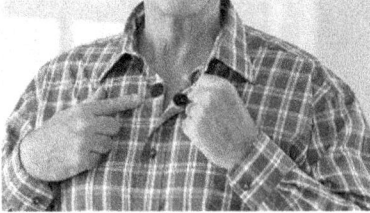

(iii)

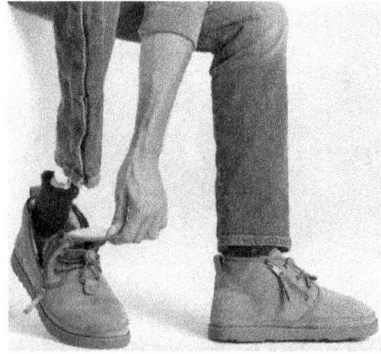

(iv)

Figure 12 i. MIGA swim – adjustable belt and snaps, ii. Buck & Buck – Velcro™ fasteners, iii. Liberare – adaptive intimates, iv. Zappos Adaptive – UGG Universal Design

(i)

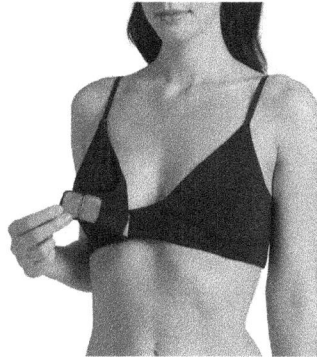

(ii)

(iii)

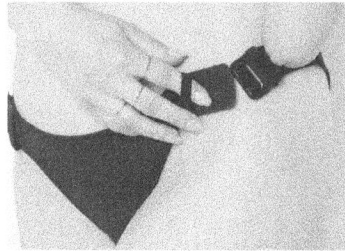

(iv)

Figure 13 i. Unhidden – unisex silk shirt, popper tape, arm port access, ii. Slick Chicks – Velcro™ brand front fastening bra, iii. FFORA – wheelchair attachment, cup holder and tubmler, iv. Liberare – side- opening underwear with magnets

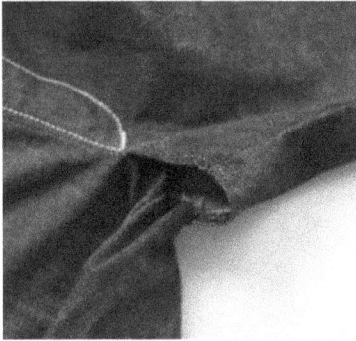

(i)

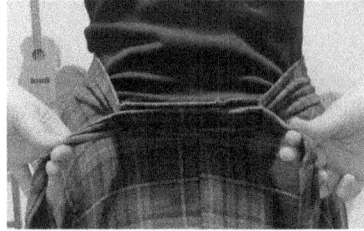

(ii)

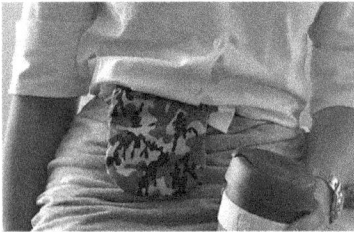

(iii)

(iv)

Figure 14 i. Alter Ur Ego – denim wheelchair jeans with catheter opening, ii. Abilitee – Ostomy bag cover, iii. Eightfold Fox – expandable waist, iv. Preventawear – sensory friendly, snap crotch children: adults

(i)

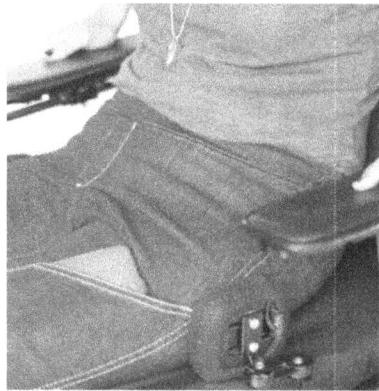

(ii)

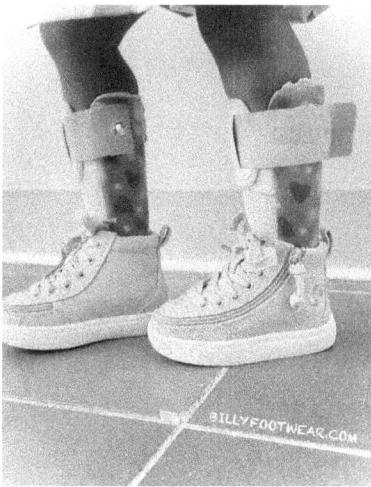

(iii)

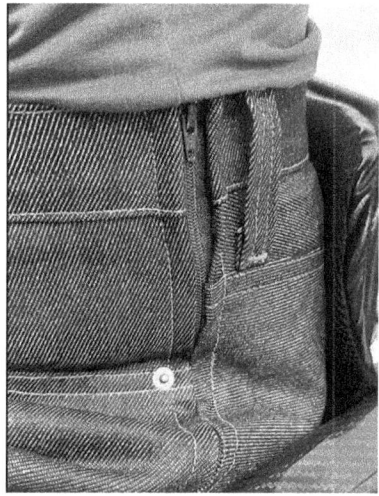

(iv)

Figure 15 i. Myself Belts Velcro™ brand belt, ii. Alter Ur Ego – tummy control wheelchair denim, iii. BILLY Footwear, iv. Sewn Adaptive – custom tailoring

Notes

1. https://www.youtube.com/watch?v=7PwvGfs6Pok

2. https://judithheumann.com/

3. https://cdrnys.org/blog/advocacy/a-short-history-of-justin-dart-jr-father-of-the-ada/

4. https://blog.mam.org/2019/05/07/functional-fashions/

5. https://www.levistrauss.com/2019/04/10/levis-an-early-adopter-of-functional-fashion/

6. https://www.youtube.com/watch?v=7PwvGfs6Pok

7. US Census Bureau, US Department of Commerce, and US Census Bureau. "Disability Characteristics." *American Community Survey, ACS 1-Year Estimates Subject Tables, Table S1810, 2023*, https://data.census.gov/table/ACSST1Y2023.S1810?q=disabiity population. [Accessed September 22, 2024].

8. Celestino, S., Garofano, A., Masiello, B. *et al.* Disability and Marketing: A bibliometric analysis and systematic literature review. *Ital. J. Mark.* 2024, 311–337 (2024). https://doi.org/10.1007/s43039-024-00098-3

9. Centers for Disease Control and Prevention, National Center on Birth Defects and Developmental Disabilities, Division of Human Development and Disability. Disability and Health Data System (DHDS) Data [online]. [Accessed 22 September 2024].

10. "Global Health Estimates." *World Health Organization (WHO)*, https://www.who.int/data/global-health-estimates. [Accessed 22 September 2024].

11. "Disability Inclusion Overview." *World Bank*, https://www.worldbank.org/en/topic/disability. [Accessed 22 September 2024].

12. https://www.ted.com/talks/mindy_scheier_how_adaptive_
    clothing_empowers_people_with_disabilities?subtitle=en

13. https://www.rollettesdance.com/

14. https://tukatech.com/

15. https://www.youtube.com/watch?v=o_xUQLFUdXc

16. https://www.deweyclothing.com/

17. https://liveffora.com/?srsltid=AfmBOopGSsPzxvQqNOG
    9KUSMtc7dCSHg02B6DDu13gB8mwECPZQXZ55x

18. https://hiddenheroes.org/resource/sew-much-comfort/

19. Rolland, John S. *Helping Couples and Families Navigate
    Illness and Disability: An Integrated Approach.* Guilford
    Publications, 2018.

20. https://cutandclarity.co/collections/disabled-stylish-col
    lection

21. https://www.jckonline.com/editorial-article/disabled-stylish-
    collab/

22. https://www.cdc.gov/

23. https://www.nih.gov/

24. https://plato.stanford.edu/entries/ancient-soul/

25. https://www.simplypsychology.org/maslow.html

26. https://www.youtube.com/watch?v=FLQcND3mszE

27. https://my.cgu.edu/student-life/student-spotlight-veronika-
    ivanova/

28. https://wid.org/this-halloween-remember-that-disability-is-
    not-a-costume/

29. https://www.broadwayworld.com/article/SPRING-AWAKENI
    NGs-Ali-Stroker-to-Offer-TEDx-Talk-with-Stories-Song-This-
    Spring-20160217#

30. https://www.ted.com/talks/kayna_hobbs_making_the_
    clothing_industry_more_inclusive?subtitle=en

31. https://www.ted.com/talks/sinead_burke_why_design_should_include_everyone?subtitle=en

32. https://www.paralympic.org/ipc/history

33. https://paralympic.ca/news/lululemon-paris-2024-kit-features-adaptive-breakthroughs-be-made-more/

34. https://skims.com/collections/skims-for-team-usa

35. https://www.uniqlo.com/se/en/contents/feature/sweden-olympic-paralympic-collection/

36. https://jewishstandard.timesofisrael.com/el-al-and-israeli-paralympic-athletes-debut-new-uniforms/

37. https://people.com/nike-unveils-50-piece-olympics-gear-team-usa-athlete-8680182

38. https://www.va.gov/disability/eligibility/special-claims/clothing-allowance/

39. https://www.ndis.gov.au/

40. https://www.canada.ca/en/employment-social-development/programs/disability-inclusion-action-plan/action-plan-2022.html

41. Merrill, David W., and Roger H. Reid. *Personal Styles and Effective Performance: Make Your Style Work for You.* Radnor, PA: Chilton Book Company, 1981.

42. SOCIAL STYLE™ is a registered trademark of The TRACOM Group. The SOCIAL STYLE Model™ is a trademark of the TRACOM Group. Learn more about SOCIAL STYLE™ and TRACOM at Tracom.com.

43. https://tracom.com/?creative&keyword&matchtype&network=x&device=c

44. https://billyfootwear.com/pages/about-us?srsltid=AfmBOorlHLw-onafk44Nfn2Yke2sSWzDuBbq7rAnxkC3kYZCxv93GHbX

45. https://www.apparelist.com/2023/10/10/nfl-launches-adaptive-apparel-collection/

46. https://paltaclothes.com/

47. https://sites.utexas.edu/tjclcr/2023/09/29/first-cripthev
ote-now-cripcandidates-social-security-disability-benefits-
and-their-impact-on-political-candidates-with-disabilities/
#:~:text=period%20of%20time.-,50,office)%20without%20
losing%20their%20benefits.

48. https://www.livekindly.com/vegan-def-leppard-drummer-
rick-allen-launches-luxury-cruelty-free-bag-range/

49. https://www.disabledlist.org/

50. https://www.shanidhanda.com/

51. https://www.apparelnews.net/news/2015/apr/16/open-
style-lab-making-apparel-accessible-all/?print

52. https://www.vollbrechtadaptiveconsulting.com/

53. https://fashionista.com/2023/11/belmont-university-junior-
design-studio-fashion-program

54. https://www.brenau.edu/news/ot-fashion-design-students-
collaborate-to-create-adaptive-clothing/

55. https://fashionista.com/2023/10/fashion-schools-teaching-
adaptive-fashion

56. https://www.fitnyc.edu/about/initiatives/dei/diversity-col
lective/grants/awards/adaptive-fashion.php

57. https://iastate.pressbooks.pub/adaptiveapparel/

58. https://www.arts.ac.uk/colleges/london-college-of-fashion/
research-at-lcf/research-networks/global-disability-innovat
ion-hub

59. https://www.arts.ac.uk/colleges/london-college-of-fashion/
research-at-lcf/research-networks/global-disability-innovat
ion-hub

60. https://www.miad.edu/academic-programs/degree-progr
ams/fashion-and-apparel-design/fashion-and-apparel-des
ign-course-information

61. https://textiles.ncsu.edu/news/2022/06/wilson-college-students-design-adaptive-fashion-for-north-carolina-spinal-cord-injury-association/

62. https://www.npr.org/2024/01/17/1225142494/parsons-school-of-design-will-launch-program-for-designers-who-identify-as-disab

63. https://www.apr.org/news/2024-02-15/ua-students-design-clothes-for-adaptive-athletes-as-part-of-grant-project

64. https://showme.missouri.edu/2023/new-mu-study-shapes-understanding-of-adaptive-clothing-customer-needs/

65. https://tam.missouri.edu/people/kerri-mcbee-black/

66. https://www.penn-mar.org/unique-fashion-show-featured-adaptive-clothing-for-people-with-disabilities/

References

"About Adaptive Apparel for Seniors & Disabled." *MagnaReady*, https://magnaready.com/pages/about-us.

"About – Alter Ur Ego." *Alter Ur Ego*, https://alterurego.co/about/.

"ABOUT." *Chelsie Hill*, https://www.chelsiehill.com/about.

About." *GCR Adaptive Project*, https://gcradaptivep.org/about/.

"About – Parsons Disabled Fashion Student Program." *Parsons Disabled Fashion Student Program*, https://disabilityfashion.parsons.edu/about/.

"Adidas Launches Uniforms for Paris 2024 Olympics & Paralympics." *YouTube*, 2024, https://www.youtube.com/watch?v=QeVr_Nfywe8.

Ali Stroker | Actor & Speaker, https://www.alistroker.com/.

(AMBIONG)AMBIONG, JASMIN. "Fashion and Blindness." *Billion Strong*, 28 February 2022, https://www.billion-strong.org/fashion-and-blindness/.

Andrews, Erin. "Official Adaptive Apparel Collection." *NFL Shop*, https://www.nflshop.com/adaptive-apparel-collection/c-2360451717+z-952151-2216459666.

ANKHGEAR, https://ankhgear.com/.

Arbaen, Hind Mohamed. "Designing Hijab (Abaya) Suitable for Women with Motor Lower Limbs Handicapped." *International Design Journal*, 2022. https://journals.ekb.eg/article_209696.html.

BEK, Klein. "Blindness - StatPearls." *NCBI*, https://www.ncbi.nlm.nih.gov/books/NBK448182/.

"Biography — JUSTIN DART." *JUSTIN DART*, https://www.justind art.com/biography.

Boyko, Alyson. "OT, Fashion Design students collaborate to create adaptive clothing." *Brenau University*, 14 February 2023, https://www.brenau.edu/news/ot-fashion-design-students-collabor ate-to-create-adaptive-clothing/.

CAYA Company - CAYA Company, https://caya.shop/.

Challenged Athletes Foundation - San Diego, https://www.challen gedathletes.org/

Cook, Judith. "Adaptive Innovations in Olympic Sportswear: A Global Perspective." *StyleAbility*, 16 July 2024, https://www.styleabil ity.co.uk/blog/project-one-5eftt-tdhmb-g5zn9-kymyh-96z7d-htmxr-ntb87-g2dlr-plesb-exjx7-b9hkm-h6e36.

Cortez-Neavel, Marta-Elena.Voyage Austin, *Rising Starts: Meet Marta-Elena Cortez-Neavel of Rosewood*   https://voyageaustin. com/interview/rising-stars-meet-marta-elena-cortez-neavel-of-rosewood.

DeVault, Nancy. "20 Adaptive Swimwear Must-Haves to Dive into the Sand & Surf." *AmeriDisability*, 19 July 2022, https://www.amer idisability.com/20-adaptive-swimwear-must-haves-to-dive-into-the-sand-surf/.

"DISABILITIES | Unlocking The Power of Clothing. UNIQLO Sustainability." *Uniqlo*, https://www.uniqlo.com/jp/en/contents/ sustainability/people/diversity/pwd/.

Donohoe, Susan. "About Kozie Clothes." *Kozie Clothes*, https:// www.kozieclothes.com/about.

Dybis, Karen. "Disabled + Stylish Collab Highlights Adaptive Fine Jewelry And Friendship." *JCK*, 11 November 2022, https://www. jckonline.com/editorial-article/disabled-stylish-collab/.

Dunn, Dana S. "Understanding ableism and negative reactions to disability." *American Psychological Association*, 14 December

2021, https://www.apa.org/ed/precollege/psychology-teacher-network/introductory-psychology/ableism-negative-reactions-disability..

Dybis, Karen, and Camilla Sjodin. "How Jewelers Can Be Adaptive, Inclusive, and Accessible." *JCK*, 21 December 2023, https://www.jckonline.com/article-long/adaptive-inclusive-accessible/.

"El Al and Israeli Paralympic Athletes Debut New Uniforms." *The Jewish Standard*, 14 June 2024, https://jewishstandard.timeso fisrael.com/el-al-and-israeli-paralympic-athletes-debut-new-uniforms/.

Inkumsah, Ashley. "This Halloween, Remember That Disability Is Not a Costume." *World Institute on Disability*, 26 October 2022, https://wid.org/this-halloween-remember-that-disability-is-not-a-costume/.

Elevate Multisport, and Deborah Carabet. "CEO & Founder." *Elevate Multisport*, https://elevatemultisport.com/about/.

"EP. 7 | Designing the Paralympic Tokyo 2020 Uniforms." *YouTube*, 17 January 2024, https://www.youtube.com/watch?v=pqBH isLv1Tk.

ESPRESO. "Adaptive Clothing for Wounded Soldiers to be Introduced in Ukraine's Armed Forces." 2004. https://global.espr eso.tv/russia-ukraine-war-adaptive-clothing-for-wounded-soldi ers-to-be-introduced-in-ukraines-armed-forces

"Fashion and Apparel Design Course Information." *Milwaukee Institute of Art and Design*, https://www.miad.edu/academic-programs/degree-programs/fashion-and-apparel-design/fash ion-and-apparel-design-course-information.

"Fashion Design Degree | Graduate Program | Drexel Westphal." *Drexel University*, https://drexel.edu/westphal/academics/gradu ate/FASH/.

"Fashion Designers – Majors at Mizzou." *Majors at Mizzou*, https://majors.missouri.edu/career/fashion-designers/.

"Fashion Design – Pathways – Beverly Hills High School." *Beverly Hills High School*, https://bhhs.bhusd.org/apps/pages/index.jsp?uREC_ID=2230420&type=d&pREC_ID=2200462.

"Fashion Merchandising Major." *Belmont University*, https://www.belmont.edu/academics/majors-programs/fashion-merchandising/.

FFORA: Designed to be Seen, https://liveffora.com/

Frischer, Brooke. "Belmont University Fashion Students Are Learning Firsthand How to Design for Underserved Markets." *Fashionista*, 29 November 2023, https://fashionista.com/2023/11/belmont-university-junior-design-studio-fashion-program.

"Freddie Rojas (@rojasclothing) • Instagram photos and videos." *Instagram*, https://www.instagram.com/rojasclothing/?hl=en.

GCR Adaptive Project - Accessible Fashion, https://gcradaptivep.org/

Giuffrida, Mary. "Wilson College Students Design Adaptive Fashion for North Carolina Spinal Cord Injury Association." *Wilson College of Textiles*, 27 June 2022, https://textiles.ncsu.edu/news/2022/06/wilson-college-students-design-adaptive-fashion-for-north-carolina-spinal-cord-injury-association/. *Girls Chronically Rock*, https://girlschronicallyrock.com/

Hathcock, Christopher. "Bracelet Helper – Lafonn." *Lafonn*, https://www.lafonn.com/products/bracelet-helper?variant=43435935695017&currency=USD#.

The Herald Times. "The Blind Make Military Uniforms." 2005, https://www.heraldtimesonline.com/story/news/2005/07/24/he-blind-make-military-uniforms/48321241/.

HHS.gov: Department of Health & Human Services, https://www.hhs.gov/.

Heumann, Judy. "Judy Heumann." *American Civil Liberties Union*, https://www.aclu.org/bio/judy-heumann.

Hobbs, Kayna. *Making the Clothing Industry More Inclusive*. Ted x, 2000, https://www.youtube.com/watch?v=U0-PBIAeUEg. iveapparel/chapter/adaptive-apparel-designers-guide-to-research/.

Holcombe, Hannah. "UA Students Design Clothes for Adaptive Athletes as Part of Grant Project." *Alabama Public Radio*, 15 February 2024, https://www.apr.org/news/2024-02-15/ua-stude nts-design-clothes-for-adaptive-athletes-as-part-of-grant-project.

GCR Adaptive Project - Accessible Fashion, https://gcradapti vep.org/.

Open Style Lab, https://www.openstylelab.org/.

Home, https://www.lpaonline.org/

https://iastate.pressbooks.pub/adaptiveapparel/chapter/adapt ive-apparel-designers-guide-to-research/.

Inkumsah, Ashley. "This Halloween, Remember That Disability Is Not A Costume." *World Institute on Disability*, 26 October 2022, https://wid.org/this-halloween-remember-that-disability-is-not-a-costume/.

"Jamal Hill." *Team USA*, https://www.teamusa.com/profiles/jamal-hill-1136097.

Jordan, Daisy. "Why Are There More Clothing Lines for Dogs Than People with Disabilities?" *Metro*, 10 April 2021, https://metro. co.uk/2021/04/10/in-focus-there-are-more-clothing-lines-for-dogs-than-disabled-people-14376043/.

Jenkins, Victoria. "About Unhidden." *Unhidden Clothing*, https:// unhiddenclothing.com/pages/about-unhidden.

Kelly, Dylan, et al. "SKIMS Joins Team USA for Olympic and Paralympic Capsule." *Hypebeast*, 24 June 2024, https://hypebeast. com/2024/6/skims-team-usa-olympic-paralympic-paris-2024-capsule-collection-campaign-release-info.

"Kerri McBee-Black, PhD // Department of Textile & Apparel Management." *Department of Textile & Apparel Management*, https://tam.missouri.edu/people/kerri-mcbee-black/.

Kessler, Ales. "'Meet Next in Fashioin designer Qaysean Williams.' The One Hand Sewing Man." 2023. *British Vogue*, https://www.vogue.co.uk/article/qaysean-williams-next-in-fashion-designer.

Kim, Sara, and World Institute on Disability. "This Halloween, Remember That Disability Is Not A Costume."

Kozie Clothes: Sensory and Adaptive Clothing for Kids, http://www.kozieclothes.com.

Latifi, Fortesa. "Disabled TikTokers Respond to SKIMS Adaptive Line." *Teen Vogue*, 23 March 2023, https://www.teenvogue.com/story/disabled-creators-skims-reaction.

Li, Shan. "How I Made It: California Fashion Assn. president Ilse Metchek." *Los Angeles Times*, 21 September 2014, https://www.latimes.com/business/la-fi-himi-metchek-20140921-story.html.

Little People UK, https://littlepeopleuk.org/.

"Liz Jackson – Women Talk Design." *Women Talk Design*, https://womentalkdesign.com/speakers/liz-jackson/.

"Los Angeles." *Braille Institute*, https://www.brailleinstitute.org/locations/los-angeles/.

"lululemon Paris 2024 kit features adaptive breakthroughs to be Made for More." *Canadian Paralympic Committee*, 10 April 2024, https://paralympic.ca/news/lululemon-paris-2024-kit-features-adaptive-breakthroughs-be-made-more/.

Maria Sol Ungar. *Welum*, https://welum.com/.

https://mydiversability.com/d30-2021-honorees/Marta%20Elena%20Cortez-Neavel.

McCartney, Stella. "adidas Brings Universal Design Principles to Kit for Paris 2024, to Optimise Fit and Performance for All." *adidas News*, 18 April 2024, https://news.adidas.com/training/adidas-brings-universal-design-principles-to-kit-for-paris-2024--to-optimise-fit-and-performance-for/s/675a0e1a-ddd7-428f-b15d-1713d59bb352.

McCartney, Stella. "adidas Reveals Industry-First Adaptive Wheelchair Basketball Uniforms." *adidas News*, 22 April 2024, https://news.adidas.com/basketball/adidas-reveals-industry-first-adaptive-wheelchair-basketball-uniforms/s/321d7fb9-926b-445a-ac4a-c6cc26a692f9.

McKinney, Ellen, and Rachel Eike. "Adaptive Apparel Design – Simple Book Publishing." *Iowa State University Digital Press*, 28 August 2023, https://iastate.pressbooks.pub/adaptiveapparel/.

McLeod, Saul. "Maslow's Hierarchy of Needs." *Simply Psychology*, 24 January 2024, https://www.simplypsychology.org/maslow.html.

"The Medical Pet Shirt – Alternative to Elizabethan Buster Collar." *Daisy Street Veterinary Centre*, 4 September 2015, https://vet-healthcentre.co.uk/news/2015/september/the-medical-pet-shirt-the-alternative-to-the.html. *Megami Store*, https://megami.store/#thefilm

Melrose Trading Post | A curated selection of handcrafted artisan goods, eclectic art and craft, vintage fashion, antique furniture and one-of-a-kind treasures at Fairfax High School every Sunday, https://melrosetradingpost.org.

MIGA Swimwear | Sustainable Swimwear | Made in USA | Live in Swim, https://migaswimwear.com/.

Mogollon, Melissa. "Fashion brands embrace adaptive clothing to empower people with disabilities." *NBC News*, 20 July 2023, https://www.nbcnews.com/now/video/fashion-brands-embrace-adaptive-clothing-to-empower-people-with-disabilities-188915781765.

Myselfbelts.com/pages/our-story.

Nieder, Alison A. "Open Style Lab: Making Apparel Accessible to All." *California Apparel News*, 16 April 2015, https://www.appareln ews.net/news/2015/apr/16/open-style-lab-making-apparel-acc essible-all/?print.

"Official Site of the National Football League." *NFL.com*, https:// www.nfl.com/playerhealthandsafety/health-and-wellness/men tal-health/.

Open Style Lab, https://www.openstylelab.org/

"Our Story – Myself Belts." *Myself Belts*, https://www.myselfbelts. com/pages/our-story

"100 Years of Swimsuits | Condé Nast Traveler." *YouTube*, 13 April 2017, https://www.youtube.com/watch?v=nXoXkm9Jpcl.

"Paralympics History - Evolution of the Paralympic Movement." *Paralympic.org*, https://www.paralympic.org/ipc/history.

"Paralympics news 2024 | Australian Paralympic team unveils 2024 uniform, by RM Williams." *Nine*, 16 May 2024, https://www.nine. com.au/sport/paralympics/news-2024-australia-unveils-paris-uniform-first-look-photos-rm-williams-20240517-p5jegx.html.

"Paralympic Team Triumph Uniform – Holyland Civilians." *Holyland Civilians*, https://holylandcivilians.com/en-us/coll ections/paralympic-team-triumph-uniform.

"Paralympic uniform featuring accessibility modifications launched at Australian Fashion Week - video Dailymotion." *Dailymotion*, 17 May 2024, https://www.dailymotion.com/video/ x8ynx5i.

"Paralyzed Veterans of America." *Home*, https://pva.org/.

"Paris 2024 Paralympics - Latest News, Schedules & Results." *Paris 2024*, https://olympics.com/en/paris-2024/paralympic-games.

"Paris 2024 Press Kit." *Uniqlo*, https://www.uniqlo.com/se/en/contents/feature/sweden-olympic-paralympic-collection/common/pdf/presskit.pdf.

"Parsons School of Design Has Partnered with Special Olympics to Design Uniforms for Athletes of All Abilities." *Special Olympics*, https://www.specialolympics.org/stories/news/parsons-school-of-design-has-partnered-with-special-olympics-to-design-uniforms-for-athletes-of-all-abilities.

"Parsons School of Design Will Launch Program for Designers Who Identify as Disabled." *NPR*, 17 January 2024, https://www.npr.org/2024/01/17/1225142494/parsons-school-of-design-will-launch-program-for-designers-who-identify-as-disab.

Penn Mar Human Services. "Unique Fashion Show Featured Adaptive Clothing for People with Disabilities."

https://www.penn-mar.org/unique-fashion-show-featured-adaptive-clothing-for-people-with-disabilities/.

"Paralyzed Veterans of America." *Home*, https://pva.org/.

"Protecting Students With Disabilities." *Department of Education*, 18 July 2023, https://www2.ed.gov/about/offices/list/ocr/504faq.html.

"Prevalence Estimates for Vision Loss and Blindness | Vision and Eye Health Surveillance System." *CDC*, 15 May 2024, https://www.cdc.gov/vision-health-data/prevalence-estimates/vision-loss-prevalence.html.

Puskarz, Hanna, and Annelie Gross. "Global Disability Innovation Hub | London College of Fashion." *University of the Arts London*, https://www.arts.ac.uk/colleges/london-college-of-fashion/research-at-lcf/research-networks/global-disability-innovation-hub.

Rolland, John. *Families, Illness, And Disability: An Integrative Treatment Model*. Basic Books, 1994.

Rollettes | wheelchair dance team | Los Angeles, CA, United States, https://www.rollettesdance.com/.

Ruggiero, Amanda. "10 NFL Players Who Overcame Barriers to Their Disabilities - Opportunity Outreach Newsletter." *Easterseals New Jersey | Home*, 1 February 2023,https://www.eastersealsnj.org/blog/10-nfl-players-who-overcame-barriers-to-their-disabilities/.

Scheer, Xochil Herrera. "About." *Tukatech*, 14 May 2024, https://tukatech.com/about/

"See Team USA's Outfits Made by Ralph Lauren for Paris Olympics." *YouTube*, 18 June 2024, https://www.youtube.com/watch?v=PbHTa8Hebfs. [Accessed 16 August 2024].

Sessoms, Janelle. "How Should Fashion Schools Address Adaptive Design?" *Fashionista*, 19 October 2023, https://fashionista.com/2023/10/fashion-schools-teaching-adaptive-fashion.

"Sew Much Comfort." *Hidden Heroes*, 9 August 2016, https://hiddenheroes.org/resource/sew-much-comfort/.

Sewn Adaptive: Home, https://sewnadaptive.com/.

Sinéad Burke, https://www.sinead-burke.com/.

Shani Dhanda: Home, https://www.shanidhanda.com/.

Silverts: Adaptive Clothing for Seniors, Elderly & Disabled, https://www.silverts.com/.

Smith, Leah. "#Ableism – Center for Disability Rights." *Center for Disability Rights*, https://cdrnys.org/blog/uncategorized/ableism/.

"SOCIAL STYLE Model™." *TRACOM Group*, https://tracom.com/social-style-training/model.

"So Yes adaptive clothing - For people with physical disabilities." *So Yes*, https://so-yes.com/en/home-so-yes-adaptive-clothing/.

"The Story of IZ Adaptive." *IZ Adaptive*, https://izadaptive.com/pages/the-story-of-iz-adaptive.

"Strengthening the Collection of Data on Disability." *World Health Organization (WHO)*, https://www.who.int/activities/collection-of-data-on-disability.

"Supplemental Security Income (SSI)." *SSA*, https://www.ssa.gov/ssi.

Tashjian, Rachel. "Will Fashion Ever be Truly Diverse?" *The Washington Post*, 4 December 2023,

https://www.washingtonpost.com/style/fashion/2023/12/04/parsons-disabled-program/.

Tavolieri, Michela. "Clothing Choices for the Blind and Visually Impaired." *Perkins School for The Blind*, https://www.perkins.org/resource/clothing-choices-blind-and-visually-impaired/.

"Team USA Paralympic Collection | www.teamusashop.com." *Team USA Shop*, https://www.teamusashop.com/team-usa/paralympic-collection/t-25843672+c-7879271650+z-90-1289629674.

TechCrunch | Startup and Technology News, http://techcrunch.com.

Threads: Senior Collection Showcase, https://threads.textiles.ncsu.edu/.

"Tommy Adaptive." *Tommy Hilfiger*, https://au.tommy.com/tommy-hilfiger-adaptive.

TRACOM *Proven Corporate Soft Skills Training Programs | Tracom Group*, https://tracom.com/.

Two Blind Brothers, https://twoblindbrothers.com/.

"An Unprecedented Paralympic Ceremony." *Paris 2024*, https://olympics.com/en/paris-2024/paralympic-games/the-games/ceremonies/opening-ceremony-paralympics.

Vogt, Christina, and Seth Gillihan. "NFL Football Players Open Up About Mental Health." *Everyday Health*, 19 January 2023, https://www.everydayhealth.com/emotional-health/football-players-whove-spoken-up-about-mental-health/.

Vollbrecht, Tracy. "Vollbrecht Adaptive Consulting." https://www.vollbrechtadaptiveconsulting.com/.

Vollbrecht, Tracy, and Vollbrecht Consulting. "History of Adaptive Fashion: Why Learning about Adaptive Fashion Is Essential to Inclusion in Fashion." *June Adaptive*, 2024.

Voyage Austin, 2024, https://voyageaustin.com/interview/rising-stars-meet-marta-elena-cortez-neavel-of-rosewood/.

Wales, Greg. "SKIMS Unveils Team USA Limited Edition Collection Ahead of 2024 Paris Olympics." *Good Morning America*, 25 June 2024, https://www.goodmorningamerica.com/shop/story/skims-unveils-team-usa-limited-edition-collection-ahead-111401268.

Welty, Matt. "The True Story Behind Nike FlyEase and Who They Pay for It." *Complex*, 27 September 2022, https://www.complex.com/sneakers/a/matt-welty/nike-flyease-kizik-skip-lei-interview.

"Why Adaptive Underwear | Our Story." *Slick Chicks*, https://slickchicksonline.com/pages/our-story

World Health Organization. "Disability." *World Health Organization (WHO)*, 7 March 2023, https://www.who.int/news-room/fact-sheets/detail/disability-and-health.

https://www.wraptmagazine.com/blog/2021/4/21/palta-more-than-just-fashion-helping-people-with-disabilities-feel-seen

"Zappos Adaptive | Functional and Fashionable Products to Make Life Easier." *Zappos*, https://www.zappos.com/c/adaptive.

Index

www.ingramcontent.com/pod-product-compliance
Lightning Source LLC
Chambersburg PA
CBHW050334270326
41926CB00016B/3455